T0220311

Cambridge Elements

Elements in Non-local Data Interactions: Foundations and Applications
edited by
Luca Calatroni
Centre National de la Recherche Scientifique (CNRS)

NONLOCAL CONTINUUM LIMITS OF p-LAPLACIAN PROBLEMS ON GRAPHS

Imad El Bouchairi
University of Caen Normandy

Jalal Fadili
ENSICAEN

Yosra Hafiene
ENSEEIHT

Abderrahim Elmoataz
University of Caen Normandy

CAMBRIDGE
UNIVERSITY PRESS

CAMBRIDGE
UNIVERSITY PRESS

Shaftesbury Road, Cambridge CB2 8EA, United Kingdom

One Liberty Plaza, 20th Floor, New York, NY 10006, USA

477 Williamstown Road, Port Melbourne, VIC 3207, Australia

314–321, 3rd Floor, Plot 3, Splendor Forum, Jasola District Centre, New Delhi – 110025, India

103 Penang Road, #05–06/07, Visioncrest Commercial, Singapore 238467

Cambridge University Press is part of Cambridge University Press & Assessment, a department of the University of Cambridge.

We share the University's mission to contribute to society through the pursuit of education, learning and research at the highest international levels of excellence.

www.cambridge.org
Information on this title: www.cambridge.org/9781009327855
DOI: 10.1017/9781009327862

© Imad El Bouchairi, Jalal Fadili, Yosra Hafiene, and Abderrahim Elmoataz 2023

This publication is in copyright. Subject to statutory exception and to the provisions of relevant collective licensing agreements, no reproduction of any part may take place without the written permission of Cambridge University Press & Assessment.

First published 2023

A catalogue record for this publication is available from the British Library.

ISBN 978-1-009-32785-5 Paperback
ISSN 2755-1296 (online)
ISSN 2755-1288 (print)

Cambridge University Press & Assessment has no responsibility for the persistence or accuracy of URLs for external or third-party internet websites referred to in this publication and does not guarantee that any content on such websites is, or will remain, accurate or appropriate.

Nonlocal Continuum Limits of p-Laplacian Problems on Graphs

Elements in Non-local Data Interactions: Foundations and Applications

DOI: 10.1017/9781009327862
First published online: April 2023

Imad El Bouchairi
University of Caen Normandy

Jalal Fadili
ENSICAEN

Yosra Hafiene
ENSEEIHT

Abderrahim Elmoataz
University of Caen Normandy

Author for correspondence: Jalal Fadili, Jalal.Fadili@ensicaen.fr

Abstract: In this Element, the authors consider fully discretized p-Laplacian problems (evolution, boundary value, and variational problems) on graphs. The motivation of nonlocal continuum limits comes from the quest for understanding collective dynamics in large ensembles of interacting particles, which is a fundamental problem in nonlinear science, with applications ranging from biology to physics, chemistry, and computer science. Using the theory of graphons, the authors give a unified treatment of all the preceding problems and establish the continuum limit for each of them together with nonasymptotic convergence rates. They also describe an algorithmic framework based on proximal splitting to solve these discrete problems on graphs.

Keywords: nonlocal p-Laplacian, evolution problem, variational problem, Dirichlet problem, numerical approximations, rates of the convergence, graphons, sparse graphs

© Imad El Bouchairi, Jalal Fadili, Yosra Hafiene, and Abderrahim Elmoataz 2023

ISBNs: 9781009327855 (PB), 9781009327862 (OC)
ISSNs: 2755-1296 (online), 2755-1288 (print)

Contents

1 Introduction

1.1 Context

Partial differential equations (PDEs) play an important role in mathematical modeling throughout various fields of science and engineering. Indeed, several problems end up modeling and solving an evolution or a boundary value problem involving different kinds of operators depending on the tasks at hand. The methods based on PDEs have also proven to provide very effective tools in data processing (signals, images, meshes, etc.), machine learning, computer vision, and biology (Aubert and Kornprobst, 2002; Chan and Shen, 2005; Osher and Paragios, 2003; Auel et al., 2017; Figalli et al., 2018; Andreu-Vaillo et al., 2010). Such methods have the advantages of better mathematical modeling, connections with physics, and better geometrical approximations. Differential operators involved in these methods are classically based on derivatives that reflect local interactions in the support domain. The nonlocal counterparts have been introduced in different settings (see, e.g., Silling, 2000; Madenci and Oterkus, 2014; Eringen and Wegner, 2003; Bažant and Jirásek, 2002; Rabczuk et al., 2019). These operators are based on an integral form, particularly with respect to space variables, that reflects nonlocal interactions between the points in the support domain. Recently, nonlocal models have been proposed in the context of image processing to design nonlocal regularization functionals and PDEs for many image processing tasks, such as denoising, deconvolution, segmentation, inpainting, and optical flow, to name a few (Kindermann et al., 2006; Gilboa and Osher, 2008, 2007; Elmoataz et al., 2015, 2012; Van Gennip et al., 2014; El Chakik et al., 2014). A main advantage for image processing is the ability to capture both the structure (geometrical parts) and textures within the same framework. In this context, nonlocal variational problems are also closely related to nonlocal filters and (nonlocal) patch-based methods (Lee, 1983; Buades et al., 2005).

To build nonlocal models, the general intuition is to replace the local operators in PDEs with newly defined nonlocal analogue operators that are expected to converge to the local ones in some appropriate continuum limit. Several works have studied this limiting behavior of nonlocal models for various notions of limits and topologies (see, for example, Silling, 2000; Andreu et al., 2008b; You et al., 2020; Radu et al., 2017). An important difficulty is that, unlike classical local PDE models, in the nonlocal setting, the boundary conditions must be defined on a region with nonzero volume outside the surface (Cortazar et al., 2008; Du et al., 2013a; Tao et al., 2017; Aksoylu and Mengesha, 2010). This is in contrast with more traditional scenarios, where boundary conditions are typically imposed on a sharp codimension one surface. The construction of such operators has been built on ideas developed in graph theory and nonlocal calculus of variations, namely nonlocal gradient, nonlocal divergence, nonlocal curl, and nonlocal Laplacian (see, e.g., Gilboa and Osher, 2008; Du et al., 2013b; Alali et al., 2015; Rabczuk et al., 2019, and references therein). Following these ideas, it has been shown that many PDE-based processes, minimizations, and computation methods can be generalized to the nonlocal setting.

1.2 p-Laplacian Problems in This Element

Among the operators introduced in the preceding setting, the nonlocal p-Laplacian operator has become popular both in the setting of Euclidean domains and on graphs and arises in a variety of practical problems in physics, engineering, biology, and economy, such as continuum mechanics, phase transition phenomena, and population dynamics (see Andreu et al., 2008a; Bates and Chmaj, 1999; Bates et al., 1997; Carrillo and Fife, 2005; Fife, 2002; Wang, 2002; Fife and Wang, 1998; and references therein). Other applications can be found in data processing, computer vision, and machine learning; see, for example, Bühler and Hein (2009); Elmoataz et al. (2014, 2008); Kawohl (2011); Gennip and Bertozzi (2012); El Alaoui et al. (2016); Trillos and Slepčev (2016); Slepcev and Thorpe (2019); Calder (2018); Garcia Trillos (2019); Garcia Trillos and Murray (2020); Calder et al. (2020); Dunlop et al. (2020); Bungert et al. (2021); Fadili et al. (2021); Laux and Lelmi (2021); Calder (2019); Flores et al. (2022); Roith and Bungert (2022).

On the continuum, the p-Laplacian operator is defined on $L^p(\Omega)$, $p \in]1, +\infty[$ as follows:

$$\Delta_p^K u(x) = -\int_\Omega K(x, y)|u(y) - u(x)|^{p-2}(u(y) - u(x))dy, \tag{1.1}$$

where Ω is a bounded set in $\mathbb{R}^d$, and $K(\cdot, \cdot)$ is a symmetric, nonnegative measurable function on Ω^2. The operator Δ_p^K can also be defined as a set-valued operator for $p = 1$ and $p = \infty$, but we will not elaborate on this for the moment. This operator can be thought of as the nonlocal analogue of the p-Laplacian operator defined on $W^{1,p}(\Omega)$ for $p \in]1, +\infty[$ as

$$\Delta_p u(x) = \operatorname{div}\left(|\nabla u(x)|^{p-2}\nabla u(x)\right),$$

which occurs also in many mathematical models and physical processes such as nonlinear diffusion/filtration and non-Newtonian flows (Bognar, 2008). The nonlocal p-Laplacian operator is the negative gradient of the p-Dirichlet energy,

$$R_p(u, K) \stackrel{\text{def}}{=} \frac{1}{2p}\int_{\Omega^2} K(x, y)|u(y) - u(x)|^p dxdy, \tag{1.2}$$

which is the nonlocal analogue to the energy functional $\frac{1}{p}\int_\Omega |\nabla u|^p$ associated to the local p-Laplacian.

Let us now introduce some classical problems governed by the nonlocal p-Laplacian operators on which we are going to focus in this chapter.

1.2.1 Nonlocal Boundary Value Problem

The nonlinear nonlocal "elliptic" boundary value problem, known as the nonlocal p-Laplacian Dirichlet problem (Gunzburger and Lehoucq, 2010; Hinds and Radu, 2012) associated to Δ_p^K, is

$$\begin{cases} -\Delta_p^K u(\boldsymbol{x}) = f(\boldsymbol{x}), & \boldsymbol{x} \in U, \\ u(\boldsymbol{x}) = g(\boldsymbol{x}), & \boldsymbol{x} \in \Gamma \stackrel{\text{def}}{=} \Omega \setminus U, \end{cases} \tag{$\mathcal{P}_{\text{nloc}}^D$}$$

where U is a bounded subset of Ω, and Γ is a "collar" surrounding U which has nonzero volume with $\Omega = U \cup \Gamma$. The nonlocal boundary value problem shares many properties with the corresponding classical elliptic boundary value problem:

$$\begin{cases} \Delta_p u(\boldsymbol{x}) = f(\boldsymbol{x}), & \boldsymbol{x} \in \Omega, \\ u(\boldsymbol{x}) = g(\boldsymbol{x}), & \boldsymbol{x} \in \partial\Omega. \end{cases} \tag{$\mathcal{P}_{\text{loc}}^D$}$$

It has been shown by Gunzburger and Lehoucq (2010) that, for $p = 2$, the problem ($\mathcal{P}_{\text{nloc}}^D$) provides a nonlocal equivalent of the problem ($\mathcal{P}_{\text{loc}}^D$). It has been shown also in You et al. (2020) that the nonlocal Neumann-type boundary value problem governed by the nonlocal p-Laplacian recovers the classical Neumann problem as the nonlocal horizon parameter vanishes.

It has been proved in Hinds and Radu (2012), using the Dirichlet principle, that the minimizers of the energy functional

$$\mathcal{F}(u) \stackrel{\text{def}}{=} R_p(u, K) + \int_\Omega f(\boldsymbol{x})u(\boldsymbol{x})d\boldsymbol{x} + \iota_{L_g^p(\Omega,U)}(u) \tag{1.3}$$

satisfy ($\mathcal{P}_{\text{nloc}}^D$) and conversely, any solution of ($\mathcal{P}_{\text{nloc}}^D$) is a minimizer of $\mathcal{F}$, where $L_g^p(\Omega, U)$ is the linear space of functions in $L^p(\Omega)$ that coincide with g on Γ, and the indicator function ι_C of a subset C is defined as

$$\iota_C(u) = \begin{cases} 0, & \text{if } u \in C, \\ +\infty, & \text{otherwise.} \end{cases}$$

1.2.2 Nonlocal Evolution Problem

Another problem governed by this nonlocal operator is the nonlinear evolution problem (Cauchy problem), known as the nonlocal p-Laplacian evolution problem with homogeneous Neumann boundary conditions (Andreu-Vaillo et al., 2010):

$$\begin{cases} \frac{\partial}{\partial t}u(x,t) = -\Delta_p^K u(x) + f(x,t), & x \in \Omega, t > 0, \\ u(x,0) = g(x), & x \in \Omega. \end{cases} \qquad (\mathcal{P}_{\mathrm{nloc}})$$

This nonlocal diffusion problem, in turn, shares many properties with the corresponding local one. For instance, if $f = 0$ and the kernel K is radially symmetric and properly rescaled with a parameter ε, it has been shown by Andreu et al. (2008b) that the solutions to the nonlocal problems $(\mathcal{P}_{\mathrm{nloc}})$ converge strongly in $L^\infty((0,T); L^p(\Omega))$, as ε goes to zero, to the solution of the well-known local p-Laplacian evolution problem

$$\begin{cases} u_t(x,t) = \frac{\partial}{\partial t}u(x,t) = \Delta_p(u(x,t)), & x \in \Omega, t > 0, \\ u(x,0) = g(x), & x \in \Omega. \end{cases} \qquad (\mathcal{P}_{\mathrm{loc}})$$

For $p = 2$, $(\mathcal{P}_{\mathrm{loc}})$ corresponds to the heat equation, while the case $p = 1$ corresponds to the total variation flow with homogeneous Neumann boundary conditions. The problem $(\mathcal{P}_{\mathrm{loc}})$ occurs in many applications such as physics, biology, or economy (Lindqvist, 2017; Drábek, 2007).

A particular case of interest is when $\Omega = \mathbb{R}^d$, $K(x,y) = J(x-y)$, where the kernel $J\colon \mathbb{R}^d \to \mathbb{R}$ is a nonnegative continuous radial function with compact support verifying $J(0) > 0$ and $\int_{\mathbb{R}^d} J(x)dx = 1$. In this case, $(\mathcal{P}_{\mathrm{nloc}})$ takes the form

$$u_t(x,t) = J * u(x,t) - u(x,t) = \int_{\mathbb{R}^d} J(x-y)(u(y,t) - u(x,t))dy, \qquad (\mathcal{P}^*_{\mathrm{nloc}})$$

where $*$ stands for the convolution. This evolution equation has been widely used recently to model diffusion processes (Andreu et al., 2008a; Bates and Chmaj, 1999; Bates et al., 1997; Carrillo and Fife, 2005; Fife, 2002; Wang, 2002; Fife and Wang, 1998). As explained in Fife (2002), when $K(x,y) = J(x-y)$ with J radially symmetric with compact support verifying $J(0) > 0$ and $\int_{\mathbb{R}^d} J(x)dx = 1$, $(\mathcal{P})$ has a nice interpretation in modeling the dispersal of organisms in space. In this case, $u(x,t)$ can be viewed as their density at point x and time t, and $J(x-y)$ is interpreted as the probability of jumping from position y to position x. In turn, the right-hand side of $(\mathcal{P})$ represents transport due to long-range dispersal mechanisms, that is, the rate at which organisms are arriving to location x from any other place. For $p = 2$ and $p = 1$, $(\mathcal{P})$ correspond respectively to the nonlocal analogues of the heat equation and the total variation flow with homogeneous Neumann boundary conditions.

1.2.3 Nonlocal Variational Problem

In this Element we will consider the following variational problem

$$\min_{u \in L^2(\Omega)} \left\{ E_\lambda(u,g,K) \stackrel{\mathrm{def}}{=} \frac{1}{2\lambda}\|u-g\|^2_{L^2(\Omega)} + R_p(u,K) \right\}, \qquad (\mathcal{VP}_{\mathrm{nloc}})$$

where the regularization term R_p is given by the nonlocal energy functional (1.2), and $\lambda > 0$ is a regularization parameter specifying the trade-off between the two competing terms. This problem was first studied by Hafiene et al. (2019).

1.3 Continuum Limits of Problems on Graphs

In the literature, numerous works, which we will review shortly, have been carried out in recent years to study continuum limits of various evolution, boundary, and variational problems on graphs. It is, however, important to stress the fact that our focus in this chapter will be on nonlocal (in contrast to local) continuum limits of problems on graphs, and for which an appropriate limit object (L^q graphon, as introduced in the recent theory of graphs) of a sequence of graphs with an increasing number of vertices will be instrumental. This is more in line with a numerical analysis standpoint.

1.3.1 Local Continuum Limits

The literature on deriving local continuum limits of some boundary value and variational problems on graphs, including with the p-Laplacian operator, is very active (see Bühler and Hein, 2009; Gennip and Bertozzi, 2012; El Alaoui et al., 2016; Trillos and Slepčev, 2016; Slepcev and Thorpe, 2019; Calder, 2018; Garcia Trillos, 2019; Garcia Trillos and Murray, 2020; Calder et al., 2020; Dunlop et al., 2020; Bungert et al., 2021; Fadili et al., 2021; Laux and Lelmi, 2021; Calder, 2019; Roith and Bungert, 2022 and others).

The motivation comes essentially from problems in data processing (e.g., point cloud processing) and machine learning (e.g., supervised learning). The idea is to take $K(\boldsymbol{x}, \boldsymbol{y}) = \varepsilon^{-d} J(|\boldsymbol{x} - \boldsymbol{y}|/\varepsilon)$, $\varepsilon > 0$, for some radially symmetric kernel J, and to consider a (geometric) random graph model whose vertices are latent random variables independently and identically sampled on Ω from a distribution having a density bounded away from zero. The goal is then to study the limit (in an appropriate topology) as the number of vertices n grows to infinity and for ε vanishing with n at an appropriate rate. This line of work is, however, fundamentally different from our perspective in this Element, where the focus is on graphons rather than geometric graphs.

1.3.2 Nonlocal Continuum Limits

The motivation of nonlocal continuum limits comes from the quest for understanding collective dynamics in large ensembles of interacting particles, which is a fundamental problem in nonlinear science with applications ranging from biology (e.g., neural and genetic networks) to physics and chemistry (e.g., interacting particle systems) and computer science (internet, data science, multiagent systems, opinion dynamics).

In particular, the work of Kaliuzhnyi-Verbovetskyi and Medvedev (2017) and Medvedev (2014b,a, 2019) focused on a nonlinear heat equation on graphs, while Hafiene et al. (2018, 2020) derived the continuum limit of the p-Laplacian evolution problem for bounded graphs and $p \in]1, \infty[$.. Nonlocal continuum limit of the p-Laplacian variational problem on graphs was established in Hafiene et al. (2019).

Motivated by applications in opinion dynamics, Ayi and Pouradier Duteil (2021) used ideas from Medvedev (2014a) to study a collective dynamics model with a time-varying kernel and Lipschitz continuous operator. They showed nonlocal continuum limits as the number of agents/vertices goes to infinity. Interestingly, those authors used such a continuum limit to derive the mean-field limit one. In fact, the graph limit approach is more general than the mean-field limit one, and this subordination of the mean-field limit to the nonlocal continuum graph limit is natural, as pointed out in Biccari et al. (2019). Mean-field limits of interacting particle systems using the theory of graphons with the p-Laplacian are an open problem that is worth investigating in the future.

Therefore, since our goal throughout the section is to study (nonlocal) graph limits through the theory of L^q graphons for which Ω must be even $[0,1]$, we will take $\Omega = [0,1]^d$. This choice will also allow us to derive nonasymptotic convergence rates in space from the error in spatial discretization of the kernel K and the data by invoking results from nonlinear approximation theory for which the choice $\Omega = [0,1]^d$ is also important. Apart from these reasons, the domain Ω can only required to be bounded and many of our tools and results in this Element will still hold.

1.4 Objectives of This Element

The main goals of this Element are to design fully discretized problems (evolution, boundary value, and variational problems) in space (graphs) and time and to show that they are provably consistent with respect to their nonlocal continuum analogues. Indeed, the discrete nonlocal problems on graphs are just approximations of the underlying nonlocal continuum problems. Thus, the following legitimate questions have to be answered separately for each problem:

(Q1) Is there any (nonlocal) continuum limit as the number of vertices grows and time step vanishes? If yes, in what sense?

(Q2) What is the rate of convergence to this limit and what is its relation to the solution of the continuum problem?

(Q3) What are the parameters involved in this convergence and what is their influence in the corresponding rate?

(Q4) Can this continuum limit help us get better insight into discrete models on graphs and their fundamental guarantees and limits?

It is our aim in this Element to give a unified treatment for these questions for the three models just presented, for both deterministic and random graphs. We consider a general class of graph structures that is versatile enough to handle both dense and sparse graphs, which in turn enlarges the scope of possible applications. This Element will not only give an overview of the main results in our previous work (Hafiene et al., 2018, 2020, 2019; El Bouchairi et al., 2020), but will also provide several new results including those in Section 5 and Section 6.

1.5 A Reading Guide

The remainder of this Element is organized as follows. Section 2 collects the necessary mathematical material used throughout the Element. In Section 3, we present a consistency analysis for the nonlocal p-Laplacian evolution problem. Our results consist of three main parts: well-posedness, error bounds for the discrete problems, and application of these results to the fully discretized problems on random graph models. For the time-discrete problem, the fully discrete versions with both forward and backward Euler approximations are presented. We prove the convergence of these schemes before comparing their corresponding problems to the continuum one. The obtained error bounds will be used in the third part to analyse error bound on fully discretized problems on sparse random graphs. In Section 4, we present our main result for the variational p-Laplacian problem: the error bound for the discrete problem. We also provide a key regularity result that will allow us to derive rates of the convergence of the discrete solution to its continuum counterpart. We finish this section by applying this result to random inhomogeneous graphs. Section 5 is dedicated to study a consistency analysis of the nonlocal p-Laplacian Dirichlet problem. First, we derive a general consistency for the discretized problem and an a priori estimate for constant boundary conditions. Relying on these error estimates, we establish the nonasymptotic rate of convergence of solutions for the discrete model on sparse random graphs to the solution of the nonlocal Dirichlet problem on the continuum. Finally, we adopt a primal-dual proximal splitting algorithm to solve the discretized problems, associated to the variational and Dirichlet problems, in graphs in Section 6; we also report some numerical results to illustrate our theoretical findings.

2 Mathematical Background

In this section, we collect the necessary mathematical material used in this Element. Let $\mathbb{R}$ denote the set of real numbers, $\mathbb{R}^+$ the set of nonnegative reals, $\overline{\mathbb{R}} = \mathbb{R} \cup \{+\infty\}$ the extended real line, and $\mathbb{R}^d$ the d-dimensional real Euclidean space. Vectors in $\mathbb{R}^m$, $m \geq 2$, will be denoted in bold small letters. We denote by $\mathbb{N}$ the set of nonnegative integers, by $\mathbb{N}^*$, the set of positive integers. We use the notation $[n] = \{1, \ldots, n\}$. For a set C, $|C|$ denotes its Lebesgue measure, and χ_C its characteristic function (taking on the value 1 on C and 0 otherwise).

2.1 Tools from Functional Analysis

Let (X, τ) be a locally convex topological vector space (LCTVS). Let $f : X \mapsto \overline{\mathbb{R}}$ be a function, of which the epigraph and domain are given by, respectively, $\mathrm{epi}(f) \stackrel{\text{def}}{=} \{(x,t) \in X \times \mathbb{R} : \ f(x) \leq t\}$ and $\mathrm{dom}(f) \stackrel{\text{def}}{=} \{x \in X : \ f(x) < +\infty\}$. The function f is said to be proper if $-\infty \notin f(S)$ and $\mathrm{dom}(f) \neq \emptyset$. A function is said to be convex (resp. lower semicontinuous or lsc) if its epigraph is a convex subset of $X \times \mathbb{R}$ (resp. a closed subset of $X \times \mathbb{R}$ with respect to the product topology of τ and the natural topology of $\mathbb{R}$).

Definition 2.1 Assume that X is a normed space. A function $f : S \subset X \mapsto \mathbb{R}$ is said to be M-Lipschitz on S if

$$\forall x, x' \in S; \ |f(x) - f(x')| \leq M\|x - x'\|_X.$$

Proposition 2.2 *Assume that X is a normed space, $x_0 \in X$, $r > 0$, $\varepsilon \in (0, r)$, and $m, M \in \mathbb{R}$. Let $f : \mathbb{B}(x_0, r) \to \mathbb{R}$ be a convex function.*

(i) If $f(x) \leq m$ on $\mathbb{B}(x_0, r)$, then $|f(x)| \leq |m| + 2|f(x_0)|$ on $\mathbb{B}(x_0, r)$.
(ii) If $|f(x)| \leq M$ on $\mathbb{B}(x_0, r)$, then f is $(\frac{2M}{\varepsilon})$-Lipschitz on $\mathbb{B}(x_0, r - \varepsilon)$.

Here $\mathbb{B}(x_0, r)$ is the ball of center x_0 and radius $r > 0$.

PROOF:
(i) See the proof of theorem 3.9 in Clason (2017).
(ii) See Dal Maso (1993), proposition 5.11. □

2.1.1 Γ-Convergence

Γ-convergence was introduced by De Giorgi in the 1970s to study the limits of variational problems. We refer the reader to Braides et al. (2002) and Dal Maso (1993) for an in-depth introduction to Γ-convergence. In this subsection we denote by (X, τ) a first countable topological space. For a sequential of equivalent definitions of Γ-convergence, we refer the reader to Attouch (1984), proposition 1.14, and Dal Maso (1993), proposition 8.1.

Definition 2.3 (Γ-convergence) We say that a sequence of functions $f_n : X \to \overline{\mathbb{R}}$, $n \in \mathbb{N}$, Γ-converges in X to $f_\infty : X \to \overline{\mathbb{R}}$ if, for all $x \in X$, we have

(i) (lim inf inequality) for every sequence $\{x_n\}_{n\in\mathbb{N}}$ τ-converging to x,

$$f_\infty(x) \leq \liminf_n f_n(x_n); \tag{2.1}$$

(ii) (lim sup inequality) there exists a sequence $\{x_n\}_{n\in\mathbb{N}}$ τ-converging to x such that

$$f_\infty(x) \geq \limsup_n f_n(x_n). \tag{2.2}$$

The function f_∞ is called the Γ-limit of $\{f_n\}_{n\in\mathbb{N}}$, and we write it as $f_\infty = \Gamma\text{-}\lim_n f_n$.

It is clear that the lim sup inequality (2.2) in Definition 2.3 can be replaced by the equality $f_\infty(x) = \lim_n f_n(x_n)$.

Definition 2.4 (Equicoercivity) A function $f : X \to \overline{\mathbb{R}}$ is (sequentially) coercive if, for all $t \in \mathbb{R}$, the τ-closure of the sublevel set $\{x \in X : f(x) \leq t\}$ is sequentially compact. A sequence $\{f_n\}_{n\in\mathbb{N}}$ is equicoercive on X if, for every $t \in \mathbb{R}$, there exists a sequentially compact subset A_t of X such that $\{x \in X : f_n(x) \leq t\} \subset A_t$ for all $n \in \mathbb{N}$.

If X is a reflexive Banach space and $f \to +\infty$ as $\|x\| \to +\infty$, then f is coercive in the weak topology of X.

Proposition 2.5 (Dal Maso, 1993, proposition 7.7) *A sequence $\{f_n\}_{n\in\mathbb{N}}$ is equicoercive if and only if there exists a lower semicontinuous coercive function $\psi : X \to \overline{\mathbb{R}}$ such that $f_n \geq \psi$ on X, for every n.*

The following theorem (fundamental theorem of Γ-convergence) concerns the convergence of the minimum values and minimizers of an equicoercive sequence of functions.

Theorem 2.6 *Let $\{f_n\}_{n\in\mathbb{N}}$ be a sequence of equicoercive functions on X that Γ-converges to f_∞. Then,* *(i)* f_∞ *is coercive.*

(ii) $\lim_n d_n = d$, *where* $d_n = \inf_{x\in X} f_n(x)$ *and* $d = \min_{x\in X} f_\infty(x)$, *that is, the minimal values converge.*

(iii) If, for every $n \in \mathbb{N}$, x_n *is a minimizer of* f_n *on* X, *then every cluster point of* $\{x_n\}_{n\in\mathbb{N}}$ *is a minimizer of* f_∞ *on* X.

PROOF: Claims (i) and (ii) follow from Dal Maso (1993), theorem 7.8. To get (iii), combine Proposition 2.5; Dal Maso (1993), corollary 7.20; and claim (ii). □

2.1.2 Mosco-Convergence

The concept of epi-convergence (Mosco-convergence) was first utilized by Wijsman (1966). Mosco (1969) was responsible for bringing to the fore important relationships between Mosco-convergence and the convergence of solutions to variational inequalities (hence the name of the convergence); see Attouch (1984) and references therein for more details. In this section, we assume that X is a reflexive Banach space. The corresponding ball centered at x and of radius r is denoted as $\mathbb{B}(x,r)$ and $\mathbb{B}_r$ when $x = 0$.

Definition 2.7 Let $\{F_n, F\colon X \to \overline{\mathbb{R}};\ n \in \mathbb{N}\}$ be a sequence of functions. The sequence $\{F_n\}_{n\in\mathbb{N}}$ is said to be Mosco-convergent to F if, for all $x \in X$:

(i) $M\text{-}\liminf_n F_n(x) \geq F(x)$; namely, for any sequence $\{x_n\}_{n\in\mathbb{N}}$ converging weakly to x, $\liminf_n F_n(x_n) \geq F(x)$.

(ii) $M\text{-}\limsup_n F_n(x) \leq F(x)$; namely there exists a sequence $\{x_n\}_{n\in\mathbb{N}}$ converging strongly to x such that $\limsup_n F_n(x_n) \leq F(x)$.

The function F is called the Mosco-limit of $\{F_n\}_{n\in\mathbb{N}}$ and we then write $F_n \xrightarrow{M} F$.

Observe that, by definition, Mosco-convergence implies Γ-convergence in the weak topology when X is a reflexive Banach space endowed with its weak topology.

Let us now recall this result, which will be useful to prove the Mosco-convergence of the sequence of integral functionals in Section 5.

Theorem 2.8 (Salinetti and Wets, 1977, theorem 2) *Let $F, F_n: X \to \mathbb{R}$, $n \in \mathbb{N}$, be a sequence of closed convex functions such that $\{F_n\}_{n\in\mathbb{N}}$ converges pointwise to F on X. Then, $F_n \xrightarrow{M} F$ if and only if the collection $\{F_n, F : X \to \overline{\mathbb{R}}; n \in \mathbb{N}\}$ is equi-lower semicontinuous.*

In the context of the nonlocal p-Laplacian boundary value problem, our consistency results will be derived, upon using Dirichlet's variational principle, from epi-convergence of the sequence of functionals $(\mathcal{VP}_n)$. In this setting, these functionals take the form of the *sum of two* proper lsc convex functionals. Whether the Γ-limit (resp. Mosco-limit) of a sum is the sum of Γ-limits (resp. Mosco-limits) is a difficult issue in general. The claim is not true in general for the Γ-limit unless stringent assumptions are imposed (see, e.g., Dal Maso, 1993, proposition 6.20). For Mosco convergence, the claim holds true for the sum of two lsc convex functions when X is a reflexive Banach space; see Azé et al. (1988). The latter result generalizes that in McLinden and Bergstrom (1981), which is valid only in finite dimension under a simple domain qualification condition. The result of Azé et al. (1988) will be instrumental in our consistency analysis, and we recall it here.

Theorem 2.9 (Azé et al., 1988, theorem 4.1) *Let $\{F_n\}_{n\in\mathbb{N}}$, F, $\{G_n\}_{n\in\mathbb{N}}$, G be lsc proper convex functions defined on X, such that $F_n \xrightarrow{M} F$ and $G_n \xrightarrow{M} G$. Assume that there exists $r > 0$ such that, for every $\zeta \in \mathbb{B}(0, r)$, there exist two sequences $\{x_n\}_{n\in\mathbb{N}}$ and $\{y_n\}_{n\in\mathbb{N}}$ of elements of X verifying the following:*

$$\begin{aligned} &\{x_n\}_{n\in\mathbb{N}} \text{ and } \{y_n\}_{n\in\mathbb{N}} \text{ are bounded with } \zeta = x_n - y_n, \\ &\limsup_n F_n(x_n) < \infty \text{ and } \limsup_n G_n(y_n) < \infty. \end{aligned} \tag{2.3}$$

Then, there exists $n_0 \in \mathbb{N}$ such that

$$F_n + G_n \text{ is proper }, \forall n \geq n_0, \quad F_n + G_n \xrightarrow{M} F + G, \quad \text{and } F + G \text{ is proper.} \tag{2.4}$$

The following result gives a sufficient condition for (2.3) to hold.

Corollary 2.10 (Azé et al., 1988, remark 1) *Let $\{F_n\}_{n\in\mathbb{N}}$, F, $\{G_n\}_{n\in\mathbb{N}}$, G and X as in Theorem 2.9 such that $F_n \xrightarrow{M} F$ and $G_n \xrightarrow{M} G$. Assume that there exist $x_0 \in \operatorname{dom} G \cap \operatorname{dom} F$ and $\rho > 0$ such that either F_n or G_n is uniformly bounded above on $\mathbb{B}(x_0, \rho)$. Then (2.3) is satisfied. In particular, (2.4) holds.*

Let us turn to the Mosco-convergence of sets.

Definition 2.11 Let $\{A_n, A;\ n \in \mathbb{N}\}$ be a sequence of subsets of X. The sequence $\{A_n\}_{n\in\mathbb{N}}$ is said to be Mosco-convergent to A if and only if the sequence (ι_{A_n}) Mosco-converges to ι_A on X.

From Definition 2.7, we immediately get the following equivalent characterization of Mosco-convergence for sets.

Proposition 2.12 *Let $\{A_n, A;\ n \in \mathbb{N}\}$ be a sequence of subsets of X. Then, the sequence $\{A_n\}_{n\in\mathbb{N}}$ is said to be Mosco-convergent to A if and only if*

(i) for any sequence $\{x_n\}_{n\in\mathbb{N}}$, where $x_n \in A_n$, converging weakly to x, implies $x \in A$;

(ii) for every $x \in A$, there exists a sequence $\{x_n\}_{n\in\mathbb{N}}$, with $x_n \in A_n$, converging strongly to x.

2.2 Tools from Nonlinear Semigroups

In this section we assume that $(X, \|\cdot\|)$ is a Banach space. Let $A\colon X \to 2^X$ be a set-valued operator. For notational convenience, the operator will sometimes be identified with its graph by denoting $(x, y) \in A$ for $y \in A(x)$. We denote by $\mathbf{Dom}(A) \stackrel{\text{def}}{=} \{x \in X :\ Ax \neq \varnothing\}$ the *domain* of A and by $\mathbf{R}(A) \stackrel{\text{def}}{=} \{Ax : x \in \mathbf{Dom}(A)\}$ its range.

Definition 2.13 (Accretive operator) An operator A in X is *accretive* if $\|x - \hat{x}\| \leq \|x - \hat{x} + \lambda(y - \hat{y})\|$ whenever $\lambda > 0$ and $(x, y), (\hat{x}, \hat{y}) \in A$.

Accretivity is a way of expressing the monotonicity of an operator in any Banach space, that is, in the absence of an inner product.

Definition 2.14 (Nonexpansive operator) An operator $A\colon X \to X$ is called *nonexpansive* if it is 1-Lipschitz continuous, that is,

$$\|A(x) - A(\hat{x})\| \leq \|x - \hat{x}\|, \quad \forall x, \hat{x} \in X.$$

Definition 2.15 (Resolvent) Let $A\colon X \to 2^X$ and $\gamma > 0$. The *resolvent* of A is defined by

$$J_{\gamma A} \stackrel{\text{def}}{=} (\mathbf{I} + \gamma A)^{-1}.$$

We have the following equivalent characterization of accretivity, the proof of which can be found in, for example, Reich and Shoiykhet (2005).

Lemma 2.16 *The operator A is accretive if and only if its resolvent is a single-valued nonexpansive map on* $\mathbf{Dom}(J_{\lambda A})$ *for* $\lambda > 0$.

Definition 2.17 (*m*-accretive operator) An operator $A: X \to 2^X$ is *m*-accretive if it is accretive and $\mathbf{Dom}(J_{\lambda A}) = X$ for some (hence all) $\lambda > 0$.

In the Hilbertian case, the notion of *m*-accretivity coincides with maximal monotonicity, which is the celebrated Minty theorem.

The accretive operators theory plays an important role in proving solution existence and uniqueness of the abstract Cauchy problem

$$\begin{cases} \dot{x} + Ax \ni f, \\ x(t_0) = x_0. \end{cases} \tag{2.5}$$

For the particular case where $f = 0$, Crandall and Liggett (1971) proved that the limit (semigroup)

$$S(t)x_0 = \lim_{n\to\infty} (J_{tA/n})^n$$

is the unique strong solution to (2.5) under some closedness assumptions on the operator A. In the case where $f \neq 0$, Bénilan (1972) proved the existence and the uniqueness of a strong solution of the Cauchy problem under some closedness assumptions on the function f and the initial data x_0; however, the exponential formula does not hold. In the context of the nonlocal p-Laplacian evolution equation that will be at the heart of Section 3, this theory will be instrumental not only in proving well-posedness but also in establishing Lipschitz continuity of the solution as a function of the initial data and the second member f. A key step in proving this is to show that the nonlocal p-Laplacian operator belongs to a rich family of operators known as *m*-completely accretive operators. This family was introduced by Bénilan and Crandall (1991).

Let S be an open set of $\mathbb{R}^d$ and let $\mathcal{M}(S)$ be the space of measurable functions from S into $\mathbb{R}$. For $u, v \in \mathcal{M}(S)$, we write

$$u \ll v \quad \text{if and only if} \quad \int_S j(u)dx \leq \int_S j(v)dx$$

for all $j \in \mathcal{J}_0 \stackrel{\text{def}}{=} \{j: \mathbb{R} \to [0, +\infty], j \text{ convex, lsc}, j(0) = 0\}$.

Definition 2.18 (Completely accretive operator) Let A be an operator in $\mathcal{M}(S)$. We say that A is *completely accretive* if the following holds:

$$u - \hat{u} \ll u - \hat{u} + \lambda(v - \hat{v}) \quad \text{for all } \lambda > 0 \text{ and all } (u, v), (\hat{u}, \hat{v}) \in A.$$

The definition of completely accretive operators does not refer explicitly to topologies or norms. However, if A is completely accretive in $\mathcal{M}(S)$ and $A \subset L^p(S) \times L^p(S)$, $p \in [1, \infty]$, then A is accretive in $L^p(S)$.

Definition 2.19 (m-completely accretive operator) An operator A on X is m-completely accretive if it is completely accretive and $Dom(J_{\lambda A}) = X$ for all $\lambda > 0$.

2.3 Tools from Approximation Theory

2.3.1 Projector and Injector Operators

Let us recall some definitions and properties of Lebesgue spaces. Let S be a bounded subset of $\mathbb{R}^d$. For $q \in [1, +\infty]$, $L^q(S)$ is the standard Banach space of Lebesgue q-integrable functions on S. For a function $F: S \times S \to \mathbb{R}$, we define the $L^{\infty,q}(S^2)$-norm as

$$\|F\|_{L^{\infty,q}(S^2)} \stackrel{\text{def}}{=} \sup_{x \in S} \|F(x, \cdot)\|_{L^q(S)}.$$

If F is symmetric, then

$$\|F\|_{L^{\infty,q}(S^2)} = \sup_{y \in S} \|F(\cdot, y)\|_{L^q(S)}.$$

The space of functions on S^2 of bounded $L^{\infty,q}(S^2)$-norm, $L^{\infty,q}(S^2)$-norm is which is, of course, a Banach space. Throughout this Element, we will often use Fubini's theorem without explicitly referring to it.

Let $n \in \mathbb{N}^*$ and denote the multi-index $\boldsymbol{i} = (i_1, i_2, \ldots, i_d) \in [n]^d$. Here we assume $\Omega = [0, 1]^d$, partitioning Ω into cells (hypercubes)

$$Q \stackrel{\text{def}}{=} \left\{ \Omega_{\boldsymbol{i}}^{(n)} \stackrel{\text{def}}{=} \prod_{k=1}^{d}]\boldsymbol{x}_{i_k - 1}, \boldsymbol{x}_{i_k}] : \ \boldsymbol{i} \in [n]^d \right\}$$

of size $h_{\boldsymbol{i}} \stackrel{\text{def}}{=} |\Omega_{\boldsymbol{i}}^{(n)}|$ and maximal mesh size

$$\delta(n) \stackrel{\text{def}}{=} \max_{\boldsymbol{i} \in [n]^d} \max_{k \in [d]} (|\boldsymbol{x}_{i_k} - \boldsymbol{x}_{i_k - 1}|).$$

When the cells are equispaced, then $h_{\boldsymbol{i}} = 1/n^d$.

We now consider the operator $P_n: L^1(\Omega) \to \mathbb{R}^{n^d}$:

$$(P_n u)_{\boldsymbol{i}} \stackrel{\text{def}}{=} \frac{1}{h_{\boldsymbol{i}}} \int_{\Omega_{\boldsymbol{i}}^{(n)}} u(\boldsymbol{x}) d\boldsymbol{x}. \tag{2.6}$$

This operator can also be seen as a piecewise constant projector of u on the space of discrete functions. For simplicity, and with a slight abuse of notation, we keep the same notation for the projector $P_n: L^1(\Omega^2) \to \mathbb{R}^{n^d \times n^d}$.

Our aim is to study the relationship between solutions of discrete approximations and the solution of the continuum model. It is then convenient to introduce an intermediate model that is the continuum extension of the discrete solution. Toward this goal, we consider the piecewise constant injector I_n of a vector $\mathbf{v} \in \mathbb{R}^{n^d}$ into $L^2(\Omega)$ defined as

$$I_n \mathbf{v}(x) \stackrel{\text{def}}{=} \sum_{i \in [n]^d} \mathbf{v}_i \chi_{\Omega_i^{(n)}}(x), \tag{2.7}$$

where we recall that χ_C is the characteristic function of the set C, that is, takes 1 on C and 0 otherwise.

We can see immediately that the operator $I_n P_n$ is the orthogonal projector on the subspace $\text{Span}\left\{\chi_{\Omega_i^{(n)}} : i \in [n]^d\right\}$ of $L^1(\Omega)$. In turn, $I_n P_n u$ is the piecewise constant approximation of u.

Lemma 2.20 *For a function $u \in L^q(\Omega)$, $q \in [1, +\infty]$, we have*

$$\|I_n P_n u\|_{L^q(\Omega)} \leq \|u\|_{L^q(\Omega)}. \tag{2.8}$$

For a function $K \in L^{\infty,q}(\Omega^2)$, $q \in [1, +\infty]$, we have

$$\|I_n P_n K\|_{L^{\infty,q}(\Omega^2)} \leq \|K\|_{L^{\infty,q}(\Omega)^2}. \tag{2.9}$$

Proof: We prove (2.9), as (2.8) is a consequence of it. Let $\mathbf{K} = P_n K$. We have, $\forall x \in \Omega$,

$$\begin{aligned}
\int_\Omega I_n P_n |K(x,y)|^q dy &= \int_\Omega \sum_{i,j} |\mathbf{K}_{i,j}|^q \chi_{\Omega_i^{(n)}}(x) \chi_{\Omega_j^{(n)}}(y) dy \\
&= \sum_{i,j} h_j \left| \frac{1}{h_i h_j} \int_{\Omega_i^{(n)} \times \Omega_j^{(n)}} K(x', y') dx' dy' \right|^q \chi_{\Omega_i^{(n)}}(x) \\
&\leq \sum_i \left(\sum_j \frac{1}{h_i} \int_{\Omega_i^{(n)} \times \Omega_j^{(n)}} |K(x', y')|^q dx' dy' \right) \chi_{\Omega_i^{(n)}}(x) \\
&= \sum_i \left(\frac{1}{h_i} \int_{\Omega_i^{(n)}} \left(\int_\Omega |K(x', y')|^q dy' \right) dx' \right) \chi_{\Omega_i^{(n)}}(x) \\
&\leq \|K\|^q_{L^{\infty,q}(\Omega^2)} \sum_i \chi_{\Omega_i^{(n)}}(x) = \|K\|^q_{L^{\infty,q}(\Omega^2)}.
\end{aligned}$$

Taking the supremum on the left-hand side yields the bound. □

2.3.2 Lipschitz Spaces on Bounded Domains

For $N \in \mathbb{N}^*$, let S be a compact subset of $\mathbb{R}^N$. We introduce the Lipschitz spaces $\text{Lip}(s, L^q(S))$, $q \in [1, +\infty]$, which contain functions with, roughly speaking, s

"derivatives" in $L^q(S)$ (DeVore and Lorentz, 1993, chapter 2, section 9). These spaces will be a key tool for us to study the full discretization, as we will be able to get nonasymptotic error estimates for random graph models when adding the assumption of belonging to these spaces to the kernel $K(\cdot,\cdot)$ and the data (f,g).

Definition 2.21 For $F \in L^q(S)$, $q \in [1,+\infty]$, we define the (first-order) $L^q(S)$ modulus of smoothness by

$$\omega(F,h)_q \stackrel{\text{def}}{=} \sup_{z\in\mathbb{R}^d, |z|<h} \left(\int_{x,x+z\in S} |F(x+z) - F(x)|^q \, dx \right)^{1/q}. \tag{2.10}$$

The Lipschitz spaces $\mathrm{Lip}(s, L^q(S))$ consist of all functions F for which

$$|F|_{\mathrm{Lip}(s,L^q(S))} \stackrel{\text{def}}{=} \sup_{h>0} h^{-s}\omega(F,h)_q < +\infty.$$

We restrict ourselves to values $s \in]0,1]$, since, for $s > 1$, only constant functions are in $\mathrm{Lip}(s, L^q(S))$. It is easy to see that $|F|_{\mathrm{Lip}(s,L^q(S))}$ is a seminorm. The space $\mathrm{Lip}(s, L^q(S))$ is endowed with the norm

$$\|F\|_{\mathrm{Lip}(s,L^q(S))} \stackrel{\text{def}}{=} \|F\|_{L^q(S)} + |F|_{\mathrm{Lip}(s,L^q(S))}\,.$$

The space $\mathrm{Lip}(s, L^q(S))$ is the Besov space $\mathrm{B}^s_{q,\infty}$ (DeVore and Lorentz, 1993, chapter 2, section 10), which is very popular in approximation theory. In particular, $\mathrm{Lip}(s, L^{1/s}(S))$ contains the space $\mathrm{BV}(S)$ of functions of bounded variation on S; see DeVore and Lorentz (1993, chapter 2, lemma 9.2). Thus, Lipschitz spaces are rich enough to contain functions with both discontinuities and fractal structure.

We now state the following approximation error bounds, whose proofs use standard arguments from approximation theory. See Hafiene et al. (2018, section 6.2.1), for details.

Lemma 2.22 *There exists a positive constant C_s, depending only on s, such that, for all $F \in \mathrm{Lip}(s, L^q(S))$, $s \in]0,1]$, $q \in [1,+\infty]$,*

$$\|F - I_n P_n F\|_{L^q(S)} \le C_s \delta(n)^s \, |F|_{\mathrm{Lip}(s,L^q(S))}, \tag{2.11}$$

where $\delta(n)$ is the maximal mesh size.

Let $p \in]1,+\infty[$. If, in addition, $F \in L^\infty(S)$, then

$$\|F - I_n P_n F\|_{L^p(S)} \le C\big(p,q,s,\|F\|_{L^\infty(S)}\big)\delta(n)^{s\min(1,q/p)}, \tag{2.12}$$

where $C\big(p,q,s,\|F\|_{L^\infty(S)}\big)$ is a positive constant depending only on p, q, s, and $\|F\|_{L^\infty(S)}$.

We denote by $\mathrm{BV}([0,T];L^q(S))$ the Banach space of functions $f\colon \Omega\times[0,T]\to\mathbb{R}$ such that

$$\mathrm{Var}_q(f) \stackrel{\mathrm{def}}{=} \sup_{0\le t_0<t_1<\cdots<t_N\le T} \sum_{i=1}^{N} \left\| f(\cdot,t_i) - f(\cdot,t_{i-1}) \right\|_{L^q(S)} < +\infty,$$

endowed with the norm $\|f\|_{\mathrm{BV}([0,T];L^q(S))} \stackrel{\mathrm{def}}{=} \|f(0)\|_{L^q(S)} + \mathrm{Var}_q(f)$.

2.4 Tools from Graph Limit Theory

2.4.1 *Preliminaries*

A weighted graph $G = (V(G), E(G), \beta)$ consists of a finite set $V(G)$ of vertices, a finite set $E(G) \subset V(G)\times V(G)$ of edges, and a weight function $\beta\colon V(G)\times V(G)\to\mathbb{R}^+$. Each node $i\in V(G)$ is an abstract representation of an element of the data structure represented by the graph. An edge $(i,j)\in E(G)$ connects a pair of vertices i and $j\in V(G)$. In this case, we write $i\sim j$, i.e., i and j are neighbors. We say that G is a connected graph if, for all $i,j\in V(G)$, there exists a sequence $i_0,i_1,\ldots,i_m\in V(G)$ such that $i = i_0\sim i_1\sim\cdots\sim i_m = j$. In this section, we consider undirected connected graphs without parallel edges, in which case the edges are symmetric. The weight function represents a similarity measure between two vertices of the graph. Since we are dealing with undirected graphs, this function is symmetric: $\forall (i,j)\in V(G)^2$, $\beta(i,j)=\beta(i,j)$. The neighborhood of a vertex i (i.e., the set of vertices adjacent to i) is denoted by $\mathcal{N}(i)$, and the degree of a vertex i is defined as $\deg_G(i) = \sum_{j\sim i}\beta(i,j)$.

2.4.2 *L^q Graphons and Graph Limits*

We now review some definitions and results of the L^q theory of sparse graphs developed in Borgs et al. (2018, 2019). This theory generalizes both existing theory of bounded graphons that are adapted to dense graph limits (Lovász, 2012), and its extension in Bollobás and Riordan (2009) to sparse graphs under a "no dense spots" assumption. Here, we in the main follow Borgs et al. (2018, 2019), in which much more detail can be found. We will be more interested in the random case, which plays a central role in our study.

Definition 2.23 Let $q\in[1,+\infty]$, where an L^q *graphon* is a measurable, symmetric function $K\in L^q([0,1]^2)$.

Here the symmetry means $K(x,y) = K(y,x)$ for all $x,y\in[0,1]$. If we do not specify q, we assume that K is in L^1 and call it simply a graphon rather than an L^1 graphon.

Every finite weighted graph G_n such that $V(G_n) = [n]$, with edge weights $\{\beta_{ij}\}_{(i,j)\in[n]^2}$, can be represented by a measurable function $K_{G_n} : [0,1]^2 \to \mathbb{R}^+$. The construction is as follows. Let Q_n be a partition of $[0,1]$ to n equal intervals $Q_n = \left\{\mathcal{I}_k^{(n)} : k \in [n]\right\}$, and for every $x \in \mathcal{I}_i^{(n)}$ and $y \in \mathcal{I}_j^{(n)}$ we set

$$K_{G_n} \overset{\text{def}}{=} \begin{cases} \beta_{ij}, & \text{if } (i,j) \in E(G_n), \\ 0, & \text{otherwise.} \end{cases} \tag{2.13}$$

This construction is not unique; however, given a graph, the set of kernels arising from (2.13) can be considered equivalent via the weakly isomorphic relation (2.15). Informally, a graphon can be thought of as a generalization of the adjacency matrix of a (weighted) graph, which has a continuum number of vertices.

Now, we introduce the important metric on the space of graphons, which is the *cut metric*. (Strictly speaking, it is merely a pseudometric, since two graphons with cut distance zero between them need not be equal.) It is defined in terms of the cut norm introduced in Frieze and Kannan (1999).

Definition 2.24 (Cut metric) For a graphon $K\colon [0,1]^2 \to \mathbb{R}$, define the *cut norm* by

$$\|K\|_{\square} \overset{\text{def}}{=} \sup_{S,T\subset[0,1]} \left| \int_{S\times T} K(x,y)dxdy \right|, \tag{2.14}$$

where S and T range over measurable subsets of $[0,1]$. Given two graphons $K, K'\colon [0,1]^2 \to \mathbb{R}$, define

$$d_{\square}(K,K') \overset{\text{def}}{=} \|K - K'\|_{\square}$$

and the *cut metric* (or *cut distance*) $\delta_{\square}$ by

$$\delta_{\square}(K,K') \overset{\text{def}}{=} \inf_{\sigma} d_{\square}(K^{\sigma},K'),$$

where σ ranges over all measure-preserving bijections $\sigma\colon [0,1] \to [0,1]$ and $K^{\sigma}(x,y) \overset{\text{def}}{=} K(\sigma(x),\sigma(y))$.

For a survey covering many properties of the cut metric, see Lovász (2012), Borgs et al. (2019), and Janson (2013), and references therein. The notions d and δ extended to any norm on the spaces of graphons. In particular, for $1 \le q \le \infty$, by definition

$$d_q(K,K') \overset{\text{def}}{=} \|K - K'\|_{L^q([0,1]^2)} \qquad \text{and} \qquad \delta_q(K,K') \overset{\text{def}}{=} \inf_{\sigma} d_q(K^{\sigma},K'),$$

with σ ranging over all measure-preserving bijections $\sigma\colon [0,1] \to [0,1]$ as before.

We now introduce the weakly isomorphic relation, denoted $\approx$, which identifies sets of graphons that all have a cut distance of zero apart (Lovász, 2012, corollary 10.34). Let K, K' be two graphons; we define the weakly isomorphic relation as follows:

$$K \approx K' \Leftrightarrow \delta_\square(K, K') = 0. \tag{2.15}$$

Theorem 2.25 (Borgs et al., 2019, theorem 2.13; Compactness of the L^q ball with respect to the cut metric) *Let $1 < q \leq \infty$ and $C > 0$; the ball $\mathcal{B}_{L^q([0,1]^2)}(C) \stackrel{\text{def}}{=} \left\{ L^q \text{ graphons } K : \|K\|_{L^q([0,1]^2)} \leq C \right\}$ is compact with respect to the cut metric $\delta_\square$ (after identifying points of distance zero).*

2.4.3 Random Graphs

The theory of random graphs was founded in the 1950s and 1960s by Erdös and Rényi (1960), who started the systematic study of the space of graphs with n labeled vertices and $M = M(n)$ edges, with all graphs equiprobable. The aim is to turn the set of all graphs with n vertices into a probability space. Intuitively, we should be able to generate a sequence of graphs $\{G_n\}_{n\in\mathbb{N}}$ randomly as follows: for each edge $(i, j) \in [n]^2$, we decide by some random experiment whether or not (i, j) will be an edge of G_n. These experiments are performed independently.

Example 2.26 (The Erdös–Renyi graphs) Let $p \in]0, 1[$ and consider the sequence of random graphs $G(n, p) = (V(G(n, p)), E(G(n, p)))$ such that $V(G(n, p)) = [n]$ and the probability $\mathbb{P}\{(i, j) \in E(G(n, p))\} = p$ for any $(i, j) \in [n]^2$. Then, for any simple graph F, $t(F, G(n, p))$ converges almost surely to $p^{|E(F)|}$ as $n \to \infty$ (Borgs et al., 2008), and $\{G(n, p)\}$ converges almost surely to the p-constant graphon, where $t(F, G(n, p))$ is the probability that a random map of $V(F)$ into $V(G)$ is a homomorphism (adjacency-preserving map).

Figure 2.1 shows a realization of the Erdös–Renyi graph model for $n = 16$, its pixel picture, and the corresponding graphon.

2.4.4 Sparse K-Random Graph Models

Let $G = (V(G), E(G))$ be a weighted graph with vertex set $V(G)$ and edge set $E(G) \subseteq V(G)^2$, respectively. In G, every edge $(i, j) \in E(G)$ (allowing loops with $i = j$) is given a weight $\beta_{ij} \in \mathbb{R}^+$.[1] We set $\beta_{ij} = 0$ whenever $(i, j) \notin E(G)$.

The idea underlying the sparse K-random graph model proposed by Borgs et al. (2019) is that each L^q graphon K gives rise to a natural random

[1] In Borgs et al. (2019), the weights are even allowed to be negative; but we will not consider this situation, which is meaningless in our context.

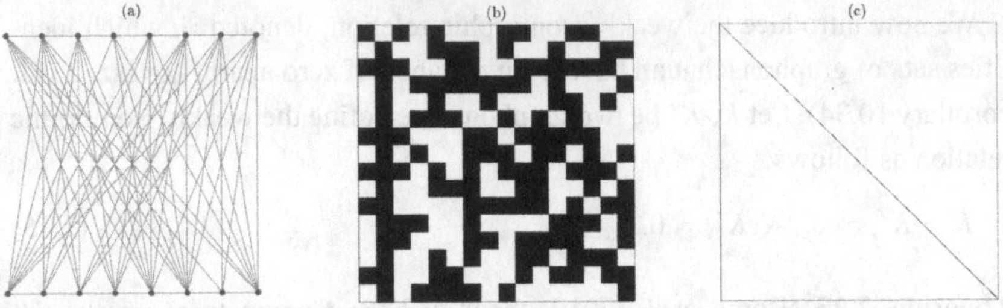

Figure 2.1 (a) A realization of the Erdös–Renyi random graph model with $p = 0.5$. (b) Its pixel picture. (c) The corresponding graphon.

graph model, which produces a sequence of sparse graphs converging to K in an appropriate metric. Inspired by their work, we propose the following construction.

Definition 2.27 Fix $n \in \mathbb{N}^*$, and let K be an L^1 graphon and $\rho_n > 0$. Take the equispaced partition of $[0,1]$ in intervals $]x_{i-1}, x_i]$, $i \in [n]$, where $x_i = i/n$. Let $\mathbf{K} \in \mathbb{R}_+^{n\times n}$ be a weight matrix such that

($\mathbf{H}_w$.1) $\left\|I_n\mathbf{K} - K\right\|_{L^1([0,1]^2)} \to 0$ as $n \to +\infty$.
($\mathbf{H}_w$.2) $\left\|I_n\mathbf{K}(x,\cdot) - K(x,\cdot)\right\|_{L^1([0,1])} \to 0$ uniformly in $x \in [0,1]$.

Generate the random graph

$$G_n = (V(G_n), E(G_n)) \stackrel{\text{def}}{=} \mathbf{G}(n, K, \rho_n)$$

as follows: join each pair $(i,j) \in [n]^2$ of vertices independently, with probability

$$\mathbb{P}\left((i,j) \in E(G_n)|\mathbf{X}\right) = \rho_n\hat{\mathbf{K}}_{ij}, \quad \text{where} \quad \hat{\mathbf{K}}_{ij} \stackrel{\text{def}}{=} \min\left(\mathbf{K}_{ij}, \rho_n^{-1}\right). \tag{2.16}$$

Remark 2.28 In the original sparse K-random graph model defined in Borgs et al. (2019), which we will adopt in Section 4 to study the nonlocal p-Laplacian variational problem with bounded assumption on the kernel considered (see Definition 2.32), the x_i's are random iid samples drawn from the uniform distribution on $[0,1]$. Moreover, $\mathbf{K}_{ij} = K(x_i, x_j)$. In this case, it follows from Borgs et al. (2019), theorem 2.14(a), which relies on Hoeffding (1961), that assumption **($\mathbf{H}_w$.1)** holds with probability 1.
Another interesting case is where $\mathbf{K} = P_nK$. Thanks to Lemma 2.20, $\left\|I_nP_n\mathbf{K}\right\|_{L^1(\Omega^2)} \le \left\|K\right\|_{L^1(\Omega^2)}$ with probability 1. Thus, the Lebesgue differentiation theorem and the dominated convergence theorem allow one to assert that $I_nP_n\mathbf{K}$ converges to K in $L^1(\Omega^2)$. In turn, assumption **($\mathbf{H}_w$.1)** holds.

For appropriate choices of ρ_n, the graph model constructed according to Definition 2.27 allows one to sample both dense and sparse graphs from the graphon K. In particular, the sparsity assumption $\rho_n \to 0$ reflects the fact that ρ_n needs to be arbitrarily close to zero in order to see the unbounded/singular part of K. The assumption that $n\rho_n \to +\infty$ means the average degree tends to infinity. To check this, the average number of edges in this graph model is

$$\mathbb{E}\left(E(\mathbf{G}(n,K,\rho_n))\right) = \rho_n n^2 \left(\|I_n\mathbf{K}\|_{L^1([0,1]^2)} - \left\|\left(I_n\mathbf{K} - \rho_n^{-1}\right)_+\right\|_{L^1([0,1]^2)}\right).$$

By assumption ($\mathbf{H}_w$.**1**), we have $\|I_n\mathbf{K}\|_{L^1([0,1]^2)} = \|K\|_{L^1([0,1]^2)} + o(1)$. Moreover, since $\rho_n \to 0$, we have from (2.17) that $\left\|\left(I_n\mathbf{K} - \rho_n^{-1}\right)_+\right\|_{L^1([0,1]^2)} = o(1)$. In turn,

$$\mathbb{E}\left(E(\mathbf{G}(n,K,\rho_n))\right) = \rho_n n^2 \left(\|K\|_{L^1([0,1]^2)} + o(1)\right).$$

As expected, this gives rise to a sparse graph whose edge density is $\rho_n \to 0$. For the average degree of this graph model, arguing similarly to the preceding discussion, and using ($\mathbf{H}_w$.**2**), we have

$$\begin{aligned}\mathbb{E}\left(\deg_{G_n}(i)\right) &= \rho_n n \left(\|I_n\mathbf{K}(x_i,\cdot)\|_{L^1([0,1])} - \left\|\left(I_n\mathbf{K}(x_i,\cdot) - \rho_n^{-1}\right)_+\right\|_{L^1([0,1])}\right)\\ &= \rho_n n \left(\int_0^1 K(x_i,y)dy + o(1)\right).\end{aligned}$$

As anticipated, the average degree is indeed unbounded, since $\rho_n n \to +\infty$. The preceding sequence of graphs generated also enjoys the following convergence result.

Proposition 2.29 *Let K be an L^1 graphon and $\mathbf{K}$ be a weight matrix such that ($\mathbf{H}_w$.1) holds. If $\rho_n > 0$ with $\rho_n \to 0$ and $n\rho_n \to +\infty$ as $n \to +\infty$, then $\rho_n^{-1}\mathbf{G}(n,K,\rho_n)$ converges almost surely to K in the cut distance metric.*

Proof: We essentially adapt the arguments in the proof of Borgs et al. (2019, theorem 2.14(b)). More precisely, since ($\mathbf{H}_w$.**1**) holds, one has to show Borgs et al. (2019), (7.1). For this, we invoke Borgs et al. (2019, lemma 7.3), by checking the condition (7.3) therein. We have by sublinearity of $(\cdot)_+$ that

$$\begin{aligned}\frac{1}{n^2}\sum_{(i,j)\in[n]^2}\left(\mathbf{K}_{ij} - \rho_n^{-1}\right)_+ &= \int_{[0,1]^2}\left(I_n\mathbf{K}(x,y) - \rho_n^{-1}\right)_+ dxdy\\ &\le \int_{[0,1]^2}\left(I_n\mathbf{K}(x,y) - K(x,y)\right)_+ dxdy + \int_{[0,1]^2}\left(K(x,y) - \rho_n^{-1}\right)_+ dxdy\\ &\le \|I_n\mathbf{K} - K\|_{L^1([0,1]^2)} + \int_{[0,1]^2}\left(K(x,y) - \rho_n^{-1}\right)_+ dxdy.\end{aligned} \tag{2.17}$$

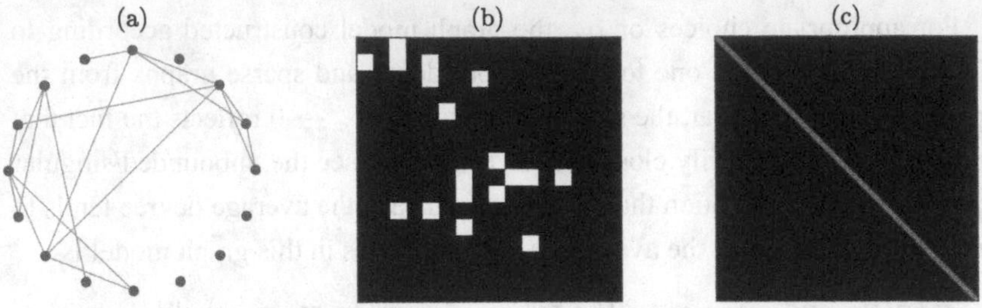

Figure 2.2 (a) A realization of the sparse graph model associated to the kernel of Example 2.30 with $\beta = 0.8$ and $\rho_n = \log(n)^{1.1}/n$. (b) Its pixel picture. (c) The corresponding kernel.

The right-hand side in (2.17) goes to 0 as $n \to +\infty$ by $(\mathbf{H_w.1})$ and since $\rho_n \to 0$. Indeed, for every $L > 0$, the limit superior of the last term is bounded by $\|(K - L)_+\|_{L^1([0,1]^2)}$, and this can be made arbitrarily small by choosing L large. □

Example 2.30 For an example that cannot be handled using L^∞ graphons, and thus does not enter in the framework of Hafiene et al. (2018, 2020), consider a K-random graph model $\mathbf{G}(n, K, \rho_n)$ constructed according to Definition 2.27 with $\mathbf{K} = P_n K$, where $K(x,y) = J(x-y)$, $J : z \in [-1,1] \mapsto 2^{-1}(1-\beta)(2-\beta)|z|^{-\beta}$, $\beta \in]0,1[$. First, observe that the radially symmetric kernel J is singular but fulfills all assumptions, that is, J is a symmetric nonnegative function in $L^1(\Omega - \Omega)$. In addition, by virtue of Remark 2.28, $(\mathbf{H_w.1})$–$(\mathbf{H_w.2})$ also hold with

$$\|K\|_{L^1([0,1]^2)} = 1 \text{ and}$$

$$\int_0^1 K(x,y)dy = 2^{-1}(2-\beta)\left(x^{1-\beta} + (1-x)^{1-\beta}\right) \in 2^{-1}(2-\beta)[1, 2^\beta].$$

Figure 2.2 shows a realization of the sparse graph model for $n = 16$ associated to this kernel, its pixel picture, and the corresponding kernel.

We also have the following convergence result in the $L^{\infty,1}$ norm that will be instrumental in Section 3.4. According to the construction in Definition 2.27, we let $\mathbf{\Lambda}_{ij}$, $(i,j) \in [n]^2, i \neq j$, be random variables such that $\rho_n \mathbf{\Lambda}_{ij}$ follows a Bernoulli distribution with parameter $\rho_n \hat{\mathbf{K}}_{ij}$. For each row $i \in [n]$, $(\mathbf{\Lambda}_{ij})_{j \in [n]}$ are independent.

Lemma 2.31 *Let K be a nonnegative $L^{\infty,1}$ graphon. Take the weight matrix $\mathbf{K} = P_n K$. Assume that $\rho_n \to 0$ and $n\rho_n = \omega\left((\log n)^\gamma\right)^2$ for some $\gamma > 1$. Then, with probability 1,*

[2] $\omega(\cdot)$ is the Landau notation, which means that $g = \omega(f) \Leftrightarrow f = o(g)$.

$$\|I_n\mathbf{\Lambda}\|_{L^{\infty,1}([0,1]^2)} - \|I_n\hat{\mathbf{K}}\|_{L^{\infty,1}([0,1]^2)} \to 0.$$

If, moreover, ($\mathbf{H}_w$.2) holds, then

$$\|I_n\mathbf{\Lambda}\|_{L^{\infty,1}([0,1]^2)} \to \|K\|_{L^{\infty,1}([0,1]^2)},$$

with probability 1.

Proof: For any $\varepsilon > 0$, we have, by the union bound,

$$\mathbb{P}\left(\left|\|I_n\mathbf{\Lambda}\|_{L^{\infty,1}([0,1]^2)} - \|I_n\hat{\mathbf{K}}\|_{L^{\infty,1}([0,1]^2)}\right| \geq \varepsilon\right) \leq \mathbb{P}\left(\max_i\left|\sum_j \rho_n(\mathbf{\Lambda}_{ij} - \hat{\mathbf{K}}_{ij})\right| \geq \varepsilon\rho_n n\right)$$
$$\leq \sum_i \mathbb{P}\left(\left|\sum_j \rho_n(\mathbf{\Lambda}_{ij} - \hat{\mathbf{K}}_{ij})\right| \geq \varepsilon\rho_n n\right).$$

Since $\left(\rho_n\mathbf{\Lambda}_{ij}\right)_j$ are independent Bernoulli variables with means $\left(\rho_n\hat{\mathbf{K}}_{ij}\right)_j$, it follows from the variant of the Chernoff bound in Borgs et al. (2019, Lemma 7.1), that for every $\varepsilon > 0$,

$$\mathbb{P}\left(\left|\|I_n\mathbf{\Lambda}\|_{L^{\infty,1}([0,1]^2)} - \|I_n\hat{\mathbf{K}}\|_{L^{\infty,1}([0,1]^2)}\right| \geq \varepsilon\right)$$
$$\leq 2\sum_i \exp\left(-\frac{1}{3}\min\left(\frac{\varepsilon\rho_n n}{\rho_n\sum_j\hat{\mathbf{K}}_{ij}}, 1\right)\varepsilon\rho_n n\right)$$
$$\leq 2n\exp\left(-\frac{1}{3}\min\left(\frac{\varepsilon}{\|I_n\hat{\mathbf{K}}\|_{L^{\infty,1}([0,1]^2)}}, 1\right)\varepsilon\rho_n n\right)$$
$$\leq 2n\exp\left(-\frac{1}{3}\min\left(\frac{\varepsilon}{\|K\|_{L^{\infty,1}([0,1]^2)}}, 1\right)\varepsilon\omega\left((\log n)^\gamma\right)\right) \leq 2n^{-\omega((\log n)^{\gamma-1})},$$

since $\gamma > 1$, and where we used (2.16) and Lemma 2.20 to show that

$$\|I_n\hat{\mathbf{K}}\|_{L^{\infty,1}([0,1]^2)} \leq \|I_n\mathbf{K}\|_{L^{\infty,1}([0,1]^2)} = \|I_nP_nK\|_{L^{\infty,1}([0,1]^2)} \leq \|K\|_{L^{\infty,1}([0,1]^2)}.$$

Invoking the (first) Borel–Cantelli lemma, we have the first claim. On the other hand,

$$\left|\|I_n\hat{\mathbf{K}}\|_{L^{\infty,1}([0,1]^2)} - \|K\|_{L^{\infty,1}([0,1]^2)}\right|$$
$$\leq \|I_n\hat{\mathbf{K}} - I_nP_nK\|_{L^{\infty,1}([0,1]^2)} + \|I_nP_nK - K\|_{L^{\infty,1}([0,1]^2)}$$
$$\leq \|(K-\rho_n^{-1})_+\|_{L^{\infty,1}([0,1]^2)} + \|(I_nP_nK - K)_+\|_{L^{\infty,1}([0,1]^2)} + \|I_nP_nK - K\|_{L^{\infty,1}([0,1]^2)}$$
$$\leq \|(K-\rho_n^{-1})_+\|_{L^{\infty,1}([0,1]^2)} + 2\|I_nP_nK - K\|_{L^{\infty,1}([0,1]^2)}.$$

Since $\rho_n \to 0$ and in view of ($\mathbf{H}_w$.**2**), the right-hand side in the preceding display goes to 0 as $n \to +\infty$. When this is combined with the first claim, we obtain the desired conclusion. □

We close this section with the description of the model of inhomogeneous random graphs that we will adopt in Section 4.4, which is a generalization of the Definition 2.27, but we restrict only on the case of bounded graphons. This random graph model is motivated by the construction of inhomogeneous random graphs in Bollobás et al. (2007) and Bollobás and Riordan (2009). It is generated as follows.

Definition 2.32 Fix $n \in \mathbb{N}^*$ and let K be a symmetric measurable function on Ω^2. Generate the graph $G_n = (V(G_n), E(G_n)) \stackrel{\text{def}}{=} G_{q_n}(n, K)$ as follows:

1) Generate n independent and identically distributed (i.i.d.) random variables $\mathbf{X} \stackrel{\text{def}}{=} (\mathbf{X}_1, \cdots, \mathbf{X}_n)$ from the uniform distribution on Ω. Let $\{\mathbf{X}_{(i)}\}_{i=1}^n$ be the order statistics of the random vector $\mathbf{X}$, that is, $\mathbf{X}_{(i)}$ is the ith smallest value.
2) Conditionally on $\mathbf{X}$, join each pair $(i, j) \in [n]^2$ of vertices independently, with probability $q_n \hat{\mathbf{K}}^{\mathbf{X}}$, that is, for every $(i, j) \in [n]^2$, $i \neq j$,

$$\mathbb{P}((i, j) \in E(G_n)|\mathbf{X}) = q_n \hat{\mathbf{K}}_{ij}^{\mathbf{X}}, \tag{2.18}$$

where

$$\hat{\mathbf{K}}_{ij}^{\mathbf{X}} \stackrel{\text{def}}{=} \min\left(\frac{1}{\left|\Omega_{nij}^{\mathbf{X}}\right|} \int_{\Omega_{nij}^{\mathbf{X}}} K(x, y) dx dy, 1/q_n\right), \tag{2.19}$$

and

$$\Omega_{nij}^{\mathbf{X}} \stackrel{\text{def}}{=}]\mathbf{X}_{(i-1)}, \mathbf{X}_{(i)}] \times]\mathbf{X}_{(j-1)}, \mathbf{X}_{(j)}] \tag{2.20}$$

where q_n is nonnegative and uniformly bounded in n.

A graph $G_{q_n}(n, K)$ generated according to this procedure is called a K-random inhomogeneous graph generated by a random sequence $\mathbf{X}$.

We denote by $\boldsymbol{x} = (\boldsymbol{x}_1, \cdots, \boldsymbol{x}_n)$ the realization of $\mathbf{X}$. To lighten the notation, we also denote

$$\Omega_{ni}^{\mathbf{X}} \stackrel{\text{def}}{=}]\mathbf{X}_{(i-1)}, \mathbf{X}_{(i)}], \quad \Omega_{ni}^{\boldsymbol{x}} \stackrel{\text{def}}{=}]\boldsymbol{x}_{(i-1)}, \boldsymbol{x}_{(i)}], \text{ and}$$
$$\Omega_{nij}^{\boldsymbol{x}} \stackrel{\text{def}}{=}]\boldsymbol{x}_{(i-1)}, \boldsymbol{x}_{(i)}] \times]\boldsymbol{x}_{(j-1)}, \boldsymbol{x}_{(j)}] \quad i, j \in [n]. \tag{2.21}$$

As the realization of the random vector **X** is fixed, we define

$$\hat{\mathbf{K}}_{ij}^{x} \stackrel{\text{def}}{=} \min\left(\frac{1}{\left|\Omega_{nij}^{x}\right|}\int_{\Omega_{nij}^{x}} K(x,y)dxdy, 1/q_n\right), \quad \forall (i,j) \in [n]^2, \quad i \neq j. \tag{2.22}$$

We put the following assumptions on the parameters of the graph sequence $\{G_{q_n}(n,K)\}_{n\in\mathbb{N}^*}$.

Assumption 2.1 *We suppose that q_n and K are such that the following hold:*

(H_w^b.1) *$G_{q_n}(n,K)$ converges almost surely and its limit is the graphon $K \in L^\infty(\Omega^2)$;*
(H_w^b.2) $\sup_{n\geq 1} q_n < +\infty$.

Graph models that verify ($\mathbf{H}_w^b$.1)–($\mathbf{H}_w^b$.2) are discussed in Hafiene et al. (2020, Proposition 2.1). They encompass the dense random graph model (i.e., with $\Theta(n^2)$ edges) extensively studied in Lovász and Szegedy (2006) and Borgs et al. (2011), for which $q_n \geq c > 0$. This graph model allows also to generate sparse (but not too sparse) graph models (see Bollobás and Riordan, 2009); that is, graphs with $o(n^2)$ but $\omega(n)$ edges, namely the average degree tends to infinity with n. For example, one can take $q_n = \exp(-\log(n)^{1-\delta}) = o(1)$, where $\delta \in]0,1[$.

3 Nonlocal p-Laplacian Evolution Problem on Graphs

3.1 Problem Statement

This section is devoted to studying consistent discretization of the following nonlocal p-Laplacian evolution problem with homogeneous Neumann boundary conditions:

$$\begin{cases} \frac{\partial}{\partial t}u(\boldsymbol{x},t) = -\Delta_p^K u(\boldsymbol{x},t) + f(\boldsymbol{x},t), & \boldsymbol{x} \in \Omega, t > 0, \\ u(\boldsymbol{x},0) = g(\boldsymbol{x}), & \boldsymbol{x} \in \Omega, \end{cases} \tag{$\mathcal{P}$}$$

where Δ_p^K is the nonlocal p-Laplacian, $p \in [1,+\infty[$, $\Omega \subset \mathbb{R}^d$ is a bounded domain, and $K\colon \Omega\times\Omega \to \mathbb{R}$ is the kernel function. Following the discussion of the introduction, in the sequel we will take $\Omega = [0,1]^d$.

In this section, we consider the following assumptions on the kernel:

(H.1) K is a nonnegative measurable function.
(H.2) K is symmetric, that is, $K(\boldsymbol{x},\boldsymbol{y}) = K(\boldsymbol{y},\boldsymbol{x})$.

(H.3) $\sup_{x\in\Omega} \int_\Omega K(x,y)dy < +\infty$.

By **(H.2)**, it is straightforward to see that

$$\sup_{x\in\Omega} \int_\Omega K(x,y)dy = \sup_{y\in\Omega} \int_\Omega K(x,y)dx,$$

and thus, **(H.3)** is equivalent to

$$\sup_{y\in\Omega} \int_\Omega K(x,y)dx < +\infty.$$

When the kernel is such that $K(x,y) = J(x-y)$, where $J\colon \mathbb{R}^d \to \mathbb{R}$, then **(H.1)**, **(H.2)**, and **(H.3)** read:

(H'.1) J is nonnegative and measurable.
(H'.2) J is symmetric, that is, $J(-x) = J(x)$.
(H'.3) $\int_{\Omega-\Omega} J(x)dx < +\infty$.

Recall that $\Omega - \Omega$ is the Minkowski sum of Ω and $-\Omega$. In the case $\Omega = [0,1]^d$, we obviously have $\Omega - \Omega = [-1,1]^d$.

The main goal of the present section is to study numerical approximations of the evolution problem $(\mathcal{P})$, which, in turn, will allow us to establish consistency estimates of the fully discretized p-Laplacian problem on sparse graphs whose limits are known not necessarily to be bounded graphons.

3.2 Well-Posedness

3.2.1 The Case $p \in]1,+\infty[$

To lighten notation, for $1 < p < +\infty$, we define the function

$$\Psi\colon x \in \mathbb{R} \mapsto |x|^{p-2}x = \operatorname{sign}(x)|x|^{p-1},$$

where we take $\operatorname{sign}(0) = 0$. The next lemma summarizes key monotonicity and continuity properties of Ψ that will be instrumental to us in the rest of this Element.

Lemma 3.1 (i) *Monotonicity: assume that the constant β satisfies $\beta \in [\max(p,2),+\infty[$. Then, for all $x,y \in \mathbb{R}$,*

$$(\Psi(y) - \Psi(x))(y-x) \geq C_1|y-x|^\beta (|y|+|x|)^{p-\beta}, \tag{3.1}$$

where the constant C_1 is sharp and given by

$$C_1 = 2^{2-p}\min(1,p-1). \tag{3.2}$$

In particular,

$$(\Psi(y) - \Psi(x))(y-x) \geq C_1 \begin{cases} |y-x|^p & p \in [2, +\infty[, \\ |y-x|^2 (|y| + |x|)^{p-2} & p \in]1, 2]. \end{cases} \tag{3.3}$$

(ii) *Continuity: assume that the constant α satisfies $\alpha \in [0, \min(1, p-1)]$. Then, for all $x, y \in \mathbb{R}$,*

$$|\Psi(y) - \Psi(x)| \leq C_2 |y-x|^\alpha (|y| + |x|)^{p-1-\alpha}, \tag{3.4}$$

where the constant C_2 is sharp and given by

$$C_2 = \max(2^{2-p}, (p-1)2^{2-p}, 1). \tag{3.5}$$

In particular,

$$|\Psi(y) - \Psi(x)| \leq C_2 \begin{cases} |y-x| (|y| + |x|)^{p-2} & p \in [2, +\infty[, \\ |y-x|^{p-1} & p \in]1, 2]. \end{cases} \tag{3.6}$$

PROOF:

(i) For (3.1), see Byström (2005, theorem 2.2). For (3.3), set $\beta = p$ for $p \geq 2$ and $\beta = 2$, and otherwise in (3.1); see also the seminal results of Glowinski and Marrocco (1975, lemma 5.1 and lemma 5.2).

(ii) For (3.4), see Byström (2005, theorem 2.1). For (3.6), set $\alpha = 1$ for $p \geq 2$ and $\alpha - p - 1$, and otherwise in (3.4); see also the seminal results of Glowinski and Marrocco (1975, lemma 5.3 and lemma 5.4).

□

We now collect some preliminary properties of the nonlocal p-Laplacian given by (1.1).

Proposition 3.2 *Assume that K satisfies* **(H.1)**, **(H.2)**, *and* **(H.3)**.

(i) *Δ_p^K is positively homogeneous of degree $p-1$.*

(ii) *If $p > 2$, $L^{p-1}(\Omega) \subset \mathrm{dom}(\Delta_p^K)$.*

(iii) *If $1 < p \leq 2$, $\mathrm{dom}(\Delta_p^K) = L^1(\Omega)$ and Δ_p^K is closed in $L^1(\Omega) \times L^1(\Omega)$.*

(iv) *Let $h\colon \mathbb{R} \to \mathbb{R}$ be a nondecreasing function. Then, for every $u, v \in L^p(\Omega)$,*

$$\begin{aligned} 0 &\leq \int_\Omega \left(\Delta_p^K u(\boldsymbol{x}) - \Delta_p^K v(\boldsymbol{x})\right) h(u(\boldsymbol{x}) - v(\boldsymbol{x})) d\boldsymbol{x} \\ &= \frac{1}{2} \int_{\Omega^2} K(\boldsymbol{x}, \boldsymbol{y}) (\Psi(u(\boldsymbol{y}) - u(\boldsymbol{x})) - \Psi(v(\boldsymbol{y}) - v(\boldsymbol{x}))) \\ &\qquad \cdot (h(u(\boldsymbol{y}) - v(\boldsymbol{y})) - h(u(\boldsymbol{x}) - v(\boldsymbol{x}))) \, d\boldsymbol{y} d\boldsymbol{x}. \end{aligned} \tag{3.7}$$

If h is bounded, then this holds for any $u, v \in \mathrm{dom}(\Delta_p^K)$.

(v) *For every $u, v \in L^p(\Omega)$,*

$$\int_\Omega \left(\Delta_p^K u(x) - \Delta_p^K v(x)\right)(u(x) - v(x))\,dx \geq \frac{C}{2}\left(\int_{\Omega^2} K(x,y)|(u(y) - u(x)) - (v(y) - v(x))|^p\,dy\,dx\right)^{\max(1,2/p)}$$

where

$$C = \begin{cases} C_1 & p \in [2, +\infty[, \\ 2^{2p-5} C_1 \|K\|_{L^{\infty,1}(\Omega^2)}^{1-2/p} \left(\|u\|_{L^p(\Omega)} + \|v\|_{L^p(\Omega)}\right)^{p-2} & p \in]1,2[. \end{cases}$$

and C_1 is the constant in (3.2)*. If $u, v \in L^\infty(\Omega)$, then*

$$\int_\Omega \left(\Delta_p^K u(x) - \Delta_p^K v(x)\right)(u(x) - v(x))\,dx \geq \frac{C}{2}\left(\int_{\Omega^2} K(x,y)|(u(y) - u(x)) - (v(y) - v(x))|^2\,dy\,dx\right)^{\max(1,p/2)},$$

where

$$C = \begin{cases} C_1 & p \in [2, +\infty[, \\ 2^{p-2} C_1 \left(\|u\|_{L^\infty(\Omega)} + \|v\|_{L^\infty(\Omega)}\right)^{p-2} & p \in]1,2[. \end{cases}$$

(vi) *For $p \in]1,2]$ and every $u, v \in L^2(\Omega)$,*

$$\int_\Omega \left(\Delta_p^K u(x) - \Delta_p^K v(x)\right)(u(x) - v(x))\,dx \geq C\|\Delta_p^K u - \Delta_p^K v\|_{L^2(\Omega)}^{p/(p-1)},$$

where $C = 2^{\frac{p-2}{2(p-1)}}\left(C_2^{1/2}\|K\|_{L^{\infty,1}(\Omega^2)}\right)^{\frac{1}{1-p}}(1 - 1/p)$, and C_2 is the constant in (3.5)*.*

(vii) *For $p \in]1, +\infty[$, Δ_p^K is completely accretive and satisfies the range condition*

$$L^p(\Omega) \subset \operatorname{ran}(\mathbf{I} + \Delta_p^K). \tag{3.8}$$

Consequently, the resolvent $J_{\lambda\Delta_p^K} \stackrel{\text{def}}{=} \left(\mathbf{I} + \lambda\Delta_p^K\right)^{-1}$, $\lambda > 0$, is single-valued on $L^p(\Omega)$ and nonexpansive in $L^q(\Omega)$ for all $q \in [1, +\infty]$.

Proof: Claims (i), (ii), and (iii) follow from Andreu et al. (2008b, remark 2.2) which still holds for our larger class of kernels K.

For (iv), see Hafiene et al. (2018, lemma A.2). Monotonicity is immediate, since h is nondecreasing.

The proof of (vii) is the same as that of Andreu et al. (2008b, theorem 2.4), where we invoke the monotonicity claim (i).

We now show (v)[3]. The case $p \in [2, +\infty[$ is immediate by inserting Lemma 3.1(i) into (3.7) with $h(x) = x$. For $p \in]1, 2]$, to lighten notation, denote the nonlocal gradient $\nabla^{\mathrm{NL}} u(\boldsymbol{x}, \boldsymbol{y}) = u(\boldsymbol{y}) - u(\boldsymbol{x})$. We then have by Lemma 3.1(i) that

$$C_1 |\nabla^{\mathrm{NL}}(u - v)(\boldsymbol{x}, \boldsymbol{y})|^2 \leq \left(\Psi(\nabla^{\mathrm{NL}} u(\boldsymbol{x}, \boldsymbol{y})) - \Psi(\nabla^{\mathrm{NL}} v(\boldsymbol{x}, \boldsymbol{y}))\right)$$
$$\left(\nabla^{\mathrm{NL}} u(\boldsymbol{x}, \boldsymbol{y}) - \nabla^{\mathrm{NL}} v(\boldsymbol{x}, \boldsymbol{y})\right) \cdot \left(|\nabla^{\mathrm{NL}} u(\boldsymbol{x}, \boldsymbol{y})| + |\nabla^{\mathrm{NL}} v(\boldsymbol{x}, \boldsymbol{y})|\right)^{2-p}. \quad (3.9)$$

Taking the power $p/2$, multiplying by K, and integrating, we get

$$C_1^{p/2} \int_{\Omega^2} K(\boldsymbol{x}, \boldsymbol{y}) |\nabla^{\mathrm{NL}}(u - v)(\boldsymbol{x}, \boldsymbol{y})|^p \, d\boldsymbol{x} d\boldsymbol{y} \leq$$
$$\int_{\Omega^2} \left(K(\boldsymbol{x}, \boldsymbol{y}) \left(\Psi(\nabla^{\mathrm{NL}} u(\boldsymbol{x}, \boldsymbol{y})) - \Psi(\nabla^{\mathrm{NL}} v(\boldsymbol{x}, \boldsymbol{y}))\right)\left(\nabla^{\mathrm{NL}} u(\boldsymbol{x}, \boldsymbol{y}) - \nabla^{\mathrm{NL}} v(\boldsymbol{x}, \boldsymbol{y})\right)\right)^{p/2}$$
$$\left(K(\boldsymbol{x}, \boldsymbol{y})^{1/p} \left(|\nabla^{\mathrm{NL}} u(\boldsymbol{x}, \boldsymbol{y})| + |\nabla^{\mathrm{NL}} v(\boldsymbol{x}, \boldsymbol{y})|\right)\right)^{(2-p)p/2} d\boldsymbol{x} d\boldsymbol{y}.$$

It is easily seen that

$$\left(K \cdot \left(\Psi(\nabla^{\mathrm{NL}} u) - \Psi(\nabla^{\mathrm{NL}} v)\right)\left(\nabla^{\mathrm{NL}} u - \nabla^{\mathrm{NL}} v\right)\right)^{p/2} \in L^{2/p}(\Omega^2),$$
$$\left(K^{1/p} \cdot \left(|\nabla^{\mathrm{NL}} u| + |\nabla^{\mathrm{NL}} v|\right)\right)^{(2-p)p/2} \in L^{2/(2-p)}(\Omega^2).$$

It then follows from the Hölder inequality and (3.7) that

$$C_1^{p/2} \int_{\Omega^2} K(\boldsymbol{x}, \boldsymbol{y}) |\nabla^{\mathrm{NL}}(u - v)(\boldsymbol{x}, \boldsymbol{y})|^p \, d\boldsymbol{x} d\boldsymbol{y} \leq$$
$$2 \left(\int_{\Omega} \left(\Delta_p^K u(\boldsymbol{x}) - \Delta_p^K v(\boldsymbol{x})\right)(u(\boldsymbol{x}) - v(\boldsymbol{x})) d\boldsymbol{x}\right)^{p/2}$$
$$\cdot \left(\int_{\Omega^2} K(\boldsymbol{x}, \boldsymbol{y}) \left(|\nabla^{\mathrm{NL}} u(\boldsymbol{x}, \boldsymbol{y})| + |\nabla^{\mathrm{NL}} v(\boldsymbol{x}, \boldsymbol{y})|\right)^p d\boldsymbol{x} d\boldsymbol{y}\right)^{(2-p)/2}.$$

We have by Jensen's inequality

$$\int_{\Omega^2} K(\boldsymbol{x}, \boldsymbol{y}) \left(|\nabla^{\mathrm{NL}} u(\boldsymbol{x}, \boldsymbol{y})| + |\nabla^{\mathrm{NL}} v(\boldsymbol{x}, \boldsymbol{y})|\right)^p d\boldsymbol{x} d\boldsymbol{y}$$
$$\leq 2^{2p-1} \|K\|_{L^{\infty,1}(\Omega^2)} \left(\|u\|_{L^p(\Omega)}^p + \|v\|_{L^p(\Omega)}^p\right),$$

whence we obtain

$$C_1 \left(\int_{\Omega^2} K(\boldsymbol{x}, \boldsymbol{y}) |\nabla^{\mathrm{NL}}(u - v)(\boldsymbol{x}, \boldsymbol{y})|^p \, d\boldsymbol{x} d\boldsymbol{y}\right)^{2/p} \leq$$

[3] This can be seen as a nonlocal analogue of Glowinski and Marrocco (1975, proposition 5.1 and proposition 5.2).

$$2^{5-2p}\left(\int_\Omega \left(\Delta_p^K u(\boldsymbol{x}) - \Delta_p^K v(\boldsymbol{x})\right)(u(\boldsymbol{x}) - v(\boldsymbol{x}))d\boldsymbol{x}\right)$$
$$\|K\|_{L^{\infty,1}(\Omega^2)}^{(2-p)/p}\left(\|u\|_{L^p(\Omega)} + \|v\|_{L^p(\Omega)}\right)^{2-p}.$$

Rearranging proves the bound. For $u, v \in L^\infty(\Omega)$ and $p \in [2, +\infty]$ we use that $L^p(\Omega) \subset L^2(\Omega)$. For $p \in]1, 2]$, we embark from (3.9) and use that for all $(\boldsymbol{x}, \boldsymbol{y}) \in \Omega^2$,

$$|\nabla^{\mathrm{NL}} u(\boldsymbol{x}, \boldsymbol{y})| + |\nabla^{\mathrm{NL}} v(\boldsymbol{x}, \boldsymbol{y})| \leq 2\left(\|u\|_{L^\infty(\Omega)} + \|v\|_{L^\infty(\Omega)}\right).$$

Multiplying (3.9) by K, integrating, and using (3.7), we conclude.

To prove (vi), we start by showing that Δ_p^K is Hölder continuous with exponent $p - 1$ on $L^2(\Omega)$. We have, by Jensen's inequality (twice) and (3.6),

$$\begin{aligned}
&\|\Delta_p^K u - \Delta_p^K v\|_{L^2(\Omega)}^2 \\
&= \int_\Omega \left|\int_\Omega K(\boldsymbol{x}, \boldsymbol{y})\left(\Psi(\nabla^{\mathrm{NL}} u(\boldsymbol{x}, \boldsymbol{y})) - \Psi(\nabla^{\mathrm{NL}} v(\boldsymbol{x}, \boldsymbol{y}))\right) d\boldsymbol{y}\right|^2 d\boldsymbol{x} \\
&\leq \|K\|_{L^{\infty,1}(\Omega^2)} \int_{\Omega^2} K(\boldsymbol{x}, \boldsymbol{y})\left(\Psi(\nabla^{\mathrm{NL}} u(\boldsymbol{x}, \boldsymbol{y})) - \Psi(\nabla^{\mathrm{NL}} v(\boldsymbol{x}, \boldsymbol{y}))\right)^2 d\boldsymbol{x}d\boldsymbol{y} \\
&\leq C_2\|K\|_{L^{\infty,1}(\Omega^2)} \int_{\Omega^2} K(\boldsymbol{x}, \boldsymbol{y})\left(\nabla^{\mathrm{NL}}(u - v)(\boldsymbol{x}, \boldsymbol{y})\right)^{2(p-1)} d\boldsymbol{x}d\boldsymbol{y} \\
&\leq 2^p C_2\|K\|_{L^{\infty,1}(\Omega^2)} \int_{\Omega^2} K(\boldsymbol{x}, \boldsymbol{y})(u(\boldsymbol{x}) - v(\boldsymbol{x}))^{2(p-1)} d\boldsymbol{x}d\boldsymbol{y} \\
&\leq 2^p C_2\|K\|_{L^{\infty,1}(\Omega^2)}^2 \left(\int_\Omega (u(\boldsymbol{x}) - v(\boldsymbol{x}))^2 d\boldsymbol{x}\right)^{p-1} \\
&= 2^p C_2\|K\|_{L^{\infty,1}(\Omega^2)}^2 \|u - v\|_{L^2(\Omega)}^{2(p-1)}.
\end{aligned} \tag{3.10}$$

We are now in a position to invoke Bauschke and Combettes (2011, corollary 18.14(i)⇒(v)) to show that the claimed inequality holds. □

Solutions of $(\mathcal{P})$ will be understood in the following sense:

Definition 3.3 Let $p \in]1, +\infty[$. A solution of $(\mathcal{P})$ in $[0, T]$ is a function

$$u \in C([0, T]; L^1(\Omega)) \cap W^{1,1}(]0, T[; L^1(\Omega))$$

that satisfies $u(\boldsymbol{x}, 0) = g(\boldsymbol{x})$ a.e. $\boldsymbol{x} \in \Omega$ and

$$\frac{\partial}{\partial t} u(\boldsymbol{x}, t) = -\Delta_p^K u(\boldsymbol{x}, t) + f(\boldsymbol{x}, t) \quad \text{a.e. in } \Omega\times]0, T[.$$

Such a solution is also a strong solution (see Andreu-Vaillo et al., 2010, definition A.3).

The main result of existence and uniqueness of a global solution, that is, a solution on $[0, T]$ for $T > 0$, is stated in the following theorem.

Theorem 3.4 *Suppose that* $p \in]1,+\infty[$ *and assumptions* **(H.1)**, **(H.2)**, *and* **(H.3)** *hold. Let* $g \in L^p(\Omega)$ *and* $f \in L^1([0,T]; L^p(\Omega))$.

(i) For any $T > 0$, *there exists a unique strong solution in* $[0,T]$ *of* $(\mathcal{P})$.
(ii) Moreover, for $q \in [1,+\infty]$, *if* $g_i \in L^q(\Omega)$ *and* $f_i \in L^1([0,T]; L^q(\Omega))$, $i = 1,2$, *and* u_i *is the solution of* $(\mathcal{P})$ *with data* (f_i, g_i), *then*

$$\|u_1(\cdot,t) - u_2(\cdot,t)\|_{L^q(\Omega)} \le \|g_1 - g_2\|_{L^q(\Omega)} + \|f_1 - f_2\|_{L^1([0,T];L^q(\Omega))}, \quad \forall t \in [0,T]. \tag{3.11}$$

Proof: The proof follows the same lines as that of Andreu et al. (2008b, theorem 1.2) extended to the case where $f \not\equiv 0$, thanks to the results of Bénilan (1972), where we invoke Proposition 3.2(ii), (iii), and (vii). □

Remark 3.5 In Andreu et al. (2008b) (see also Andreu-Vaillo et al., 2010, chapte 6), the authors impose the following stringent assumptions: $K(\boldsymbol{x},\boldsymbol{y}) = J(\boldsymbol{x} - \boldsymbol{y})$, where J is nonnegative, continuous, radially symmetric, compactly supported, $J(0) > 0$, and $\int_{\mathbb{R}^d} J(\boldsymbol{x})d\boldsymbol{x} < +\infty$. Actually, these assumptions are not needed for existence and uniqueness. The particular form $J(\boldsymbol{x} - \boldsymbol{y})$ of the kernel is not needed. Continuity with radial symmetry and support compactness play a pivotal role in studying convergence to the local p-Laplacian problem in Andreu et al. (2008b, theorem 1.5). In addition, $J(0) > 0$ was mandatory to prove a Poincaré-type inequality in Andreu et al. (2008b, proposition 4.1). Even for the form $J(\boldsymbol{x} - \boldsymbol{y})$, our assumptions **(H'.1)**, **(H'.2)**, and **(H'.3)** are weaker than those of Andreu et al. (2008b). This discussion remains true also for the case $p = 1$.

3.2.2 The Case $p = 1$

We will need to define the subdifferential of the absolute value function on $\mathbb{R}$, which is the well-known set-valued mapping $\partial|\cdot|: \mathbb{R} \to 2^{\mathbb{R}}$,

$$\partial|\cdot|(x) = \begin{cases} 1 & x > 0, \\ [-1,1] & x = 0, \\ -1 & x < 0. \end{cases}$$

It will be convenient to denote the 1-Laplacian Δ_1^K. This is a set-valued operator in $L^1(\Omega) \times L^1(\Omega)$ such that $\eta \in \Delta_1^K u$ if and only if

$$\eta(\boldsymbol{x}) = -\int_\Omega K(\boldsymbol{x},\boldsymbol{y}) w(\boldsymbol{x},\boldsymbol{y}) d\boldsymbol{y} \quad \text{a.e. in } \Omega,$$

for a subgradient function w satisfying $\|w\|_{L^\infty(\Omega^2)} \leq 1$, $w(x,y) = -w(y,x)$, and

$$w(x,y) \in \partial|\cdot|(u(y) - u(x)).$$

Solutions of $(\mathcal{P})$ will be understood in the following sense.

Definition 3.6 A solution of $(\mathcal{P})$ for $p = 1$ in $[0,T]$ is a function

$$u \in C([0,T]; L^1(\Omega)) \cap W^{1,1}(]0,T[; L^1(\Omega)),$$

that satisfies $u(x,0) = g(x)$ for a.e. $x \in \Omega$ and

$$\frac{\partial}{\partial t}u(x,t) = -\eta(x,t) + f(x,t) \quad \text{a.e. in } \Omega\times]0,T[,$$

where $\eta(\cdot,t) \in \Delta_1^K u(\cdot,t)$.

Observe that for $p = 1$, the evolution problem $(\mathcal{P})$ reads

$$\begin{cases} \frac{\partial}{\partial t}u(x,t) = \int_\Omega K(x,y)\,\mathrm{sign}(u(y,t) - u(x,t))dy + f(x,t), & x \in \Omega, t > 0, \\ u(x,0) = g(x), \quad x \in \Omega, \end{cases}$$

where

$$\mathrm{sign}(x) = \begin{cases} \frac{x}{|x|} & x \neq 0, \\ 0 & x = 0. \end{cases}$$

Thus, it satisfies

$$\frac{\partial}{\partial t}u(\cdot,t) \in -\Delta_1^K u(\cdot,t) + f(\cdot,t).$$

In the same vein as Proposition 3.2, the 1-Laplacian enjoys the following properties.

Proposition 3.7 *Assume that K satisfies* **(H.1)**, **(H.2)**, *and* **(H.3)**.

(i) $\mathrm{dom}(\Delta_1^K) = L^1(\Omega)$ *and (the graph of)* Δ_1^K *is closed in* $L^1(\Omega) \times L^1(\Omega)$.
(ii) *Let* $h \in C^1(\mathbb{R})$ *be a nondecreasing function. Then, for every* $u_i \in L^1(\Omega)$ *and any* $\eta_i \in \Delta_1^K u_i$, $i = 1,2$,

$$\begin{aligned} 0 &\leq \int_\Omega (\eta_1(x) - \eta_2(x))\,(h(u_1(x) - u_2(x)))\,dx \\ &= \frac{1}{2}\int_{\Omega^2} K(x,y)\,(w_1(x,y) - w_2(x,y)) \\ &\qquad \cdot (h(u_1(y) - u_2(y)) - h(u_1(x) - u_2(x)))\,dxdy. \end{aligned} \tag{3.12}$$

where w_i are the corresponding subgradient functions defined earlier. In particular,

$$\int_{\Omega^2} K(x,y)w_i(x,y)u_i(x)dxdy = -\frac{1}{2}\int_{\Omega^2} K(x,y)|u_i(y)-u_i(x)|dxdy.$$

(iii) Δ_1^K *is completely accretive and satisfies the range condition*

$$L^\infty(\Omega) \subset \mathrm{ran}(\mathbf{I}+\Delta_1^K). \tag{3.13}$$

PROOF: For (i), see Andreu et al. (2008b, remark 2.8), which still holds for our class of kernels K.

The proof of (iii) is again the same as that of Andreu et al. (2008b, theorem 2.9), where we invoke the monotonicity claim (ii), to which we turn now. For any $v \in L^1(\Omega)$, we have the integration by parts formula

$$\begin{aligned}
&\int_{\Omega^2} K(x,y)w_i(x,y)(v(y)-v(x))dxdy \\
&= -\int_{\Omega^2} K(y,x)w_i(y,x)v(y)dydx - \int_{\Omega^2} K(x,y)w_i(x,y)v(x))dxdy \\
&= -2\int_{\Omega^2} K(x,y)w_i(x,y)v(x)dxdy.
\end{aligned} \tag{3.14}$$

Taking $v(x) = h(u_1(x)-u_2(x))$ in (3.14) with w_1 and w_2, and then taking the difference, we arrive at

$$\begin{aligned}
&-2\int_\Omega\left(\int_\Omega K(x,y)(w_1(x,y)-w_2(x,y))dy\right)h(u_1(x)-u_2(x))dx \\
&= 2\int_\Omega (\eta_1(x)-\eta_2(x))\,(h(u_1(x)-u_2(x)))\,dx \\
&= \int_{\Omega^2} K(x,y)\,(w_1(x,y)-w_2(x,y))\,(h(u_1(y)-u_2(y))-h(u_1(x)-u_2(x)))\,dxdy.
\end{aligned}$$

By the mean-value theorem applied to h, we get

$$\begin{aligned}
&= 2\int_\Omega (\eta_1(x)-\eta_2(x))\,(h(u_1(x)-u_2(x)))\,dx \\
&= \int_{\Omega^2} K(x,y)\,(w_1(x,y)-w_2(x,y))\,h'(\zeta(x,y))\left(\nabla^{\mathrm{NL}}(u_1-u_2)(x,y)\right)dxdy \\
&= \int_{\Omega^2} K(x,y)h'(\zeta(x,y))\,(w_1(x,y)-w_2(x,y))\left(\nabla^{\mathrm{NL}}(u_1-u_2)(x,y)\right)dxdy,
\end{aligned}$$

where $\zeta(x,y)$ is an intermediate value between $u_1(y)-u_2(y)$ and $u_1(x)-u_2(x)$. Since h is increasing, that $w_i(x,y) \in \partial|\cdot|(u_i(y)-u_i(x))$, and $\partial|\cdot|$ is a monotone operator, we get the claimed monotonicity.

To get the particular identity, we specialize (3.14) by taking $v = u_i$, which entails

$$\begin{aligned}&-\int_{\Omega^2} K(\boldsymbol{x},\boldsymbol{y})w_i(\boldsymbol{x},\boldsymbol{y})(u_i(\boldsymbol{y}) - u_i(\boldsymbol{x}))d\boldsymbol{x}d\boldsymbol{y}\\&= 2\int_{\Omega^2} K(\boldsymbol{x},\boldsymbol{y})w_i(\boldsymbol{x},\boldsymbol{y})u_i(\boldsymbol{x})d\boldsymbol{x}d\boldsymbol{y}.\end{aligned}$$

We finally use the equivalent characterization of $\partial|\cdot|$, which originates from Fenchel's identity since $|\cdot|$ is positively homogeneous:

$$\partial|\cdot|(x) = \{\xi \in \mathbb{R} : |\xi| \le 1 \text{ and } \xi x = |x|\}.$$

Applying this identity with $x = u_i(\boldsymbol{y}) - u_i(\boldsymbol{x})$ and $\xi = w_i(\boldsymbol{x},\boldsymbol{y})$ gives the claim. □

Theorem 3.8 *Suppose that $p = 1$, and assumptions* ***(H.1)***, ***(H.2)***, *and* ***(H.3)*** *hold. Let $g \in L^1(\Omega)$ and $f \in L^1([0,T]; L^1(\Omega))$. For any $T > 0$, there exists a unique solution in $[0,T]$ of $(\mathcal{P})$ in the sense of Definition 3.6.*

PROOF: The proof is an adaptation of Andreu et al. (2008b, theorem 1.4) to the case where $f \not\equiv 0$, thanks to the results of Bénilan (1972), where we invoke Proposition 3.7(i) and (iii). □

3.3 Error Bounds for the Discrete Problem

We establish in this section error bounds for fully discrete (in time and space) approximations of $(\mathcal{P})$. For that, let $0 < t_1 < t_2 < \cdots < t_{N-1} < t_N = T$ be a partition (not necessarily equispaced) of $[0,T]$. Let $\tau_{k-1} \stackrel{\text{def}}{=} |t_k - t_{k-1}|$ and denote $\tau = \max_{k\in[N]} \tau_k$.

Let $\mathbf{K} \in \mathbb{R}^{n^d \times n^d}$ and $\mathbf{g} \in \mathbb{R}^{n^d}$ be discrete approximations of, respectively, the kernel K and initial data g in $(\mathcal{P})$, on a regular mesh of size $\delta(n)$, that is, $h_i = |\Omega_i^{(n)}| = 1/n^d$. Typically, one can take $\mathbf{K} = P_n K$ and $\mathbf{g} = P_n g$. For $1 < p < \infty$, the discrete p-Laplacian operator with kernel $\mathbf{K}$ is

$$\widehat{\boldsymbol{\Delta}}_p^{\mathbf{K}} : \mathbf{u} \in \mathbb{R}^{n^d} \mapsto -\sum_{j\in[n]^d} h_j \mathbf{K}_{ij} |\mathbf{u}_j - \mathbf{u}_i|^{p-2}(\mathbf{u}_j - \mathbf{u}_i) = -\sum_{j\in[n]^d} h_j \mathbf{K}_{ij} \Psi(\mathbf{u}_j - \mathbf{u}_i).$$

In the same way, we define the discrete 1-Laplacian operator as the set-valued operator $\widehat{\boldsymbol{\Delta}}_1^{\mathbf{K}} : \mathbb{R}^{n^d} \to 2^{\mathbb{R}^{n^d}}$ such that $\eta \in \widehat{\boldsymbol{\Delta}}_1^{\mathbf{K}}\mathbf{u}$ if and only if

$$\eta_i = -\sum_{j\in[n]^d} h_j \mathbf{K}_{ij} \mathbf{w}_{ij},$$

where $\|\mathbf{w}\|_\infty \le 1$, $\mathbf{w}_{ij} = -\mathbf{w}_{ji}$, and

$$\mathbf{w}_{ij} \in \partial|\cdot|(\mathbf{u}_j - \mathbf{u}_i).$$

By construction, we have the following simple lemma whose proof is immediate.

Lemma 3.9 *For any* $\mathbf{K} \in \mathbb{R}^{n^d \times n^d}$ *and* $\mathbf{u} \in \mathbb{R}^{n^d}$, *the following holds:*

(i) If $1 < p < +\infty$,

$$I_n \widehat{\boldsymbol{\Delta}}_p^{\mathbf{K}}(\mathbf{u}) = \Delta_p^{I_n\mathbf{K}}(I_n\mathbf{u}).$$

(ii) If $p = 1$,

$$I_n\eta(x) = -\int_\Omega I_nK(x,y)I_n\mathbf{w}(x,y)dy, \quad \textit{where}$$

$$I_n\mathbf{w}(x,y) \in \partial|\cdot|(I_n\mathbf{u}(y) - I_n\mathbf{u}(x)).$$

Moreover, $\|I_n\mathbf{w}\|_{L^\infty(\Omega^2)} \le 1$ *and* $I_n\mathbf{w}(x,y) = -I_n\mathbf{w}(y,x)$.

3.3.1 Forward/Explicit Euler Discretization

We start with $p \in]1,2]$ and consider a totally discrete problem with forward/explicit Euler scheme in time,

$$\begin{cases} \dfrac{\mathbf{u}^k - \mathbf{u}^{k-1}}{\tau_{k-1}} = -\widehat{\boldsymbol{\Delta}}_p^{\mathbf{K}}\mathbf{u}^{k-1} + \mathbf{f}, \quad k \in [N], \\ \mathbf{u}^0 = \mathbf{g}, \end{cases} \tag{$\mathcal{P}_p^{\mathrm{TDF}}$}$$

where $\mathbf{u}^k, \mathbf{f} \in \mathbb{R}^{n^d}$. We have implicitly assumed that f does not depend on time, which is a standard assumption in the context of explicit discretization.

Since our aim is to compare the solutions of problems $(\mathcal{P})$ and $(\mathcal{P}_p^{\mathrm{TDF}})$, we introduce the following continuum extensions in space and/or time of $\{\mathbf{u}^k\}_{k\in[N]}$ as

$$u_n^k = I_n\mathbf{u}^k, k \in [N], \text{ and } f_n = I_n\mathbf{f},$$

$$\breve{u}_n(x,t) = \frac{t_k - t}{\tau_{k-1}}u_n^{k-1}(x) + \frac{t - t_{k-1}}{\tau_{k-1}}u_n^k(x), \quad (x,t) \in \Omega\times]t_{k-1}, t_k], k \in [N],$$

$$\bar{u}_n(x,t) = \sum_{k=1}^N u_n^{k-1}(x)\chi_{]t_{k-1},t_k]}(t), \quad (x,t) \in \Omega\times]0,T].$$

Then, in the same vein as Lemma 3.9, it is easy to see that $(\mathcal{P}_p^{\mathrm{TDF}})$ is equivalent to the following evolution problem:

$$\begin{cases} \frac{\partial}{\partial t}\breve{u}_n(\boldsymbol{x},t) = -\Delta_p^{I_n\mathbf{K}}\bar{u}_n(\boldsymbol{x},t) + f_n(\boldsymbol{x}), & (\boldsymbol{x},t) \in \Omega\times]0,T], \\ \breve{u}_n(\boldsymbol{x},0) = I_n\mathbf{g}(\boldsymbol{x}), & \boldsymbol{x} \in \Omega. \end{cases} \tag{3.15}$$

Before turning to the consistency result, we collect some useful estimates.

Lemma 3.10 *Consider problem* ($\mathcal{P}_p^{\mathrm{TDF}}$) *with kernel* $\mathbf{K}$*, data* $(\mathbf{f},\mathbf{g})$ *and variable step-size* $\tau_k \le 2C\left\|\Delta_p^{I_n\mathbf{K}}u_n^k - f_n\right\|_{L^2(\Omega)}^{\frac{2-p}{p-1}}$*, where* C *is the constant in Proposition 3.2(vi). Assume that* $I_n\mathbf{g} \in L^2(\Omega)$ *and* $I_n\mathbf{K}$ *satisfies* **(H.1)**, **(H.2)**, *and* **(H.3)**. *Suppose also that for each* $n \in \mathbb{N}$, $\mathbf{f}$ *is such that* ($\mathcal{P}_p^{\mathrm{TDF}}$) *has a stationary solution* $\mathbf{u}^\star$ *and that* $\sup_{n\in\mathbb{N}}\left\|I_n\mathbf{g} - I_n\mathbf{u}^\star\right\|_{L^2(\Omega)} < +\infty$. *Then,*

$$\bar{u}_n(\cdot,t) \in L^2(\Omega), \forall t \in [0,T], \quad \textit{and} \quad \sup_{t\in[0,T],n\in\mathbb{N}}\left\|\bar{u}_n(\cdot,t) - I_n\mathbf{u}^\star\right\|_{L^2(\Omega)} < +\infty.$$

Remark 3.11

(1) Condition on the time-step τ_k can be seen as an abstract nonlinear CFL condition. It is better than the one in Hafiene et al. (2018) since we here exploit the Hölder continuity of $\Delta_p^{I_n\mathbf{K}}$ on $L^2(\Omega)$ for $p \in]1,2]$; see Proposition 3.2(vi). For $p = 2$, where $\Delta_2^{I_n\mathbf{K}}$ is a linear Lipschitz continuous operator on $L^2(\Omega)$, the condition reads $\tau_k \le 2C$. Such a condition for explicit time-discretization of evolution problems with accretive and Lipschitz continuous operators is known; see, for example, Nochetto and Savaré (2006). It is also consistent with known convergence results for finding zeros of so-called cocoercive operators on Hilbert spaces; see Bauschke and Combettes (2011).

(2) The assumption on $\mathbf{f}$ and $\mathbf{K}$ implies that $f_n \in L^2(\Omega)$. Indeed, (3.10) entails

$$\left\|f_n\right\|_{L^2(\Omega)} = \left\|\Delta_p^{I_n\mathbf{K}}(I_n\mathbf{u}^\star)\right\|_{L^2(\Omega)} \le 2^p C_2\left\|K\right\|_{L^{\infty,1}(\Omega^2)}^2\left\|I_n\mathbf{u}^\star\right\|_{L^2(\Omega)}^{p-1}.$$

(3) The assumption made on $\mathbf{f}$ is trivially true when $\mathbf{f} = \mathbf{0}$, since $\mathbf{0}$ is a stationary solution in this case. In turn, using Lemma 2.20, one can see that the uniform boundedness conditions on $\mathbf{g}$ and $\mathbf{K}$ are fulfilled if $\mathbf{g} = P_n g$ and $\mathbf{K} = P_n K$, where $g \in L^2(\Omega)$ and K satisfies **(H.1)**–**(H.3)**.

Proof: We show the claim by an induction argument. Since $\Delta_p^{I_n\mathbf{K}}(I_n\mathbf{u}^\star) = f_n$, we have

$$\begin{aligned} &\left\|u_n^1 - I_n\mathbf{u}^\star\right\|_{L^2(\Omega)}^2 - \left\|I_n\mathbf{g} - I_n\mathbf{u}^\star\right\|_{L^2(\Omega)}^2 \\ &= -2\tau_0\int_\Omega\left(\Delta_p^{I_n\mathbf{K}}(I_n\mathbf{g})(\boldsymbol{x}) - f_n(\boldsymbol{x})\right)\left(I_n\mathbf{g}(\boldsymbol{x}) - I_n\mathbf{u}^\star\right)d\boldsymbol{x} \\ &\quad + \tau_0^2\left\|\Delta_p^{I_n\mathbf{K}}(I_n\mathbf{g}) - f_n\right\|_{L^2(\Omega)}^2 \end{aligned}$$

$$= -2\tau_0 \int_\Omega \left(\Delta_p^{I_n\mathbf{K}}(I_n\mathbf{g})(x) - \Delta_p^{I_n\mathbf{K}}(I_n\mathbf{u}^\star)(x)\right)(I_n\mathbf{g}(x) - I_n\mathbf{u}^\star)\,dx$$
$$+ \tau_0^2 \left\|\Delta_p^{I_n\mathbf{K}}(I_n\mathbf{g}) - f_n\right\|_{L^2(\Omega)}^2.$$

By assumption on g, $\mathbf{u}^\star$, and τ_k, we can invoke Proposition 3.2(vi) to get

$$\left\|u_n^1 - I_n\mathbf{u}^\star\right\|_{L^2(\Omega)}^2 - \left\|I_n\mathbf{g} - I_n\mathbf{u}^\star\right\|_{L^2(\Omega)}^2$$
$$\leq -2C\tau_0 \left\|\Delta_p^{I_n\mathbf{K}}(I_n\mathbf{g}) - f_n\right\|_{L^2(\Omega)}^{p/(p-1)} + \tau_0^2 \left\|\Delta_p^{I_n\mathbf{K}}(I_n\mathbf{g}) - f_n\right\|_{L^2(\Omega)}^2$$
$$\leq -\tau_0 \left\|\Delta_p^{I_n\mathbf{K}}(I_n\mathbf{g}) - f_n\right\|_{L^2(\Omega)}^2 \left(2C\left\|\Delta_p^{I_n\mathbf{K}}(I_n\mathbf{g}) - f_n\right\|_{L^2(\Omega)}^{(2-p)/(p-1)} - \tau_0\right) \leq 0.$$

Suppose now that, for any $k > 1$,

$$\left\|u_n^k - I_n\mathbf{u}^\star\right\|_{L^2(\Omega)}^2 \leq \left\|I_n\mathbf{g} - I_n\mathbf{u}^\star\right\|_{L^2(\Omega)}^2,$$

and thus $u_n^k \in L^2(\Omega)$. We can then use Proposition 3.2(vi) as previously to see that

$$\left\|u_n^{k+1} - I_n\mathbf{u}^\star\right\|_{L^2(\Omega)}^2 - \left\|I_n\mathbf{g} - I_n\mathbf{u}^\star\right\|_{L^2(\Omega)}^2$$
$$\leq -\tau_k \left\|\Delta_p^{I_n\mathbf{K}}(u_n^k) - f_n\right\|_{L^2(\Omega)}^2 \cdot \left(2C\left\|\Delta_p^{I_n\mathbf{K}}(u_n^k) - f_n\right\|_{L^2(\Omega)}^{(2-p)/(p-1)} - \tau_k\right) \leq 0.$$

Thus, the sequence $\left\{\left\|u_n^k\right\|_{L^2(\Omega)}\right\}_{k\in[N]}$ is bounded, and so is $\left\|\bar{u}_n(\cdot,t)\right\|_{L^2(\Omega)}$ for $t \in [0,T]$ by its definition. We also have

$$\sup_{\substack{t\in[0,T],\\ n\in\mathbb{N}}} \left\|\bar{u}_n(\cdot,t) - I_n\mathbf{u}^\star\right\|_{L^2(\Omega)} = \sup_{\substack{(n,N)\in\mathbb{N}^2,\\ k\in[N]}} \left\|u_n^k - I_n\mathbf{u}^\star\right\|_{L^2(\Omega)}$$
$$\leq \sup_{n\in\mathbb{N}} \left\|I_n\mathbf{g} - I_n\mathbf{u}^\star\right\|_{L^2(\Omega)} < +\infty.$$

□

Lemma 3.12 *In addition to the assumptions of Lemma 3.10, suppose that* $\sup_{n\in\mathbb{N}} \left\|I_n\mathbf{K}\right\|_{L^{\infty,1}(\Omega^2)} < +\infty$. *Then*

$$\sup_{t\in[0,T],n\in\mathbb{N}} \left\|\check{u}_n(\cdot,t) - \bar{u}_n(\cdot,t)\right\|_{L^2(\Omega)} \leq C\tau,$$

where C is a positive constant that does not depend on (n, N, T).

PROOF: It is easy to see that for $t \in]t_{k-1}, t_k]$, $k \in \mathbb{N}$,

$$\left\|\check{u}_n(\cdot,t) - \bar{u}_n(\cdot,t)\right\|_{L^2(\Omega)} = (t - t_{k-1})\left\|\frac{u_n^k - u_n^{k-1}}{\tau_{k-1}}\right\|_{L^2(\Omega)}$$
$$= (t - t_{k-1})\left\|\Delta_p^{I_n\mathbf{K}} u_n^{k-1} - \Delta_p^{I_n\mathbf{K}} I_n\mathbf{u}^\star\right\|_{L^2(\Omega)}$$
$$\leq \tau\left\|\Delta_p^{I_n\mathbf{K}}\bar{u}_n(\cdot,t) - \Delta_p^{I_n\mathbf{K}} I_n\mathbf{u}^\star\right\|_{L^2(\Omega)}.$$

As $\Delta_p^{I_n\mathbf{K}}$ is Hölder continuous on $L^2(\Omega)$ with exponent $p-1$ (see (3.10)), we get

$$\|\breve{u}_n(\cdot,t)-\bar{u}_n(\cdot,t)\|_{L^2(\Omega)} \leq \tau 2^{p/2} C_2^{1/2} \|K\|_{L^{\infty,1}(\Omega^2)} \|\bar{u}_n(\cdot,t) - I_n\mathbf{u}^\star\|_{L^2(\Omega)}^{p-1}.$$

We then take the supremum over t and n, and use Lemma 3.10 to conclude. □

We are now in a position to state the error bound for the totally discrete problem $(\mathcal{P}_p^{\mathrm{TDF}})$.

Theorem 3.13 *Suppose that $p \in]1,2]$. Let u be a solution of $(\mathcal{P})$ with kernel K and data (f,g), where f is time-independent, and $\{\mathbf{u}^k\}_{k\in[N]}$ is the sequence generated by $(\mathcal{P}_p^{\mathrm{TDF}})$ with $\mathbf{K}=P_nK$, $\mathbf{g}=P_ng$, $\mathbf{f}=P_nf$, and τ_k as prescribed in Lemma 3.10. Assume that K satisfies* **(H.1)**, **(H.2)**, *and $K\in L^{\infty,2}(\Omega^2)$, and that f,g belong either to $L^2(\Omega)$ or $L^\infty(\Omega)$. Then, the following hold.*

(i) u is the unique solution of $(\mathcal{P})$, $\{\mathbf{u}^k\}_{k\in[N]}$ is uniquely defined, and $\left\{\|I_n\mathbf{u}^k\|_{L^2(\Omega)}\right\}_{k\in[N]}$ is bounded (uniformly in n when $\mathbf{f}=\mathbf{0}$).

(ii) We have the error estimate

$$\sup_{\substack{k\in[N],\\ t\in]t_{k-1},t_k]}} \|I_n\mathbf{u}^{k-1}-u(\cdot,t)\|_{L^2(\Omega)} \leq \exp(T/2)\Bigg(\|I_nP_ng-g\|_{L^2(\Omega)} + CT^{1/2}\left(\tau^{1/(3-p)} + \|f_n-f\|_{L^2(\Omega)} + \begin{cases}\|I_nP_nK-K\|_{L^{\infty,2}(\Omega^2)} & g\in L^2(\Omega)\\ \|I_nP_nK-K\|_{L^2(\Omega^2)}, & g\in L^\infty(\Omega)\end{cases}\right)\Bigg), \tag{3.16}$$

for τ sufficiently small, where C is a positive constant that depends only on p, g, f, and K.

(iii) If, moreover, $f,g\in L^\infty(\Omega)\cap \mathrm{Lip}(s,L^2(\Omega))$ and $K\in\mathrm{Lip}(s,L^2(\Omega^2))$, then

$$\sup_{\substack{k\in[N],\\ t\in]t_{k-1},t_k]}} \|I_n\mathbf{u}^{k-1}-u(\cdot,t)\|_{L^2(\Omega)} \leq C\exp(T/2)\left((1+T^{1/2})\delta(n)^s + T^{1/2}\tau^{1/(3-p)}\right), \tag{3.17}$$

for τ sufficiently small, where C is a positive constant that depends only on p, g, f, K, and s.

Proof: In the proof, C is any positive constant that may depend only on p, g, f, K, and/or s, and that may be different at each line.

(i) Since $L^{\infty,2}(\Omega^2)\subset L^{\infty,1}(\Omega^2)$, assumption **(H.3)** holds for K. We also have the embeddings $L^\infty(\Omega)\subset L^p(\Omega)$ and $L^2(\Omega)\subset L^p(\Omega)$ for $p\in]1,2]$. Thus,

$g \in L^p(\Omega)$ and $f \in L^1([0,T];L^p(\Omega))$. Existence and uniqueness of the solution u in the sense of Definition 3.3 is a consequence of Theorem 3.4. The claimed well-posedness of the sequence $\{\mathbf{u}^k\}_{k\in[N]}$ is a consequence of Lemma 3.10 and Remark 3.11(3).

(ii) Denote $\check{\xi}_n(\boldsymbol{x},t) = \check{u}_n(\boldsymbol{x},t) - u(\boldsymbol{x},t)$, $\bar{\xi}_n(\boldsymbol{x},t) = \bar{u}_n(\boldsymbol{x},t) - u(\boldsymbol{x},t)$, $g_n = I_nP_ng$ and $K_n = I_nP_nK$. We thus have a.e.

$$\frac{\partial \check{\xi}_n(\boldsymbol{x},t)}{\partial t} = -\left(\Delta_p^{K_n}(\bar{u}_n(\boldsymbol{x},t)) - \Delta_p^{K_n}(u(\boldsymbol{x},t))\right) - \left(\Delta_p^{K_n}(u(\boldsymbol{x},t)) - \Delta_p^{K}(u(\boldsymbol{x},t))\right) + (f_n(\boldsymbol{x}) - f(\boldsymbol{x})).$$

Multiplying both sides by $\check{\xi}_n(\boldsymbol{x},t)$, integrating, and rearranging the terms, we get

$$\begin{aligned}\frac{1}{2}\frac{\partial}{\partial t}\|\check{\xi}_n(\cdot,t)\|^2_{L^2(\Omega)} = &-\int_\Omega \left(\Delta_p^{K_n}\bar{u}_n(\boldsymbol{x},t) - \Delta_p^{K_n}u(\boldsymbol{x},t)\right)(\bar{u}_n(\boldsymbol{x},t) - u(\boldsymbol{x},t))d\boldsymbol{x}\\ &-\int_\Omega \left(\Delta_p^{K_n}u(\boldsymbol{x},t) - \Delta_p^{K}u(\boldsymbol{x},t)\right)\check{\xi}_n(\boldsymbol{x},t)d\boldsymbol{x}\\ &-\int_\Omega \left(\Delta_p^{K_n}\bar{u}_n(\boldsymbol{x},t) - \Delta_p^{K_n}u(\boldsymbol{x},t)\right)(\check{u}_n(\boldsymbol{x},t) - \bar{u}_n(\boldsymbol{x},t))\,d\boldsymbol{x}\\ &+\int_\Omega (f_n(\boldsymbol{x}) - f(\boldsymbol{x}))\check{\xi}_n(\boldsymbol{x},t)d\boldsymbol{x}.\end{aligned} \tag{3.18}$$

Since $f,g \in L^p(\Omega)$ in both cases, so is $u(\cdot,t)$, thanks to (3.11). We also have $\bar{u}_n(\cdot,t) \in L^2(\Omega) \subset L^p(\Omega)$ by Lemma 3.10. We are then in a position to use Proposition 3.2(iv) with $h(x) = x$ to assert that the first term on the right-hand side of (3.18) is nonpositive. Let us now bound the second term.

- Case $g \in L^\infty(\Omega)$: in this case $\|u\|_{C([0,T];L^\infty(\Omega))} \leq \|g\|_{L^\infty(\Omega)} + \|f\|_{L^1([0,T];L^\infty(\Omega))}$, thanks to (3.11), and we get from the Cauchy–Schwartz inequality that

$$\begin{aligned}&\left|\int_{\Omega^2}(K_n(\boldsymbol{x},\boldsymbol{y}) - K(\boldsymbol{x},\boldsymbol{y}))\Psi(u(\boldsymbol{y},t) - u(\boldsymbol{x},t))\xi_n(\boldsymbol{x},t)d\boldsymbol{x}d\boldsymbol{y}\right|\\ &\leq 2^{p-1}\|u(\cdot,t)\|^{p-1}_{L^\infty(\Omega)}\int_{\Omega^2}|K_n(\boldsymbol{x},\boldsymbol{y}) - K(\boldsymbol{x},\boldsymbol{y})||\xi_n(\boldsymbol{x},t)|d\boldsymbol{x}d\boldsymbol{y}\\ &\leq 2^{p-1}\left(\|g\|_{L^\infty(\Omega)} + \|f\|_{L^1([0,T];L^\infty(\Omega))}\right)^{p-1}\|K_n - K\|_{L^2(\Omega^2)}\\ &\quad\|\xi_n(\cdot,t)\|_{L^2(\Omega)}\\ &= C\|K_n - K\|_{L^2(\Omega^2)}\|\xi_n(\cdot,t)\|_{L^2(\Omega)}.\end{aligned}$$

- Case $g \in L^2(\Omega)$: applying again the Cauchy–Schwartz inequality and Jensen's inequality to the concave function $x \in \mathbb{R}^+ \mapsto x^{p-1}$, we obtain

$$
\begin{aligned}
&\left|\int_{\Omega^2} (K_n(\boldsymbol{x},\boldsymbol{y}) - K(\boldsymbol{x},\boldsymbol{y}))\Psi(u(\boldsymbol{y},t) - u(\boldsymbol{x},t))\xi_n(\boldsymbol{x},t)d\boldsymbol{x}d\boldsymbol{y}\right| \\
&\leq \left(\int_{\Omega^2} |u(\boldsymbol{y},t) - u(\boldsymbol{x},t)|^{2(p-1)} d\boldsymbol{x}d\boldsymbol{y}\right)^{\frac{1}{2}} \\
&\quad \left(\int_{\Omega^2} |K_n(\boldsymbol{x},\boldsymbol{y}) - K(\boldsymbol{x},\boldsymbol{y})|^2 |\xi_n(\boldsymbol{x},t)|^2 d\boldsymbol{x}d\boldsymbol{y}\right)^{\frac{1}{2}} \\
&\leq \left(\int_{\Omega^2} |u(\boldsymbol{y},t) - u(\boldsymbol{x},t)|^{2(p-1)} d\boldsymbol{x}d\boldsymbol{y}\right)^{1/2} \left\|K_n - K\right\|_{L^{\infty,2}(\Omega^2)} \\
&\quad \left\|\xi_n(\cdot,t)\right\|_{L^2(\Omega)} \\
&\overset{Jensen}{\leq} \left(\int_{\Omega^2} |u(\boldsymbol{y},t) - u(\boldsymbol{x},t)|^{2} d\boldsymbol{x}d\boldsymbol{y}\right)^{(p-1)/2} \left\|K_n - K\right\|_{L^{\infty,2}(\Omega^2)} \\
&\quad \left\|\xi_n(\cdot,t)\right\|_{L^2(\Omega)} \\
&\leq 2^{p-1}\left(\|g\|_{L^2(\Omega)} + \|f\|_{L^1([0,T];L^2(\Omega))}\right)^{p-1} \left\|K_n - K\right\|_{L^{\infty,2}(\Omega^2)} \\
&\quad \left\|\xi_n(\cdot,t)\right\|_{L^2(\Omega)} \\
&= C\left\|K_n - K\right\|_{L^{\infty,2}(\Omega^2)} \left\|\xi_n(\cdot,t)\right\|_{L^2(\Omega)},
\end{aligned}
$$

where we used (3.11) in the last inequality.

Applying Young's inequality for the two cases, we have

$$
\begin{aligned}
&\left|\int_\Omega \left(\Delta_p^{K_n} u(\boldsymbol{x},t) - \Delta_p^{K} u(\boldsymbol{x},t)\right) \check{\xi}_n(\boldsymbol{x},t)d\boldsymbol{x}\right| \\
&\leq \begin{cases} C\left\|K_n - K\right\|_{L^{\infty,2}(\Omega^2)} \left\|\check{\xi}_n(\cdot,t)\right\|_{L^2(\Omega)}, & g \in L^2(\Omega) \\ C\left\|K_n - K\right\|_{L^{2}(\Omega^2)} \left\|\check{\xi}_n(\cdot,t)\right\|_{L^2(\Omega)}, & g \in L^\infty(\Omega), \end{cases} \\
&\leq \frac{1}{6}\left\|\check{\xi}_n(\cdot,t)\right\|^2_{L^2(\Omega)} + \begin{cases} C\left\|K_n - K\right\|^2_{L^{\infty,2}(\Omega^2)}, & g \in L^2(\Omega) \\ C\left\|K_n - K\right\|^2_{L^{2}(\Omega^2)}, & g \in L^\infty(\Omega). \end{cases}
\end{aligned}
$$

For the third term in (3.18), we invoke Lemma 3.12 to get

$$
\begin{aligned}
&\left|\int_\Omega \left(\Delta_p^{K_n} \bar{u}_n(\boldsymbol{x},t) - \Delta_p^{K_n} u(\boldsymbol{x},t)\right)(\check{u}_n(\boldsymbol{x},t) - \bar{u}_n(\boldsymbol{x},t))\,d\boldsymbol{x}\right| \\
&\leq \left\|\Delta_p^{K_n} \bar{u}_n(\cdot,t) - \Delta_p^{K_n} u(\cdot,t)\right\|_{L^2(\Omega)} \left\|\check{u}_n(\cdot,t) - \bar{u}_n(\cdot,t)\right\|_{L^2(\Omega)} \\
&\leq C\left\|\Delta_p^{K_n} \bar{u}_n(\cdot,t) - \Delta_p^{K_n} u(\cdot,t)\right\|_{L^2(\Omega)}\tau.
\end{aligned}
$$

We then use the fact that $\Delta_p^{I_n\mathbf{K}}$ is Hölder continuous on $L^2(\Omega)$ with exponent $p-1$ (see (3.10)), to obtain

$$
\left\|\Delta_p^{K_n} \bar{u}_n(\cdot,t) - \Delta_p^{K_n} u(\cdot,t)\right\|_{L^2(\Omega)} \leq C\left\|\bar{\xi}_n(\cdot,t)\right\|^{p-1}_{L^2(\Omega)} \leq C\left(\left\|\check{\xi}_n(\cdot,t)\right\|^{p-1}_{L^2(\Omega)} + \tau^{p-1}\right),
$$

where we used Lemma 3.12 to go from $\bar{\xi}_n$ to $\check{\xi}_n$, and that $p \in]1,2]$. It then follows by the Cauchy–Schwartz inequality that

$$\begin{aligned}
&\left|\int_\Omega \left(\Delta_p^{K_n}\bar{u}_n(x,t) - \Delta_p^{K_n}u(x,t)\right)(\check{u}_n(x,t) - \bar{u}_n(x,t))\,dx\right| \\
&\leq C\left(\|\check{\xi}_n(\cdot,t)\|_{L^2(\Omega)}^{p-1}\tau + \tau^p\right) \\
&\leq \frac{1}{6}\|\check{\xi}_n(\cdot,t)\|_{L^2(\Omega)}^2 + C(\tau^{2/(3-p)} + \tau^p).
\end{aligned}$$

Using Young's inequality to bound the last term in (3.18), and combining the bounds on the three other terms, we have shown that

$$\frac{\partial}{\partial t}\|\check{\xi}_n(\cdot,t)\|_{L^2(\Omega)}^2 \leq \|\check{\xi}_n(\cdot,t)\|_{L^2(\Omega)}^2 + C\left(\tau^{2/(3-p)} + \tau^p + \|f_n - f\|_{L^2(\Omega)}^2 + \begin{cases}\|K_n - K\|_{L^{\infty,2}(\Omega^2)}^2, & g \in L^2(\Omega) \\ \|K_n - K\|_{L^2(\Omega^2)}^2, & g \in L^\infty(\Omega)\end{cases}\right).$$

Using Gronwall's lemma and taking the square root, we get

$$\|\check{u}_n - u\|_{C([0,T];L^2(\Omega))} \leq \exp(T/2)\left(\|I_nP_ng - g\|_{L^2(\Omega)} + CT^{1/2}\left(\tau^{1/(3-p)} + \tau^{p/2} + \|f_n - f\|_{L^2(\Omega)} + \begin{cases}\|I_nP_nK - K\|_{L^{\infty,2}(\Omega^2)} & g \in L^2(\Omega) \\ \|I_nP_nK - K\|_{L^2(\Omega^2)}, & g \in L^\infty(\Omega)\end{cases}\right)\right). \quad (3.19)$$

Since $1/2 < 1/(3-p) \leq p/2$ for $p \in]1,2]$, the dependence on τ scales as $O(\tau^{1/(3-p)})$ for τ sufficiently small (or N large enough). Inserting (3.19) into

$$\begin{aligned}
\sup_{\substack{k\in[N],\\ t\in]t_{k-1},t_k]}} \|u_n^{k-1} - u(\cdot,t)\|_{L^2(\Omega)} &= \|\bar{u}_n - u\|_{C([0,T];L^2(\Omega))} \\
&\leq \|\check{u}_n - u\|_{C([0,T];L^2(\Omega))} + C\tau
\end{aligned} \quad (3.20)$$

completes the proof of the error bound.

(iii) Plug (2.11) into (3.16). □

Remark 3.14 Error bounds in $L^p(\Omega)$ were derived in Hafiene et al. (2018) for forward Euler discretization. Their rate is better than ours and is provided for the range $p \in]1,+\infty[$. Unfortunately, we believe that their proof contains invalid arguments that can be fixed but only for $p \in]1,2]$.

We now turn to the case $p = 1$ and consider the discrete system

$$\begin{cases} \dfrac{\mathbf{u}^k - \mathbf{u}^{k-1}}{\tau_{k-1}} = -\boldsymbol{\eta}^{k-1} + \mathbf{f}, & k \in [N], \\ \mathbf{u}^0 = \mathbf{g}, \end{cases} \tag{$\mathcal{P}_1^{\mathrm{TDF}}$}$$

where

$$\boldsymbol{\eta}^k = -\sum_{j\in[n]^d} h_j \mathbf{K}_{ij}\, \mathrm{sign}(\mathbf{u}_j^k - \mathbf{u}_i^k), \quad \text{and thus} \quad \boldsymbol{\eta}^k \in \widehat{\boldsymbol{\Delta}}_1^{\mathbf{K}} \mathbf{u}^k.$$

We consider the continuum extensions in space and/or time of $\{\mathbf{u}^k\}_{k\in[N]}$ as before, namely u_n^k, $\check{u}_n$ and $\bar{u}_n$, $f_n = I_n\mathbf{f}$, and the space-time continuum extension of $\{\boldsymbol{\eta}^k\}_{k\in[N]}$:

$$\begin{aligned} \bar{\eta}_n(\boldsymbol{x},t) &= \sum_{k=1}^{N} (I_n\boldsymbol{\eta}^{k-1})(\boldsymbol{x})\chi_{]t_{k-1},t_k]}(t) \\ &= -\int_\Omega I_n\mathbf{K}(\boldsymbol{x},\boldsymbol{y})\, \mathrm{sign}(\bar{u}_n(\boldsymbol{y},t) - \bar{u}_n(\boldsymbol{x},t))d\boldsymbol{y}, \quad (\boldsymbol{x},t) \in \Omega\times]0,T]. \end{aligned}$$

In view of Lemma 3.9, these extensions satisfy the evolution problem

$$\begin{cases} \frac{\partial}{\partial t}\check{u}_n(\boldsymbol{x},t) = -\bar{\eta}_n(\boldsymbol{x},t) + f_n(\boldsymbol{x}), & (\boldsymbol{x},t) \in \Omega\times]0,T], \\ \check{u}_n(\boldsymbol{x},0) = I_n\mathbf{g}(\boldsymbol{x}), & \boldsymbol{x} \in \Omega, \end{cases} \tag{3.21}$$

and

$$\bar{\eta}_n(\boldsymbol{x},t) \in \Delta_1^{I_n\mathbf{K}} \bar{u}_n(\boldsymbol{x},t).$$

We have the following counterpart estimates of Lemma 3.10.

Lemma 3.15 *Consider problem ($\mathcal{P}_1^{\mathrm{TDF}}$) with kernel* $\mathbf{K}$*, data* $(\mathbf{f},\mathbf{g})$*, and variable step size*

$$\tau_k = \frac{\alpha_k}{\max\left(\left\|I_n\boldsymbol{\eta}^k - f_n\right\|_{L^2(\Omega)}, 1\right)}, \quad \textit{where} \quad \sum_{k\in\mathbb{N}} \alpha_k^2 < +\infty.$$

Assume that $I_n\mathbf{g} \in L^2(\Omega)$ *and* $I_n\mathbf{K}$ *satisfies* ***(H.1)–(H.2)*** *and* ***(H.3)****. Suppose also that for each* $n \in \mathbb{N}$, $\mathbf{f}$ *is such that* ($\mathcal{P}_p^{\mathrm{TDF}}$) *has a stationary solution* $\mathbf{u}^\star$ *and that* $\sup_{n\in\mathbb{N}} \left\|I_n\mathbf{g} - I_n\mathbf{u}^\star\right\|_{L^2(\Omega)} < +\infty$*. Then*

$$\bar{u}_n(\cdot,t) \in L^2(\Omega), \forall t \in [0,T], \quad \textit{and} \quad \sup_{t\in[0,T],n\in\mathbb{N}} \left\|\bar{u}_n(\cdot,t) - I_n\mathbf{u}^\star\right\|_{L^2(\Omega)} < +\infty.$$

Remark 3.16 The condition on the time step τ_k is reminiscent of subgradient descent and has been used in Hafiene et al. (2018). The assumptions on $(\mathbf{f},\mathbf{g},\mathbf{K})$

are again verified when $\mathbf{f} = 0$, $\mathbf{g} = P_n g$, and $\mathbf{K} = P_n K$, where $g \in L^2(\Omega)$ and K satisfies **(H.1)**–**(H.3)**.

PROOF: Define the series $s_k \stackrel{\text{def}}{=} \sum_{i=0}^k \alpha_i^2$. As in Lemma 3.10, we proceed by induction using the monotonicity of the 1-Laplacian (Proposition 3.7(ii)). Indeed, since $f_n \in \Delta_p^{I_n\mathbf{K}}(I_n\mathbf{u}^\star)$, we have

$$\begin{aligned}\left\|u_n^1 - I_n\mathbf{u}^\star\right\|_{L^2(\Omega)}^2 &= \left\|I_n\mathbf{g} - I_n\mathbf{u}^\star\right\|_{L^2(\Omega)}^2 \\ &- 2\tau_0 \int_\Omega \left(\Delta_p^{I_n\mathbf{K}}(I_n\mathbf{g})(x) - \Delta_p^{I_n\mathbf{K}}(I_n\mathbf{u}^\star)(x)\right)\left(I_n\mathbf{g}(x) - I_n\mathbf{u}^\star\right) dx + \alpha_0^2.\end{aligned}$$

By assumption on $\mathbf{g}$, $\mathbf{u}^\star$, we can invoke Proposition 3.7(ii) to get

$$\left\|u_n^1 - I_n\mathbf{u}^\star\right\|_{L^2(\Omega)}^2 \le \left\|I_n\mathbf{g} - I_n\mathbf{u}^\star\right\|_{L^2(\Omega)}^2 + s_0.$$

Suppose now that, for any $k > 1$,

$$\left\|u_n^k - I_n\mathbf{u}^\star\right\|_{L^2(\Omega)}^2 \le \left\|I_n\mathbf{g} - I_n\mathbf{u}^\star\right\|_{L^2(\Omega)}^2 + s_{k-1},$$

and thus $u_n^k \in L^2(\Omega)$. We can then invoke again Proposition 3.7(ii) to see that

$$\begin{aligned}&\left\|u_n^{k+1} - I_n\mathbf{u}^\star\right\|_{L^2(\Omega)}^2 - \left\|u_n^k - I_n\mathbf{u}^\star\right\|_{L^2(\Omega)}^2 \\ &= -2\tau_k \int_\Omega \left(\Delta_p^{I_n\mathbf{K}}(u_n^k)(x) - \Delta_p^{I_n\mathbf{K}}(I_n\mathbf{u}^\star)(x)\right)\left(u_n^k(x) - I_n\mathbf{u}^\star\right) dx + \alpha_k^2 \\ &\le \alpha_k^2.\end{aligned}$$

This shows that for all $k \in \mathbb{N}$,

$$\left\|u_n^k - I_n\mathbf{u}^\star\right\|_{L^2(\Omega)}^2 \le \left\|I_n\mathbf{g} - I_n\mathbf{u}^\star\right\|_{L^2(\Omega)}^2 + s_\infty,$$

and thus $\left\{\left\|I_n\mathbf{u}^k\right\|_{L^2(\Omega)}\right\}_{k\in[N]}$ is bounded. In turn, so is $\left\|\bar{u}_n(\cdot,t)\right\|_{L^2(\Omega)}$ for $t \in [0,T]$ by its definition. Moreover,

$$\begin{aligned}\sup_{t\in[0,T],n\in\mathbb{N}} \left\|\bar{u}_n(\cdot,t) - I_n\mathbf{u}^\star\right\|_{L^2(\Omega)} &= \sup_{(n,N)\in\mathbb{N}^2,k\in[N]} \left\|u_n^k - I_n\mathbf{u}^\star\right\|_{L^2(\Omega)} \\ &\le \sup_{n\in\mathbb{N}} \left\|I_n\mathbf{g} - I_n\mathbf{u}^\star\right\|_{L^2(\Omega)} + s_\infty^{1/2} < +\infty.\end{aligned}$$

□

We also have the following analogue of Lemma 3.12.

Lemma 3.17 *In addition to the assumptions of Lemma 3.15, suppose that* $\sup_{n\in\mathbb{N}} \left\|I_n\mathbf{K}\right\|_{L^{\infty,1}(\Omega^2)} < +\infty$. *Then,*

$$\sup_{t\in[0,T],n\in\mathbb{N}} \left\|\breve{u}_n(\cdot,t) - \bar{u}_n(\cdot,t)\right\|_{L^2(\Omega)} \le C\tau,$$

where C is a positive constant that does not depend on (n,N,T).

PROOF: Arguing as the beginning of Lemma 3.12, we get for any $t \in]t_{k-1}, t_k]$, $k \in \mathbb{N}$,

$$\|\breve{u}_n(\cdot,t) - \bar{u}_n(\cdot,t)\|_{L^2(\Omega)} \leq \tau \|\bar{\eta}_n(x,t) - f_n\|_{L^2(\Omega)}.$$

By the Hölder inequality, we have

$$\|\bar{\eta}_n(x,t)\|^2_{L^2(\Omega)} = \int_\Omega \left| \int_\Omega I_n\mathbf{K}(x,y)\,\mathrm{sign}(\bar{u}_n(y,t) - \bar{u}_n(x,t))dy \right|^2 dx$$
$$\leq \int_\Omega \left(\int_\Omega I_n\mathbf{K}(x,y)dy \right)^2 dx \leq \|I_n\mathbf{K}\|^2_{L^{\infty,1}(\Omega^2)}.$$

The same bound also holds on $\|f_n\|_{L^2(\Omega)}$. We then take the supremum over t and n to conclude. □

Theorem 3.18 *Let u be a solution of $(\mathcal{P})$ with kernel K and data (f, g), where f is time-independent, and $\{\mathbf{u}^k\}_{k\in[N]}$ is the sequence generated by $(\mathcal{P}_1^{\mathrm{TDF}})$ with $\mathbf{K} = P_nK$, $\mathbf{g} = P_ng$, $\mathbf{f} = P_nf$, and τ_k as prescribed in Lemma 3.15. Assume that K satisfies (**H.1**), (**H.2**), and $K \in L^{\infty,2}(\Omega^2)$, and that $f, g \in L^2(\Omega)$. Then, the following hold.*

(i) u is the unique solution of $(\mathcal{P})$, $\{\mathbf{u}^k\}_{k\in[N]}$ is uniquely defined and $\left\{\|I_n\mathbf{u}^k\|_{L^2(\Omega)}\right\}_{k\in[N]}$ is bounded (uniformly in n when $\mathbf{f} = 0$).

(ii) We have the error estimate

$$\sup_{k\in[N], t\in]t_{k-1},t_k]} \|I_n\mathbf{u}^{k-1} - u(\cdot,t)\|_{L^2(\Omega)} \leq \exp(T/2) \Bigg(\|I_nP_ng - g\|_{L^2(\Omega)}$$
$$+ CT^{1/2} \left(\tau^{1/2} + \|f_n - f\|_{L^2(\Omega)} + \|I_nP_nK - K\|_{L^2(\Omega^2)} \right) \Bigg) \quad (3.22)$$

where C is a positive constant that depends only on K.

(iii) If, moreover, $f, g \in \mathrm{Lip}(s, L^2(\Omega))$ and $K \in \mathrm{Lip}(s, L^2(\Omega^2))$, then

$$\sup_{\substack{k\in[N],\\ t\in]t_{k-1},t_k]}} \|I_n\mathbf{u}^{k-1} - u(\cdot,t)\|_{L^2(\Omega)} \leq C\exp(T/2)\left((1 + T^{1/2})\delta(n)^s + T^{1/2}\tau^{1/2}\right),$$
$$(3.23)$$

where C is a positive constant that depends only on g, f, K, and s.

PROOF: C is any positive constant that may depend only on g, f, K, and s, and that may be different at each line. We use the same notation as in the proof of Theorem 3.13.

(i) Existence and uniqueness of u follow from Theorem 3.8, since $g, f \in L^2(\Omega) \subset L^1(\Omega)$ and $K \in L^{\infty,2}(\Omega^2) \subset L^{\infty,1}(\Omega^2)$. Well-posedness of $\{\mathbf{u}^k\}_{k\in[N]}$ follows from Lemma 3.15 and Remark 3.16.

(ii) We have

$$\frac{\partial \check{\xi}_n(x,t)}{\partial t} = \int_\Omega K_n(x,y)\,(\bar{w}_n(x,y,t) - w(x,y,t))\,dy + \int_\Omega (K_n(x,y) - K(x,y))w(x,y,t)dy + (f_n(x) - f(x)),$$

where w is the subgradient function associated to u (see Definition 3.6), and $\bar{w}_n(x,y,t) = \operatorname{sign}(\bar{u}_n(y,t) - \bar{u}_n(x,t))$. Multiplying both sides by $\check{\xi}_n(x,t)$, integrating, and rearranging the terms, we get

$$\begin{aligned}\frac{1}{2}\frac{\partial}{\partial t}\|\check{\xi}_n(\cdot,t)\|^2_{L^2(\Omega)} &= \int_{\Omega^2} K_n(x,y)\,(\bar{w}_n(x,y,t) - w(x,y,t))\,(\bar{u}_n(x,t) - u(x,t))dxdy \\ &+ \int_{\Omega^2} (K_n(x,y) - K(x,y))w(x,y,t)\check{\xi}_n(x,t)dxdy \\ &+ \int_\Omega K_n(x,y)\,(\bar{w}_n(x,y,t) - w(x,y,t))\,(\check{u}_n(x,t) - \bar{u}_n(x,t))\,dxdy \\ &+ \int_\Omega (f_n(x) - f(x))\,\check{\xi}_n(x,t)dx.\end{aligned} \tag{3.24}$$

As $u(\cdot,t) \in L^1$ and $\bar{u}_n(\cdot,t) \in L^2(\Omega) \subset L^1(\Omega)$ by Lemma 3.15, the monotonicity claim in Proposition 3.7(ii) yields that the first term in (3.24) is nonpositive. The second term can be easily bounded as

$$\left|\int_{\Omega^2} (K_n(x,y) - K(x,y))w(x,y,t)\check{\xi}_n(x,t)dxdy\right| \leq \|K_n - K\|_{L^2(\Omega^2)}\|\check{\xi}_n(\cdot,t)\|_{L^2(\Omega)} \leq \frac{1}{4}\|\check{\xi}_n(\cdot,t)\|^2_{L^2(\Omega)} + \|K_n - K\|^2_{L^2(\Omega^2)}.$$

and the third term, using Lemma 3.17, as

$$\left|\int_\Omega K_n(x,y)\,(\bar{w}_n(x,y,t) - w(x,y,t))\,(\check{u}_n(x,t) - \bar{u}_n(x,t))\,dxdy\right| \leq 2\|K\|^2_{L^{\infty,2}(\Omega^2)}\tau.$$

Bounding the last term by Young's inequality, we obtain

$$\frac{\partial}{\partial t}\|\check{\xi}_n(\cdot,t)\|^2_{L^2(\Omega)} \leq \|\check{\xi}_n(\cdot,t)\|^2_{L^2(\Omega)} + 2\|f_n - f\|^2_{L^2(\Omega)} + 2\|K_n - K\|^2_{L^2(\Omega^2)} + C\tau.$$

Using Gronwall's lemma and (3.20), we get the claimed bound.

(iii) Insert (2.11) into (3.22). □

3.3.2 Backward/Implicit Euler Discretization

Forward Euler discretization was able to deal only with $p \in [1,2]$. For backward Euler discretization, we will tackle $p \in]1,+\infty[$.

We consider the fully discrete problem with backward Euler time scheme

$$\begin{cases} \dfrac{\mathbf{u}^k - \mathbf{u}^{k-1}}{\tau_{k-1}} = -\widehat{\boldsymbol{\Delta}}_p^{\mathbf{K}} \mathbf{u}^k + \mathbf{f}^k, & k \in [N], \\ \mathbf{u}^0 = \mathbf{g}, \end{cases} \qquad (\mathcal{P}_p^{\mathrm{TDB}})$$

where $\mathbf{u}^k, \mathbf{f}^k \in \mathbb{R}^{n^d}$. This can also be written equivalently as

$$\mathbf{u}^k = J_{\tau_{k-1}\widehat{\boldsymbol{\Delta}}_p^{\mathbf{K}}}(\mathbf{u}^{k-1} + \tau_{k-1}\mathbf{f}^k).$$

This is known as the proximal iteration and is at the heart of so-called mild solutions as well as existence and uniqueness of solutions to $(\mathcal{P})$ through the nonlinear semigroups theory; see Crandall and Liggett (1971); Bénilan (1972); Koabayashi (1975); Bénilan and Crandall (1991). Denoting as before $u_n^k = I_n\mathbf{u}^k$ and $f_n^k = I_n\mathbf{f}^k$, the space continuum extensions of $\mathbf{u}^k$ and $\mathbf{f}^k$, we also have

$$u_n^k = J_{\tau_{k-1}\Delta_p^{I_n\mathbf{K}}}(u_n^{k-1} + \tau_{k-1}f_n^k).$$

We also define the time-space continuum extensions

$$\check{u}_n(\boldsymbol{x},t) = \frac{t_k - t}{\tau_{k-1}} u_n^{k-1}(\boldsymbol{x}) + \frac{t - t_{k-1}}{\tau_{k-1}} u_n^k(\boldsymbol{x}), \quad (\boldsymbol{x},t) \in \Omega\times]t_{k-1},t_k], k \in [N],$$

$$\bar{u}_n(\boldsymbol{x},t) = \sum_{k=1}^{N} u_n^k(\boldsymbol{x})\chi_{]t_{k-1},t_k]}(t), \ \bar{f}_n(\boldsymbol{x},t) = \sum_{k=1}^{N} f_n^k(\boldsymbol{x})\chi_{]t_{k-1},t_k]}(t), \ (\boldsymbol{x},t) \in \Omega\times]0,T].$$

Observe that the difference with the explicit Euler case lies in the definition of $\bar{u}_n$. From $(\mathcal{P}_p^{\mathrm{TDB}})$ one clearly sees that $\check{u}_n$ and $\bar{u}_n$ then satisfy again (3.15), with $\bar{f}_n(\boldsymbol{x},t)$ replacing $f_n(\boldsymbol{x})$.

The following estimates hold.

Lemma 3.19 *Consider problem $(\mathcal{P}_p^{\mathrm{TDB}})$ with kernel* $\mathbf{K}$ *and data* $(\mathbf{f},\mathbf{g})$ *and step sizes $\tau_k > 0$ for all k. Assume that $I_n\mathbf{K}$ satisfies* **(H.1)–(H.2)** *and* **(H.3)**, *that $I_n\mathbf{g} \in L^{\max(p,q)}(\Omega)$, for some $q \in [1,+\infty]$, and $\sup_{n\in\mathbb{N}} \|I_n\mathbf{g}\|_{L^q(\Omega)} < +\infty$, and that $\bar{f}_n \in L^1([0,T]; L^{\max(p,q)}(\Omega))$ and $\sup_{n\in\mathbb{N}} \|\bar{f}_n\|_{L^1([0,T];L^q(\Omega))} < +\infty$. Then,*

$$\bar{u}_n(\cdot,t) \in L^{\max(p,q)}(\Omega), \forall t \in [0,T], \quad \textit{and} \quad \sup_{t\in[0,T],n\in\mathbb{N}} \|\bar{u}_n(\cdot,t)\|_{L^q(\Omega)} < +\infty.$$

PROOF: Recall from Proposition 3.2(vii) that $J_{\lambda\Delta_p^{I_n\mathbf{K}}}, \lambda > 0$, is single-valued on $L^p(\Omega)$ and nonexpansive on $L^q(\Omega)$ for all $q \in [1, +\infty]$. Therefore, by induction, we have that, for any $k \in [N]$,

$$\begin{aligned}\|u_n^k\|_{L^p(\Omega)} &\leq \|I_n g\|_{L^p(\Omega)} + \sum_{i=0}^{k} \tau_i \|f_n^i\|_{L^p(\Omega)} \leq \|I_n g\|_{L^p(\Omega)} + \sum_{i=0}^{N} \tau_i \|f_n^i\|_{L^p(\Omega)} \\ &= \|I_n g\|_{L^p(\Omega)} + \|\bar{f}_n\|_{L^1([0,T];L^p(\Omega))}.\end{aligned}$$

Thus, $u_n^k \in L^p(\Omega)$, for all $k \in [N]$. In turn, $J_{\tau_k \Delta_p^{I_n\mathbf{K}}}(u_n^k)$ is single-valued for all k, and arguing as previously, its nonexpansiveness yields

$$\|u_n^k\|_{L^q(\Omega)} \leq \|I_n g\|_{L^q(\Omega)} + \|\bar{f}_n\|_{L^1([0,T];L^q(\Omega))}.$$

Taking the supremum over k and n and using the definition of $\bar{u}_n$ and the assumptions on g and f, we conclude. □

Lemma 3.20 *Suppose that the assumptions of Lemma 3.19 are satisfied with $q = 2$ when $p \in]1, 2]$, $q = 2(p-1)$ when $p \geq 2$. Assume in addition that $\sup_{n\in\mathbb{N}} \|I_n\mathbf{K}\|_{L^{\infty,1}(\Omega^2)} < +\infty$ and $\sup_{n\in\mathbb{N}} \|\bar{f}_n\|_{\mathrm{BV}([0,T];L^2(\Omega))} < +\infty$. Then,*

$$\sup_{t\in[0,T], n\in\mathbb{N}} \|\breve{u}_n(\cdot,t) - \bar{u}_n(\cdot,t)\|_{L^2(\Omega)} \leq C\tau,$$

where C is a positive constant that does not depend on (n, N, T).

PROOF: For $t \in]t_{k-1}, t_k]$, $k \in \mathbb{N}$, we have

$$\begin{aligned}\|\breve{u}_n(\cdot,t) - \bar{u}_n(\cdot,t)\|_{L^2(\Omega)} &= (t_k - t)\left\|\frac{u_n^{k-1} - u_n^k}{\tau_{k-1}}\right\|_{L^2(\Omega)} \\ &\leq \tau \|\Delta_p^{I_n\mathbf{K}} u_n^k - f_n^k\|_{L^2(\Omega)} \\ &\leq \tau \left(\|\Delta_p^{I_n\mathbf{K}} \bar{u}_n(\cdot,t_k)\|_{L^2(\Omega)} + \sum_{i=1}^{k} \|\bar{f}_n(\cdot,t_i) - \bar{f}_n(\cdot,t_{i-1})\|_{L^2(\Omega)} + \|\bar{f}_n(\cdot,0)\|_{L^2(\Omega)} \right) \\ &\leq \tau \left(\|\Delta_p^{I_n\mathbf{K}} \bar{u}_n(\cdot,t_k)\|_{L^2(\Omega)} + \|\bar{f}_n\|_{\mathrm{BV}([0,T];L^2(\Omega))} \right).\end{aligned} \tag{3.25}$$

For $p \in]1, 2]$, we have from (3.10) that

$$\|\Delta_p^{I_n\mathbf{K}} \bar{u}_n(\cdot,t_k)\|_{L^2(\Omega)} \leq 2^{p/2} C_2^{1/2} \|K\|_{L^{\infty,1}(\Omega^2)} \|\bar{u}_n(\cdot,t)\|_{L^2(\Omega)}^{p-1}.$$

For $p \geq 2$, it is easy to to show with simple arguments as before that

$$\|\Delta_p^{I_n\mathbf{K}} \bar{u}_n(\cdot,t_k)\|_{L^2(\Omega)} \leq 2^{p-3/2} \|K\|_{L^{\infty,1}(\Omega^2)} \|\bar{u}_n(\cdot,t)\|_{L^{2(p-1)}(\Omega)}^{p-1}.$$

Inserting the last two estimates in (3.25), taking the supremum over t and n over both sides, and applying Lemma 3.19, we conclude. □

Remark 3.21 As observed in the case of explicit time-discretization, the uniform (over n) boundedness assumption made in the previous two lemmas holds true if $\mathbf{g} = P_n g$, $\mathbf{K} = P_n K$, and $\mathbf{f}^k = \tau_k^{-1} \int_{t_{k-1}}^{t_k} P_n f(\cdot,t)dt$, where g, f, and K verify simple assumptions. Indeed, in this case we have, thanks to Lemma 2.20, that for any $q \in [1,+\infty]$,

$$\sup_{n\in\mathbb{N}} \left\|I_n\mathbf{g}\right\|_{L^q(\Omega)} \le \left\|g\right\|_{L^q(\Omega)}, \quad \sup_{n\in\mathbb{N}} \left\|I_n\mathbf{K}\right\|_{L^{\infty,q}(\Omega^2)} \le \left\|K\right\|_{L^{\infty,q}(\Omega^2)},$$

$$\sup_{n\in\mathbb{N}} \left\|\bar{f}_n\right\|_{L^1([0,T];L^q(\Omega))} \le \left\|f\right\|_{L^1([0,T];L^q(\Omega))} \text{ and}$$

$$\sup_{n\in\mathbb{N}} \left\|\bar{f}_n\right\|_{\mathrm{BV}([0,T];L^q(\Omega))} \le \left\|f\right\|_{\mathrm{BV}([0,T];L^q(\Omega))}.$$

In fact, the condition $f \in \mathrm{BV}([0,T];L^q(\Omega))$ is sufficient to ensure that

$$\sup_{n\in\mathbb{N}} \left\|\bar{f}_n\right\|_{L^1([0,T];L^q(\Omega))} < +\infty \text{ and } \sup_{n\in\mathbb{N}} \left\|\bar{f}_n\right\|_{\mathrm{BV}([0,T];L^q(\Omega))} < +\infty.$$

Indeed, arguing as in Brézis (1973, lemma A.1), this condition implies $f \in L^\infty([0,T];L^q(\Omega))$. In turn, using Lemma 2.20, we get

$$\begin{aligned}\left\|\bar{f}_n\right\|_{L^1([0,T];L^q(\Omega))} &\le \left\|f\right\|_{L^1([0,T];L^q(\Omega))} \\ &\le \left\|f\right\|_{L^\infty([0,T];L^q(\Omega))} \le \left\|f\right\|_{\mathrm{BV}([0,T];L^q(\Omega))}.\end{aligned}$$

We are now in a position to state the error bound for the fully discrete problem with backward/implicit Euler time discretization.

Theorem 3.22 *Suppose that $p \in]1,+\infty[$. Let u be a solution of $(\mathcal{P})$ with kernel K and data (f,g), and $\{\mathbf{u}^k\}_{k\in[N]}$ be the sequence generated by $(\mathcal{P}_p^{\mathrm{TDB}})$ with $\mathbf{K} = P_n K$, $\mathbf{g} = P_n g$, $\mathbf{f}^k = \tau_k^{-1} \int_{t_{k-1}}^{t_k} P_n f(\cdot,t)dt$. Assume that K satisfies **(H.1)**, **(H.2)**, and $K \in L^{\infty,2}(\Omega^2)$, and that f, g satisfy one of the following conditions:*

(a) $p \in]1,2[$, $g \in L^2(\Omega)$, and $f \in L^1([0,T];L^2(\Omega))$,
(b) $p \ge 2$, $g \in L^{2(p-1)}(\Omega)$ and $f \in L^1([0,T];L^{2(p-1)}(\Omega))$,
(c) $g, g_n \in L^\infty(\Omega)$ and $f, f_n \in L^1([0,T];L^\infty(\Omega))$,

and that $f \in \mathrm{BV}([0,T];L^2(\Omega))$. Then, the following hold:

(i) u is the unique solution of $(\mathcal{P})$, $\{\mathbf{u}^k\}_{k\in[N]}$ is uniquely defined, and $\left\{\left\|I_n\mathbf{u}^k\right\|_{L^2(\Omega)}\right\}_{k\in[N]}$ is bounded uniformly in n.
(ii) We have the error estimate

$$\sup_{\substack{k\in[N],\\ t\in]t_{k-1},t_k]}} \left\|I_n\mathbf{u}^k - u(\cdot,t)\right\|_{L^2(\Omega)} \leq \exp(T/2)\left(\left\|I_nP_ng - g\right\|_{L^2(\Omega)} + \left\|\bar{f}_n - f\right\|_{L^1([0,T];L^2(\Omega))}\right.$$

$$\left. + CT^{1/2}\begin{cases} \tau^{1/(3-p)} + \left\|I_nP_nK - K\right\|_{L^{\infty,2}(\Omega^2)} & \textit{under (a)} \\ \tau^{p/(2p-1)} + \left\|I_nP_nK - K\right\|_{L^{\infty,2}(\Omega^2)} & \textit{under (b)} \\ \tau^{1/(3-p)} + \left\|I_nP_nK - K\right\|_{L^2(\Omega^2)} & \textit{under (c) when } p \in]1,2] \\ \tau + \left\|I_nP_nK - K\right\|_{L^2(\Omega^2)} & \textit{under (c) when } p \geq 2 \end{cases}\right), \tag{3.26}$$

for τ sufficiently small, where C is a positive constant that depends only on p, g, f, and K.

(iii) *If, moreover, $g \in L^\infty(\Omega) \cap \mathrm{Lip}(s, L^2(\Omega))$, $K \in \mathrm{Lip}(s, L^2(\Omega^2))$, and $f \in L^1([0,T]; L^\infty(\Omega)) \cap \mathrm{Lip}(s, L^2(\Omega \times [0,T]))$, then*

$$\sup_{k\in[N],t\in]t_{k-1},t_k]} \left\|I_n\mathbf{u}^k - u(\cdot,t)\right\|_{L^2(\Omega)} \leq C\exp(T/2)\left((1+T^{1/2})\delta(n)^s \right.$$

$$\left. + T^{1/2}\left(\begin{cases} \tau^{\min(s,1/(3-p))} & \textit{when } p \in]1,2] \\ \tau^s & \textit{when } p \geq 2 \end{cases}\right)\right), \tag{3.27}$$

for τ sufficiently small, where C is a positive constant that depends only on p, g, f, K, and s. The term τ^s in the dependence on τ disappears when f is time-independent.

PROOF: In the proof, C is any positive constant that may depend solely on p, g, f, K, and/or s, and that may be different at each line.

(i) Since $L^{\infty,2}(\Omega^2) \subset L^{\infty,1}(\Omega^2)$, assumption **(H.3)** holds for K. We also have the embeddings
   - $L^2(\Omega) \subset L^p(\Omega)$ under (a),
   - $L^{2(p-1)}(\Omega) \subset L^p(\Omega)$ under (b), and
   - $L^\infty(\Omega) \subset L^p(\Omega)$ under (c).

   Thus, $g \in L^p(\Omega)$ and $f \in L^1([0,T]; L^p(\Omega))$. Existence and uniqueness of the solution u in the sense of Definition 3.3 is a consequence of Theorem 3.4. Well-posedness of the sequence $\{\mathbf{u}^k\}_{k\in[N]}$ is a consequence of Lemma 3.19 and Remark 3.21.

(ii) For $p \in]1,2]$, the proof of the error bound is exactly the same as that of (3.16) in Theorem 3.13 using the modified definition of $\bar{u}_n$ and that now f is time-dependent, and thus we replace f_n there by $\bar{f}_n$. We also denote $g_n = I_nP_ng$ and $K_n = I_nP_nK$.

For $p \geq 2$, the argument is also similar, and the main change consists in bounding appropriately the third term in (3.18). We then invoke Lemma 3.20 to show that

$$\left|\int_\Omega \left(\Delta_p^{K_n}\bar{u}_n(x,t) - \Delta_p^{K_n}u(x,t)\right)(\check{u}_n(x,t) - \bar{u}_n(x,t))\,dx\right| \leq C\|\Delta_p^{K_n}\bar{u}_n(\cdot,t) - \Delta_p^{K_n}u(\cdot,t)\|_{L^2(\Omega)}\tau,$$

where C is indeed a finite constant owing to the assumption on f and Remark 3.21. We now use Lemma 3.1(ii) to get the bound

$$\begin{aligned}
&\|\Delta_p^{K_n}\bar{u}_n(\cdot,t) - \Delta_p^{K_n}u(\cdot,t)\|_{L^2(\Omega)}^2 \\
&= \int_\Omega\left|\int_\Omega K_n(x,y)(\Psi(\bar{u}_n(y,t) - \bar{u}_n(x,t)) - \Psi(u(y,t) - u(x,t)))\,dy\right|^2 dx \\
&\leq \int_\Omega\left(\int_\Omega K_n(x,y)|\bar{\xi}_n(y,t) - \bar{\xi}_n(x,t))| \right.\\
&\qquad \left. \cdot (|\bar{u}_n(y,t) - \bar{u}_n(x,t)| + |u(y,t) - u(x,t)|)^{p-2}\,dy\right)^2 dx.
\end{aligned} \tag{3.28}$$

For case (c), we infer from Lemma 3.19 (with $q = +\infty$) and Lemma 2.20 that

$$\begin{aligned}
&\|\Delta_p^{K_n}\bar{u}_n(\cdot,t) - \Delta_p^{K_n}u(\cdot,t)\|_{L^2(\Omega)}^2 \\
&\leq \left(4\left(\|g\|_{L^\infty(\Omega)} + \|f\|_{L^1([0,T];L^\infty(\Omega))}\right)\right)^{2(p-2)} \\
&\qquad \cdot \int_\Omega\left(\int_\Omega K_n(x,y)|\bar{\xi}_n(y,t) - \bar{\xi}_n(x,t))|dy\right)^2 dx \\
&\leq \left(4\left(\|g\|_{L^\infty(\Omega)} + \|f\|_{L^1([0,T];L^\infty(\Omega))}\right)\right)^{2(p-2)} \\
&\qquad \cdot \|K\|_{L^{\infty,2}(\Omega^2)}\int_{\Omega^2} K_n(x,y)|\bar{\xi}_n(y,t) - \bar{\xi}_n(x,t))|^2 dx\,dy \\
&\leq 4\left(4\left(\|g\|_{L^\infty(\Omega)} + \|f\|_{L^1([0,T];L^\infty(\Omega))}\right)\right)^{2(p-2)}\|K\|_{L^{\infty,2}(\Omega^2)}^2\|\bar{\xi}_n(\cdot,t)\|_{L^2(\Omega)}^2.
\end{aligned} \tag{3.29}$$

It then follows by the Cauchy–Schwartz inequality that

$$\begin{aligned}
&\left|\int_\Omega \left(\Delta_p^{K_n}\bar{u}_n(x,t) - \Delta_p^{K_n}u(x,t)\right)(\check{u}_n(x,t) - \bar{u}_n(x,t))\,dx\right| \\
&\leq C\|\bar{\xi}_n(\cdot,t)\|_{L^2(\Omega)}\tau \leq C\left(\|\check{\xi}_n(\cdot,t)\|_{L^2(\Omega)}\tau + \tau^2\right) \leq \frac{1}{6}\|\check{\xi}_n(\cdot,t)\|_{L^2(\Omega)}^2 + C\tau^2.
\end{aligned}$$

Inserting this in (3.18), using again Young's inequality for the last term, we have shown that when $p \geq 2$ and (c) holds,

$$\frac{\partial}{\partial t}\|\check{\xi}_n(\cdot,t)\|^2_{L^2(\Omega)} \leq \|\check{\xi}_n(\cdot,t)\|^2_{L^2(\Omega)} + C\Big(\tau^2 + \|\bar{f}_n(\cdot,t) - f(\cdot,t)\|^2_{L^2(\Omega)} + \|K_n - K\|^2_{L^2(\Omega^2)}\Big).$$

Using Gronwall's lemma, taking the square root, and using (3.20), we get the error bound in this case.

It remains to consider the case (b), when $p \geq 2$. For this, we embark from (3.28) and use the continuity of Ψ in Lemma 3.1 (i) (see (3.4)) with $\alpha = 1/p$. Combining this with the Jensen and Hölder inequalities, we get

$$\begin{aligned}
&\|\Delta_p^{K_n}\bar{u}_n(\cdot,t) - \Delta_p^{K_n}u(\cdot,t)\|^2_{L^2(\Omega)} \\
&\leq \|K\|_{L^{\infty,1}(\Omega^2)}\int_{\Omega^2}\Big(K_n(\boldsymbol{x},\boldsymbol{y})|\bar{\xi}_n(\boldsymbol{y},t) - \bar{\xi}_n(\boldsymbol{x},t))|^{2/p}\Big) \\
&\quad\cdot(|\bar{u}_n(\boldsymbol{y},t) - \bar{u}_n(\boldsymbol{x},t)| + |u(\boldsymbol{y},t) - u(\boldsymbol{x},t)|)^{2(p-1)-2/p}\,d\boldsymbol{x}d\boldsymbol{y} \\
&\leq \|K\|_{L^{\infty,1}(\Omega^2)}\Big(\int_{\Omega^2}K_n(\boldsymbol{x},\boldsymbol{y})|\bar{\xi}_n(\boldsymbol{y},t) - \bar{\xi}_n(\boldsymbol{x},t))|^2 d\boldsymbol{x}d\boldsymbol{y}\Big)^{1/p} \\
&\quad\cdot\Big(\int_{\Omega^2}K_n(\boldsymbol{x},\boldsymbol{y})\,(|\bar{u}_n(\boldsymbol{y},t) - \bar{u}_n(\boldsymbol{x},t)|+|u(\boldsymbol{y},t) - u(\boldsymbol{x},t)|)^{2p-2/(p-1)}d\boldsymbol{x}d\boldsymbol{y}\Big)^{\frac{p-1}{p}} \\
&\leq \|K\|_{L^{\infty,1}(\Omega^2)}\Big(4\int_{\Omega^2}K_n(\boldsymbol{x},\boldsymbol{y})|\bar{\xi}_n(\boldsymbol{x},t))|^2 d\boldsymbol{x}d\boldsymbol{y}\Big)^{1/p} \\
&\quad\Big(2^{2p-2/(p-1)}\int_{\Omega^2}K_n(\boldsymbol{x},\boldsymbol{y})\,(|\bar{u}_n(\boldsymbol{x},t)|+|u(\boldsymbol{x},t)|)^{2p-2/(p-1)}d\boldsymbol{x}d\boldsymbol{y}\Big)^{\frac{p-1}{p}} \\
&\leq 4\|K\|^2_{L^{\infty,1}(\Omega^2)}\Big(\int_{\Omega^2}|\bar{\xi}_n(\boldsymbol{x},t))|^2 d\boldsymbol{x}d\boldsymbol{y}\Big)^{1/p} \\
&\quad\cdot\Big(\int_{\Omega^2}(|\bar{u}_n(\boldsymbol{x},t)| + |u(\boldsymbol{x},t)|)^{2p-2/(p-1)}\,d\boldsymbol{x}d\boldsymbol{y}\Big)^{(p-1)/p}.
\end{aligned}$$

Observe that $L^{2p-2/(p-1)}(\Omega) \subset L^{2(p-1)}(\Omega)$; hence, by the Hölder inequality and Lemma 3.19 with $q = 2(p-1)$ and Lemma 2.20, the last term in the preceding display can be bounded as

$$\begin{aligned}
&\Big(\int_{\Omega^2}(|\bar{u}_n(\boldsymbol{x},t)| + |u(\boldsymbol{x},t)|)^{2p-2/(p-1)}\,d\boldsymbol{x}d\boldsymbol{y}\Big)^{(p-1)/p} \\
&\leq \||\bar{u}_n(\boldsymbol{x},t)| + |u(\boldsymbol{x},t)|\|^{2(p-1)-2/p}_{L^{2(p-1)}(\Omega)} \\
&\leq \Big(\|g\|_{L^{2(p-1)}(\Omega)} + \|f\|_{L^1([0,T];L^{2(p-1)}(\Omega))}\Big)^{2(p-1)-2/p}.
\end{aligned}$$

We then arrive at

$$\left\|\Delta_p^{K_n}\bar{u}_n(\cdot,t) - \Delta_p^{K_n}u(\cdot,t)\right\|_{L^2(\Omega)}^2 \leq C\left\|K\right\|_{L^{\infty,1}(\Omega^2)}^2\left\|\bar{\xi}_n\right\|_{L^2(\Omega)}^{2/p}.$$

Hence,

$$\begin{aligned}
&\left|\int_\Omega \left(\Delta_p^{K_n}\bar{u}_n(x,t) - \Delta_p^{K_n}u(x,t)\right)(\check{u}_n(x,t) - \bar{u}_n(x,t))\,dx\right| \\
&\leq C\left\|\bar{\xi}_n(\cdot,t)\right\|_{L^2(\Omega)}^{1/p}\tau \\
&\leq C\left(\left\|\check{\xi}_n(\cdot,t)\right\|_{L^2(\Omega)}^{1/p}\tau + \tau^{(p+1)/p}\right) \\
&\leq \frac{1}{6}\left\|\check{\xi}_n(\cdot,t)\right\|_{L^2(\Omega)}^2 + C(\tau^{2p/(2p-1)} + \tau^{(p+1)/p}).
\end{aligned}$$

Inserting this into (3.18), using again Young's inequality for the last term,

$$\begin{aligned}
\frac{\partial}{\partial t}\left\|\check{\xi}_n(\cdot,t)\right\|_{L^2(\Omega)}^2 \leq \left\|\check{\xi}_n(\cdot,t)\right\|_{L^2(\Omega)}^2 + C\Bigg(&\tau^{2p/(2p-1)} + \tau^{(p+1)/p} \\
&+ \left\|\bar{f}_n(\cdot,t) - f(\cdot,t)\right\|_{L^2(\Omega)}^2 + \left\|K_n - K\right\|_{L^2(\Omega^2)}^2\Bigg).
\end{aligned}$$

Hence, using Gronwall's lemma, taking the square root, and using (3.20), we get the error bound in this case, after observing that the dependence on τ scales as $O(\tau^{p/(2p-1)})$ for τ sufficiently small (or N large enough) since $1/2 < p/(2p-1) \leq (p+1)/(2p)$ for $p \geq 2$.

(iii) Plug (2.11) into (3.26) after observing that

$$\begin{aligned}
\left\|\bar{f}_n - f\right\|_{L^1([0,T];L^2(\Omega))} &\leq T^{1/2}\left\|\bar{f}_n - f\right\|_{L^2([0,T];L^2(\Omega))} \\
&= T^{1/2}\left\|\bar{f}_n - f\right\|_{L^2(\Omega\times[0,T])} \leq CT^{1/2}\max(\tau^s, \delta(n)^s).
\end{aligned}$$

For the scaling in τ, we use that $s \in]0,1]$. □

Another way to derive error bounds for ($\mathcal{P}_p^{\mathrm{TDB}}$) is as follows. To lighten notation, denote $g_n = I_nP_ng$, $f_n(\cdot,t) = I_nP_nf(\cdot,t)$ for $t \in [0,T]$, and $K_n = I_nP_n\mathbf{K}$. Let u_n be a solution to ($\mathcal{P}$) with data (f_n, g_n) and kernel K_n. Under the assumptions of Theorem 3.22 on (f, g, K), u_n is unique. Then one has

$$\left\|\check{u}_n - u\right\|_{C([0,T];L^2(\Omega))} \leq \left\|\check{u}_n - u_n\right\|_{C([0,T];L^2(\Omega))} + \left\|u_n - u\right\|_{C([0,T];L^2(\Omega))}.$$

Theorem 3.3.1 in El Bouchairi et al. (2020) provides a bound on the last term of the right-hand side in the preceding display, which captures the space-discretization error, which reads

$$\begin{aligned}
\left\|u_n - u\right\|_{C([0,T];L^2(\Omega))} \leq \left\|g_n - g\right\|_{L^2(\Omega)} + &\left\|f_n - f\right\|_{L^1([0,T];L^2(\Omega))} \\
&+ CT\left\|K_n - K\right\|_{L^2(\Omega^2)}.
\end{aligned}$$

Bounds for the first term, which corresponds to the time-discretization error, were derived in $C([0,T];L^p(\Omega))$ by Crandall and Liggett in their seminal paper (1971) for constant time step size and $f=0$, and then extended to non-uniform time partitions in Koabayashi (1975); see also Nochetto and Savaré (2006). More precisely, using Nochetto and Savaré (2006, Theorem 1) and the fact that $\check{u}_n(\cdot,0)=u_n(\cdot,0)=g_n$, the following bound holds:

$$\begin{aligned}\|\check{u}_n-u_n\|_{C([0,T];L^p(\Omega))} \leq& \|\bar{f}_n-f_n\|_{L^1([0,T];L^p(\Omega))}\\ &+2T^{1/2}\left(\|f_n^1-\Delta_p^{K_n}g_n\|_{L^p(\Omega)}+\mathrm{Var}_p(\bar{f}_n)\right)\tau^{1/2},\end{aligned}$$

where $\mathrm{Var}_p(f)$ is the p-variation of the function $f(\cdot,\cdot)$ with respect to the second variable.

The first term can be bounded as follows (for constant step size to simplify):

$$\begin{aligned}\|\bar{f}_n-f_n\|_{L^1([0,T];L^p(\Omega))} &= \sum_{k=1}^{N}\int_{t_{k-1}}^{t_k}\|\tau_k^{-1}\int_{t_{k-1}}^{t_k}f_n(\cdot,s)ds-f_n(\cdot,t)\|_{L^p(\Omega)}dt\\ &\leq \tau^{-1}\sum_{k=1}^{N}\int_{t_{k-1}}^{t_k}\int_{t_{k-1}}^{t_k}\|f(\cdot,s)-f(\cdot,t)\|_{L^p(\Omega)}dsdt\\ &\leq \tau^{-1}\int_{-\tau}^{\tau}\left(\int_0^T\|f(\cdot,t+s)-f(\cdot,t)\|_{L^p(\Omega)}dt\right)ds\\ &\leq \tau^{-1}\int_{-\tau}^{\tau}s\mathrm{Var}_p(f)ds=\tau\mathrm{Var}_p(f),\end{aligned}$$

where we used Lemma 2.20 in the first inequality and Brézis (1973, Lemma A.1) in the last one. Overall, this shows that the time discretization error $\|\check{u}_n-u_n\|_{C([0,T];L^p(\Omega))}$ scales as $O\left((T\tau)^{1/2}\right)$ for τ sufficiently small. The rate $O(\tau^{1/2})$ is known to be optimal for general accretive operators in Banach spaces (see Nochetto and Savaré, 2006). In turn, by standard comparisons of $L^q(\Omega)$ norms (assuming that (c) holds so that boundedness of $\check{u}_n$ and u_n is in force), this strategy gives us a bound that scales as

$$\|\check{u}_n-u_n\|_{C([0,T];L^p(\Omega))}=\begin{cases}O\left(\tau^{1/2}\right) & p\geq 2,\\ O\left(\tau^{p/4}\right) & p\in]1,2].\end{cases}$$

This is strictly worse than the rates in τ obtained from (3.26). There is, however, no contradiction in this, and the reason is that the strategy outlined previously is too general and does not exploit all properties of the operator Δ_p^K, among which is its continuity that was key in deriving better rates in τ. In this sense, our present results are optimal. We also remark that our rates are consistent with those in Hafiene et al. (2018) for $p\geq 2$.

3.4 Application to Random Graph Sequences

In this section, we study continuum limits of fully discrete problems on the random graph model of Definition 2.27 with backward/implicit Euler time discretization. Explicit discretization can also be treated following our results in Section 3.3.1, but we will not elaborate further on it for the sake of brevity.

Recall the notations in Section 2.4.4, in which case we now set $\Omega = [0,1]$. Recall also the construction of the random graph model in Definition 2.27, where each edge (i,j) is independently set to 1 with probability (2.16). This entails that the random matrix $\mathbf{\Lambda}$ is symmetric. However, it is worth emphasizing that the entries of $\mathbf{\Lambda}$ are not independent, but only the entries in each row are mutually independent.[4] This observation will be instrumental in deducing our error bound.

We consider the fully discrete problem on K-random graphs $\mathbf{G}(n,K,\rho_n)$ with backward Euler time scheme

$$\begin{cases} \dfrac{\mathbf{u}^k - \mathbf{u}^{k-1}}{\tau_{k-1}} = \dfrac{1}{\rho_n n} \displaystyle\sum_{j:(i,j)\in E(\mathbf{G}(n,K,\rho_n))} \Psi(\mathbf{u}_j - \mathbf{u}_i) + \mathbf{f}^k, \quad k \in [N], \\ \mathbf{u}^0 = \mathbf{g}, \end{cases} \qquad (\mathcal{P}_p^{\mathrm{TDB},\mathbf{G}})$$

where $\mathbf{u}^k, \mathbf{f}^k \in \mathbb{R}^n$. It is important to keep in mind that, since $\mathbf{G}(n,K,\rho_n)$ is a random variable taking values in the set of simple graphs, the evolution problem $(\mathcal{P}_p^{\mathrm{TDB},\mathbf{G}})$ must be understood in this sense. Observe that the normalization in $(\mathcal{P}_p^{\mathrm{TDB},\mathbf{G}})$ by $\rho_n n$ corresponds to the average degree (see Section 2.4.4 for details).

Problem $(\mathcal{P}_p^{\mathrm{TDB},\mathbf{G}})$ can be equivalently written as

$$\begin{cases} \dfrac{\mathbf{u}^k - \mathbf{u}^{k-1}}{\tau_{k-1}} = -\widehat{\Delta}_p^{\mathbf{\Lambda}} \mathbf{u}^k + \mathbf{f}^k, \quad k \in [N], \\ \mathbf{u}^0 = \mathbf{g}. \end{cases}$$

We define the time-space continuum extensions $\check{u}_n$ and $\bar{u}_n$ and as in the preceding section. One then sees that they satisfy

$$\begin{cases} \frac{\partial}{\partial t}\check{u}_n(x,t) = -\Delta_p^{I_n \mathbf{\Lambda}} \bar{u}_n(x,t) + \bar{f}_n(x,t), \quad (x,t) \in \Omega \times]0,T], \\ \check{u}_n(x,0) = I_n \mathbf{g}(x), \quad x \in \Omega. \end{cases} \tag{3.30}$$

Toward our goal of establishing error bounds, we define $\mathbf{v}$ as the solution of the fully discrete problem $(\mathcal{P}_p^{\mathrm{TDB}})$ with data $(\mathbf{f}, \mathbf{g})$ and discrete kernel $\hat{\mathbf{K}}$.

[4] This feature was already used in the proof of Lemma 2.31.

Its time-space continuum extensions, $\check{v}_n$ and $\bar{v}_n$, defined similarly as earlier, fulfill

$$\begin{cases} \frac{\partial}{\partial t}\check{v}_n(x,t) = -\Delta_p^{I_n\hat{\mathbf{K}}}\bar{v}_n(x,t) + \bar{f}_n(x,t), & (x,t) \in \Omega\times]0,T], \\ \check{v}_n(x,0) = I_n\mathbf{g}(x), & x \in \Omega. \end{cases} \tag{3.31}$$

We have

$$\left\|\check{u}_n - u\right\|_{C([0,T];L^2(\Omega))} \leq \left\|\check{u}_n - \check{v}_n\right\|_{C([0,T];L^2(\Omega))} + \left\|\check{v}_n - u\right\|_{C([0,T];L^2(\Omega))}. \tag{3.32}$$

This bound is composed of two terms: the first one captures the error of random sampling, and the second that of (space and time) discretization. We start by bounding the first term by comparing (3.30) and (3.31).

Lemma 3.23 *Assume that* $(\mathbf{f}^k, \mathbf{g}, \mathbf{K}, f, g, K)$ *verify the assumptions of Theorem 3.22. Assume also that* $\rho_n \to 0$ *and* $n\rho_n = \omega\left((\log n)^\gamma\right)$ *for some* $\gamma > 1$. *Then, for any* $\beta \in]0,1[$,

$$\left\|\check{u}_n - \check{v}_n\right\|_{C([0,T];L^2(\Omega))} \leq C\exp(T/2)T^{1/2} \left((\rho_n n)^{-\beta/2} + \begin{cases} \tau^{1/(3-p)} & p \in]1,2], \\ \tau & p \geq 2. \end{cases} \right), \tag{3.33}$$

with probability at least $1 - (\rho_n n)^{-(1-\beta)}$. *In particular,*

$$\left\|\check{u}_n - \check{v}_n\right\|_{C([0,T];L^2(\Omega))} \leq C\exp\left(\frac{T}{2}\right)T^{\frac{1}{2}} \left(o\left((\log n)^{-\gamma\beta/2}\right) + \begin{cases} \tau^{1/(3-p)} & p \in]1,2] \\ \tau & p \geq 2. \end{cases} \right). \tag{3.34}$$

with probability at least $1 - o\left((\log n)^{-\gamma(1-\beta)}\right)$.

Proof: Denote $\check{\xi}_n(x,t) = \check{v}_n(x,t) - \check{u}_n(x,t)$, $\bar{\xi}_n(x,t) = \bar{v}_n(x,t) - \bar{u}_n(x,t)$, $g_n = I_n\Gamma_n g$, $\hat{\mathbf{K}} - I_n\hat{\mathbf{K}}$, and $\Lambda_n = I_n\mathbf{\Lambda}$. We thus have from (3.30) and (3.31) that a.e.

$$\begin{aligned} \frac{\partial\check{\xi}_n(x,t)}{\partial t} &= -\left(\Delta_p^{\hat{\mathbf{K}}}(\bar{v}_n(x,t)) - \Delta_p^{\Lambda_n}(\bar{u}_n(x,t))\right) \\ &= -\left(\Delta_p^{\hat{\mathbf{K}}}(\bar{v}_n(x,t)) - \Delta_p^{\Lambda_n}(\bar{v}_n(x,t))\right) \\ &\quad - \left(\Delta_p^{\Lambda_n}(\bar{v}_n(x,t)) - \Delta_p^{\Lambda_n}(\bar{u}_n(x,t))\right). \end{aligned}$$

Multiplying both sides by $\check{\xi}_n(x,t)$, integrating, and rearranging the terms, we get

$$\frac{1}{2}\frac{\partial}{\partial t}\|\check{\xi}_n(\cdot,t)\|^2_{L^2(\Omega)} = -\int_\Omega \left(\Delta_p^{\Lambda_n}\bar{v}_n(x,t) - \Delta_p^{\Lambda_n}\bar{u}_n(x,t)\right)(\bar{v}_n(x,t)-\bar{u}_n(x,t))dx$$
$$-\int_\Omega \left(\Delta_p^{\hat{\mathbf{K}}}\bar{v}_n(x,t) - \Delta_p^{\Lambda_n}\bar{v}_n(x,t)\right)\check{\xi}_n(x,t)dx$$
$$-\int_\Omega \left(\Delta_p^{\Lambda_n}\bar{v}_n(x,t) - \Delta_p^{\Lambda_n}\bar{u}_n(x,t)\right)((\check{v}_n(x,t)-\bar{v}_n(x,t)) - (\check{u}_n(x,t)-\bar{u}_n(x,t)))\,dx. \tag{3.35}$$

Under our condition on $n\rho_n$, Lemma 2.31 tells us that with probability 1,

$$\|\Lambda_n\|_{L^{\infty,1}(\Omega^2)} = \|\hat{\mathbf{K}}\|_{L^{\infty,1}(\Omega^2)} + o(1) \le \|I_n P_n K\|_{L^{\infty,1}(\Omega^2)} + o(1)$$
$$\le \|K\|_{L^{\infty,1}(\Omega^2)} + o(1),$$

so, in particular, $\|\Lambda_n\|_{L^{\infty,1}(\Omega^2)}$ is uniformly bounded with probability 1. Λ_n is also positive and symmetric. Since $g \in L^q(\Omega)$ and $f \in L^1([0,T];L^q(\Omega)) \cap \mathrm{BV}([0,T];L^2(\Omega))$, $q \in \{2, 2(p-1), +\infty\}$, the conclusions of Lemma 3.19 and Lemma 3.20 remain true, which shows that, with probability 1,

$$\sup_{\substack{t\in[0,T],\\ n\in\mathbb{N}}} \|\bar{u}_n(\cdot,t)\|_{L^q(\Omega)} < +\infty \quad\text{and}\quad \sup_{\substack{t\in[0,T],\\ n\in\mathbb{N}}} \|\check{u}_n(\cdot,t) - \bar{u}_n(\cdot,t)\|_{L^2(\Omega)} \le C\tau.$$

The same claim holds for $\check{v}_n$ and $\bar{v}_n$ since $\|\hat{\mathbf{K}}\|_{L^{\infty,1}(\Omega^2)} \le \|K\|_{L^{\infty,1}(\Omega^2)} < +\infty$ and $\hat{\mathbf{K}}$ is positive and symmetric, that is, $\hat{\mathbf{K}}$ obeys **(H.1)**–**(H.3)**. Thus, Proposition 3.2(iv) entails that the first term on the right-hand side of (3.35) is nonpositive with probability 1. Let us now bound the second term. Denote the random variables $\mathbf{Z}_i \stackrel{\text{def}}{=} \frac{1}{n}\sum_{j\in[n]}(\mathbf{\Lambda}_{ij} - \hat{\mathbf{K}}_{ij})\Psi(\mathbf{v}_j - \mathbf{v}_i)$. By the Cauchy–Schwartz inequality, we have

$$\left|\int_\Omega \left(\Delta_p^{\Lambda_n}\bar{u}_n(x,t) - \Delta_p^{\hat{\mathbf{K}}}\bar{u}_n(x,t)\right)\check{\xi}_n(x,t)dx\right| \le C\|I_n\mathbf{Z}\|_{L^2(\Omega)}\|\check{\xi}_n(\cdot,t)\|_{L^2(\Omega)}.$$

For the last term in (3.35), we argue as in the proof of Theorem 3.22 to show that, with probability 1,

$$\left|\int_\Omega \left(\Delta_p^{\Lambda_n}\bar{u}_n(x,t) - \Delta_p^{\Lambda_n}\bar{v}_n(x,t)\right)((\check{u}_n(x,t)-\bar{u}_n(x,t)) - (\check{v}_n(x,t)-\bar{v}_n(x,t)))\,dx\right|$$
$$\le C\begin{cases}\|\check{\xi}_n(\cdot,t)\|^{p-1}_{L^2(\Omega)}\tau + \tau^p & p \in]1,2],\\ \|\check{\xi}_n(\cdot,t)\|_{L^2(\Omega)}\tau + \tau^2 & p \ge 2.\end{cases}$$

Collecting all these bounds, after using Young's inequality, we have shown that (again with probability 1),

$$\frac{\partial}{\partial t}\|\check{\xi}_n(\cdot,t)\|^2_{L^2(\Omega)} \le \|\check{\xi}_n(\cdot,t)\|^2_{L^2(\Omega)} + C\left(\|I_n\mathbf{Z}\|^2_{L^2(\Omega)} + \begin{cases}\tau^{2/(3-p)} + \tau^p & p \in]1,2],\\ \tau^2 & p \ge 2.\end{cases}\right)$$

Using Gronwall's lemma and taking the square root, we get, for τ sufficiently small,

$$\left\|\breve{u}_n-\breve{v}_n\right\|_{C([0,T];L^2(\Omega))} \le C\exp\left(\frac{T}{2}\right)T^{\frac{1}{2}}\left(\left\|I_n\mathbf{Z}\right\|_{L^2(\Omega)}+\begin{cases}\tau^{1/(3-p)} & p\in]1,2],\\ \tau & p\ge 2.\end{cases}\right). \tag{3.36}$$

It remains to bound the random variable $\left\|I_n\mathbf{Z}\right\|_{L^2(\Omega)}$. For this purpose, we have by the Markov inequality that, for $\varepsilon > 0$,

$$\mathbb{P}\left(\left\|I_n\mathbf{Z}\right\|_{L^2(\Omega)} \ge \varepsilon\right) = \mathbb{P}\left(n^{-1}\sum_i \mathbf{Z}_i^2 \ge \varepsilon^2\right) \le \varepsilon^{-2}n^{-1}\sum_i \mathbb{E}\left(\mathbf{Z}_i^2\right).$$

By independence of $\left(\mathbf{\Lambda}_{ij}\right)_{j\in[n]}$, for each $i \in [n]$, we get

$$\begin{aligned}\mathbb{E}\left(\mathbf{Z}_i^2\right) &= (\rho_n n)^{-2}\sum_{j\in[n]}\mathrm{Var}\left(\rho_n\mathbf{\Lambda}_{ij}\right)\left(\Psi(\mathbf{v}_j-\mathbf{v}_i)\right)^2\\ &\le (\rho_n n^2)^{-1}\sum_{j\in[n]}\hat{\mathbf{K}}_{ij}|\mathbf{v}_j-\mathbf{v}_i|^{2(p-1)}.\end{aligned}$$

In turn,

$$\begin{aligned}\mathbb{P}\left(\left\|I_n\mathbf{Z}\right\|_{L^2(\Omega)} \ge \varepsilon\right) &\le (\varepsilon^2\rho_n n)^{-1}\frac{1}{n^2}\sum_{i,j\in[n]}\hat{\mathbf{K}}_{ij}|\mathbf{v}_j-\mathbf{v}_i|^{2(p-1)}\\ &= (\varepsilon^2\rho_n n)^{-1}\int_{\Omega^2}\hat{\mathbf{K}}(x,y)|\bar{v}_n(y)-\bar{v}_n(x)|^{2(p-1)}dydx.\end{aligned}$$

If condition (a) holds, then by the symmetry of the kernel, the Jensen inequality, and the Hölder inequality, one gets

$$\begin{aligned}\int_{\Omega^2}\hat{\mathbf{K}}(x,y)|\bar{v}_n(y)-\bar{v}_n(x)|^{2(p-1)}dydx &\le 4\int_{\Omega^2}\hat{\mathbf{K}}(x,y)|\bar{v}_n(x)|^{2(p-1)}dydx\\ &\le 4\left\|\hat{\mathbf{K}}\right\|_{L^{\infty,1}(\Omega^2)}\left\|\bar{v}_n\right\|_{L^2(\Omega)}^{2(p-1)}.\end{aligned}$$

Under condition (b), by the symmetry of the kernel and the Jensen inequality again, we have

$$\begin{aligned}\int_{\Omega^2}\hat{\mathbf{K}}(x,y)|\bar{v}_n(y)-\bar{v}_n(x)|^{2(p-1)}dydx &\le 2^{2(p-1)}\int_{\Omega^2}\hat{\mathbf{K}}(x,y)|\bar{v}_n(x)|^{2(p-1)}dydx\\ &\le 2^{2(p-1)}\left\|\hat{\mathbf{K}}\right\|_{L^{\infty,1}(\Omega^2)}\left\|\bar{v}_n\right\|_{L^{2(p-1)}(\Omega)}^{2(p-1)}.\end{aligned}$$

Similarly, under condition (c), we have

$$\int_{\Omega^2} \hat{\mathbf{K}}(x,y)|\bar{v}_n(y) - \bar{v}_n(x)|^{2(p-1)} dy dx \leq 2^{2(p-1)} \|\bar{v}_n\|_{L^\infty(\Omega)}^{2(p-1)} \|\hat{\mathbf{K}}\|_{L^1(\Omega^2)}$$

$$\leq 2^{2(p-1)} \|\hat{\mathbf{K}}\|_{L^{\infty,1}(\Omega^2)} \|\bar{v}_n\|_{L^\infty(\Omega)}^{2(p-1)}.$$

Since $\|\hat{\mathbf{K}}\|_{L^{\infty,1}(\Omega^2)} \leq \|K\|_{L^{\infty,1}(\Omega^2)}$ (see (2.9) in Lemma 2.20), we have

$$\mathbb{P}\left(\|I_n \mathbf{Z}\|_{L^2(\Omega)} \geq \varepsilon\right) \leq C(\varepsilon^2 \rho_n n)^{-1} \|K\|_{L^{\infty,1}(\Omega^2)},$$

where

$$C = \begin{cases} 4 \sup_n \|\bar{v}_n\|_{L^2(\Omega)}^{2(p-1)}, & \text{under (a)}, \\ 2^{2(p-1)} \sup_n \|\bar{v}_n\|_{L^{2(p-1)}(\Omega)}^{2(p-1)}, & \text{under (b)}, \\ 2^{2(p-1)} \sup_n \|\bar{v}_n\|_{L^\infty(\Omega)}^{2(p-1)}, & \text{under (c)}, \end{cases}$$

and $C < +\infty$, thanks to Lemma 3.19.

Taking $\varepsilon = \left(\frac{C\|K\|_{L^{\infty,1}(\Omega^2)}}{(\rho_n n)^\beta}\right)^{1/2}$, we get

$$\mathbb{P}\left(\|I_n \mathbf{Z}\|_{L^2(\Omega)} \geq \varepsilon\right) \leq \frac{1}{(\rho_n n)^{1-\beta}}.$$

Plugging the latter into (3.36) completes the proof. □

Remark 3.24 Lemma 3.23 gives a deviation bound that holds with a controlled probability. One may ask if almost sure convergence could be obtained. A straightforward approach would be to invoke the Borel–Cantelli lemma as done in Hafiene et al. (2020, remark 3.4(iv)) for the case of graphons. But this argument does not apply here to the more complex setting of L^q-graphons, given that the probability of success in the statement of Lemma 3.23 does not converge sufficiently fast. Even this cannot be made faster, as ρ_n has to converge to 0. Thus, it is not clear at this stage whether this is even possible to achieve or not. We leave this question to future research.

We finally obtain the following error bound on fully discretized problems on sparse random graphs.

Theorem 3.25 *Suppose that $p \in]1, +\infty[$. Let u be a solution of $(\mathcal{P})$ with kernel K and data (f, g), and $\{\mathbf{u}^k\}_{k\in[N]}$ is the sequence generated by $(\mathcal{P}_p^{\mathrm{TDB},\mathbf{G}})$ with $\mathbf{K} = P_n K$, $\mathbf{g} = P_n g$, and $\mathbf{f}^k = \tau_k^{-1} \int_{t_{k-1}}^{t_k} P_n f(\cdot, t) dt$. Assume that (f, g, K) satisfy the assumptions of Theorem 3.22, and that those of Lemma 3.23 also hold.*

1. *For any $\beta \in]0, 1[$, with probability at least $1 - (\rho_n n)^{-(1-\beta)}$,*

$$\sup_{\substack{k\in[N],\\ t\in]t_{k-1},t_k]}} \left\|I_n\mathbf{u}^k - u(\cdot,t)\right\|_{L^2(\Omega)} \le \exp(T/2)\Bigg(\left\|I_nP_ng - g\right\|_{L^2(\Omega)} + \left\|\bar{f}_n - f\right\|_{L^1([0,T];L^2(\Omega))}$$

$$+ CT^{1/2}(\rho_n n)^{-\beta/2} + CT^{1/2}\Bigg($$

$$\cdot\begin{cases} \tau^{1/(3-p)} + \left\|(K-\rho_n^{-1})_+\right\|_{L^{\infty,2}(\Omega^2)} + \left\|I_nP_nK - K\right\|_{L^{\infty,2}(\Omega^2)} & \text{under (a)} \\ \tau^{p/(2p-1)} + \left\|(K-\rho_n^{-1})_+\right\|_{L^{\infty,2}(\Omega^2)} + \left\|I_nP_nK - K\right\|_{L^{\infty,2}(\Omega^2)} & \text{under (b)} \\ \tau^{1/(3-p)} + \left\|(K-\rho_n^{-1})_+\right\|_{L^2(\Omega^2)} + \left\|I_nP_nK - K\right\|_{L^2(\Omega^2)} & \text{under (c), } p\in]1,2] \\ \tau + \left\|(K-\rho_n^{-1})_+\right\|_{L^2(\Omega^2)} + \left\|I_nP_nK - K\right\|_{L^2(\Omega^2)} & \text{under (c), } p\ge 2. \end{cases}\Bigg)\Bigg), \tag{3.37}$$

for τ sufficiently small, where C is a positive constant that depends only on p, g, f, and K.

2. *If, moreover, $g \in L^\infty(\Omega)\cap \mathrm{Lip}(s, L^2(\Omega))$, $K \in \mathrm{Lip}(s, L^2(\Omega^2))$, and $f \in L^1([0,T];L^\infty(\Omega)) \cap \mathrm{Lip}(s, L^2(\Omega\times[0,T]))$, then, for any $\delta \in]0,1[$, with probability at least $1-(\rho_n n)^{-(1-\beta)}$,*

$$\sup_{\substack{k\in[N],\\ t\in]t_{k-1},t_k]}} \left\|I_n\mathbf{u}^k - u(\cdot,t)\right\|_{L^2(\Omega)} \le C\exp(T/2)\Bigg((1+T^{1/2})n^{-s} + T^{1/2}\left\|(K-\rho_n^{-1})_+\right\|_{L^2(\Omega^2)}$$

$$+ T^{1/2}(\rho_n n)^{-\beta/2} + T^{1/2}\left(\begin{cases} \tau^{\min(s,1/(3-p))} & \text{when } p\in]1,2] \\ \tau^s & \text{when } p\ge 2 \end{cases}\right)\Bigg), \tag{3.38}$$

for τ sufficiently small, where C is a positive constant that depends only on p, g, f, K, and s, and $\left\|(K-\rho_n^{-1})_+\right\|_{L^2(\Omega^2)} = o(1)$. The term τ^s in the dependence on τ disappears when f is time-independent.

PROOF: In view of (3.32), we shall use Theorem 3.22 to bound the second term, and a bound on the first term is provided by Lemma 3.23. Since $I_n\hat{\mathbf{K}}(x,y) \le I_n\mathbf{K}(x,y) = I_nP_nK(x,y)$, the assumptions on $\mathbf{K}$ transfer to $\hat{\mathbf{K}}$, and the second term of (3.32) can then be bounded using (3.26), replacing I_nP_nK there by $I_n\hat{\mathbf{K}}$. Observe that

$$\begin{aligned} \left\|I_n\hat{\mathbf{K}} - K\right\|_{L^2(\Omega^2)} &= \left\|\min(I_nP_nK, \rho_n^{-1}) - K\right\|_{L^2(\Omega^2)} \\ &\le \left\|\min(I_nP_nK, \rho_n^{-1}) - I_nP_nK\right\|_{L^2(\Omega^2)} + \left\|I_nP_nK - K\right\|_{L^2(\Omega^2)} \\ &= \left\|(I_nP_nK - \rho_n^{-1})_+\right\|_{L^2(\Omega^2)} + \left\|I_nP_nK - K\right\|_{L^2(\Omega^2)} \\ &\le \left\|(K - \rho_n^{-1})_+\right\|_{L^2(\Omega^2)} + 2\left\|I_nP_nK - K\right\|_{L^2(\Omega^2)}, \end{aligned}$$

and similarly for the $L^{\infty,2}$ norm. The fact that $\left\|(K-\rho_n^{-1})_+\right\|_{L^2(\Omega^2)} = o(1)$ is because $\rho_n \to 0$ by the same argument as the end of the proof of Proposition 2.29. This completes the proof. □

4 Nonlocal p-Laplacian Variational Problem on Graphs

4.1 Problem Statement

Let $\Omega \subset \mathbb{R}$ be a bounded domain, and without loss of generality, throughout this section $\Omega = [0,1]$, and the kernel K is a symmetric, nonnegative, measurable and bounded function on Ω^2. We consider the following variational problem for $p \in [1,+\infty[$:

$$\min_{u\in L^2(\Omega)} \left\{ E_\lambda(u,g,K) \stackrel{\text{def}}{=} \frac{1}{2\lambda}\|u-g\|_{L^2(\Omega)}^2 + R_p(u,K) \right\}. \qquad (\mathcal{VP}^{\lambda,p})$$

The nonlocal regularizer R_p is defined as

$$R_p(u,K) \stackrel{\text{def}}{=} \begin{cases} \frac{1}{2p}\int_{\Omega^2} \left|\nabla_K^{\text{NL}} u(x,y)\right|^p dxdy & \text{if } |\cdot|^p \circ \nabla_K^{\text{NL}} u \in L^1(\Omega^2), \\ +\infty & \text{otherwise.} \end{cases} \qquad (4.1)$$

Here λ is a positive regularization parameter that balances the relative importance of the smoothness of the minimizer and fidelity to the initial data. The chief goal of this section is to study numerical approximations of the nonlocal variational problem $(\mathcal{VP}^{\lambda,p})$, which, in turn, will allow us to establish consistency estimates of the discrete counterpart of this problem on bounded graphons.

In the context of image processing, smoothing and denoising are key processing tasks. Among the existing methods, the variational ones, based on nonlocal regularization such as $(\mathcal{VP}^{\lambda,p})$, provide a popular and versatile framework to achieve these goals. In image processing, such variational problems are in general formulated and studied on the continuum and then discretized on sampled images. On the other hand, many data sources, such as point clouds or meshes, are discrete by nature. Thus, handling such data necessitates a discrete counterpart of $(\mathcal{VP}^{\lambda,p})$, which reads

$$\min_{\mathbf{u}\in\mathbb{R}^n} \left\{ \mathbf{E}_\lambda(\mathbf{u},\mathbf{g},\mathbf{K}) \stackrel{\text{def}}{=} \frac{1}{2\lambda n}\|\mathbf{u}-\mathbf{g}\|_2^2 + \mathbf{R}_p(\mathbf{u},\mathbf{K}) \right\}, \qquad (\mathcal{VP}^d_{\text{nloc}})$$

where

$$\mathbf{R}_p(\mathbf{u},\mathbf{K}) \stackrel{\text{def}}{=} \frac{1}{2n^2 p} \sum_{i,j=1}^{n} \mathbf{K}_{ij} |\mathbf{u}_j - \mathbf{u}_i|^p. \qquad (4.2)$$

Our aim is to study the relationship between the variational problems $(\mathcal{VP}^{\lambda,p})$ and $(\mathcal{VP}^d_{\text{nloc}})$. More specifically, we aim at deriving error estimates between the corresponding minimizers, respectively $u^\star$ and $\mathbf{u}^\star$.

4.2 Well-Posedness

We start by proving existence and uniqueness of the minimizers for $(\mathcal{VP}^{\lambda,p})$ and $(\mathcal{VP}^{d}_{\text{nloc}})$.

Theorem 4.1 *Suppose that $p \in [1, +\infty[$, K is a nonnegative measurable mapping, and $g \in L^2(\Omega)$. Then, $E_\lambda(\cdot, g, K)$ has a unique minimizer in*

$$\left\{u \in L^2(\Omega) : R_p(u, K) \leq (2\lambda)^{-1}\|g\|^2_{L^2(\Omega)}\right\},$$

and $\mathbf{E}_\lambda(\cdot, \mathbf{g}, \mathbf{K})$ has a unique minimizer.

PROOF: The arguments are standard (coercivity, lower semicontinuity, and strict convexity), but we provide a self-contained proof (only for $E_\lambda(\cdot, g, K)$). First observe that from Bauschke and Combettes (2011, proposition 9.32 and proposition 9.5), we infer that $R_p(\cdot, K)$ in (4.1) is proper convex and lower semicontinuous. Let $\{u_k^\star\}_{k\in\mathbb{N}}$ be a minimizing sequence in $L^2(\Omega)$. By optimality and Jensen's inequality, we have

$$\begin{aligned}\|u_k^\star\|^2_{L^2(\Omega)} &\leq 2\left(2\lambda E_\lambda(u_k^\star, g, K) + \|g\|^2_{L^2(\Omega)}\right) \leq 2\left(2\lambda E_\lambda(0, g, K) + \|g\|^2_{L^2(\Omega)}\right) \\ &= 4\|g\|^2_{L^2(\Omega)} < +\infty.\end{aligned} \tag{4.3}$$

Moreover,

$$R_p(u_k^\star, K) \leq E_\lambda(u_k^\star, g, K) \leq E_\lambda(0, g, K) = \frac{1}{2\lambda}\|g\|^2_{L^2(\Omega)} < +\infty. \tag{4.4}$$

Thus, $\|u_k^\star\|_{L^2(\Omega)}$ is bounded uniformly in k so that the Banach–Alaoglu theorem for $L^2(\Omega)$ and compactness provide a weakly convergent subsequence (not relabeled) with a limit $\bar{u} \in L^2(\Omega)$. By lower semicontinuity of the $L^2(\Omega)$ norm and that of $R_p(\cdot, K)$, $\bar{u}$ must be a minimizer. The uniqueness follows from strict convexity of $\|\cdot\|^2_{L^2(\Omega)}$ and convexity of $R_p(\cdot, K)$. □

Remark 4.2 Theorem 4.1 can be extended to linear inverse problems, where the data fidelity in $E_\lambda(0, g, K)$ is replaced by $\|g - \mathrm{A}u\|^2_{L^2(\Sigma)}$, and where A is a continuous linear operator. The case where $\mathrm{A} : L^2(\Omega) \to L^2(\Sigma)$ is injective is immediate. The general case is more intricate and would necessitate appropriate assumptions on A and a Poincaré-type inequality. For instance, if $\mathrm{A} : L^p(\Omega) \to L^2(\Sigma)$, and the kernel of A intersects constant functions trivially, then using the Poincaré inequality in Andreu-Vaillo et al. (2010, proposition 6.19), one can show existence and uniqueness in $L^p(\Omega)$, and thus in $L^2(\Omega)$ if $p \geq 2$. We omit the details here, as these are beyond the scope of this work.

We now turn to provide a useful characterization of the minimizers $u^\star$ and $\mathbf{u}^\star$. We stress that the minimization problem $(\mathcal{VP}^{\lambda,p})$ that we deal with is considered over $L^2(\Omega)$ ($L^2(\Omega) \subset L^p(\Omega)$ only for $p \in [1,2]$, since Ω is bounded), over which the function $R_p(\cdot, K)$ may not be finite (see (4.1)). In correspondence, we will consider the subdifferential of the proper lower semicontinuous convex function $R_p(\cdot, K)$ on $L^2(\Omega)$ defined as

$$\partial R_p(u,K) \stackrel{\text{def}}{=} \left\{\eta \in L^2(\Omega) : R_p(v,K) \geq R_p(u,K) + \langle \eta, v-u \rangle_{L^2(\Omega)}, \forall v \in L^2(\Omega)\right\},$$

and $\partial R_p(u,K) = \emptyset$ if $R_p(u,K) = +\infty$.

Lemma 4.3 *Suppose that the assumptions of Theorem 4.1 hold. Then $u^\star$ is the unique solution to $(\mathcal{VP}^{\lambda,p})$ if and only if*

$$u^\star = \text{prox}_{\lambda R_p(\cdot,K)}(g) \stackrel{\text{def}}{=} (\mathbf{I} + \lambda \partial R_p(\cdot, K))^{-1}(g). \tag{4.5}$$

Moreover, the proximal mapping $\text{prox}_{\lambda R_p(\cdot,K)}$ is nonexpansive on $L^2(\Omega)$, that is, for $g_1, g_2 \in L^2(\Omega)$, the corresponding minimizers $u_1^\star, u_2^\star \in L^2(\Omega)$ obey

$$\|u_1^\star - u_2^\star\|_{L^2(\Omega)} \leq \|g_1 - g_2\|_{L^2(\Omega)}. \tag{4.6}$$

A similar claim is easily obtained for $(\mathcal{VP}^d_{\text{nloc}})$ as well.

Proof: The proof is again classical. By the first-order optimality condition and since the squared $L^2(\Omega)$-norm is Fréchet differentiable, $u^\star$ is the unique solution to $(\mathcal{VP}^{\lambda,p})$ if and only if the following monotone inclusion holds:

$$0 \in u^\star - g + \lambda \partial R_p(u^\star, K).$$

The first claim then follows. Writing the subgradient inequality for $u_1^\star$ and $u_2^\star$, we have

$$R_p(u_2^\star, K) \geq R_p(u_1^\star, K) + \frac{1}{\lambda}\langle g_1 - u_1^\star, u_2^\star - u_1^\star \rangle_{L^2(\Omega)},$$
$$R_p(u_1^\star, K) \geq R_p(u_2^\star, K) + \frac{1}{\lambda}\langle g_2 - u_2^\star, u_1^\star - u_2^\star \rangle_{L^2(\Omega)}.$$

Adding these two inequalities, we get

$$\|u_2^\star - u_1^\star\|^2_{L^2(\Omega)} \leq \langle u_2^\star - u_1^\star, g_2 - g_1 \rangle_{L^2(\Omega)},$$

and we conclude upon applying the Cauchy–Schwartz inequality. □

We now formally derive the directional derivative of $R_p(\cdot, K)$ when $p \in]1, +\infty[$. For this the symmetry assumption on K is needed as well. Let $v \in L^2(\Omega)$. Then the following derivative exists:

$$\begin{aligned}\frac{d}{dt} R_p(u + tv, K)|_{t=0} &= \frac{1}{2}\int_{\Omega^2} K(x,y) \left|\nabla^{\text{NL}} u(x,y)\right|^{p-2} \\ &\quad \times (\nabla^{\text{NL}}(u - v)(x,y)) dx dy \\ &= \langle \Delta_p^K(u), v \rangle_{L^2(\Omega)}.\end{aligned}$$

We get the last equality by applying Proposition 3.2 (iv), where h is the identity function and $v = 0$. This shows that under the preceding assumptions, $R_p(\cdot, K)$ is Fréchet differentiable (hence Gâteaux differentiable) on $L^2(\Omega)$ with Fréchet gradient Δ_p^K.

4.3 Error Estimate for the Discrete Variational Problem

The chief goal of this section is to bound the difference between the unique minimizer of the continuum functional $E_\lambda(\cdot, g, K)$ defined on $L^2(\Omega)$ and the piecewise-continuous extension of the minimizer of $\mathbf{E}_\lambda(\cdot, \mathbf{g}, \mathbf{K})$. We are now ready to state the main result of this section.

Theorem 4.4 *Suppose that $g \in L^2(\Omega)$ and K is a nonnegative measurable, symmetric, and bounded mapping. Let $u^\star$ and $\mathbf{u}^\star$ be the unique minimizers of $(\mathcal{VP}^{\lambda,p})$ and $(\mathcal{VP}^d_{\mathrm{nloc}})$, respectively. Then, we have the following error bounds:*

(i) If $p \in [1, 2]$, then

$$\left\|I_n\mathbf{u}^\star - u^\star\right\|^2_{L^2(\Omega)} \le C\left(\left\|g - I_n\mathbf{g}\right\|^2_{L^2(\Omega)} + \left\|g - I_n\mathbf{g}\right\|_{L^2(\Omega)} + \lambda\left\|K - I_n\mathbf{K}\right\|_{L^{\frac{2}{2-p}}(\Omega^2)} + \lambda\left\|u^\star - I_nP_nu^\star\right\|_{L^{\frac{2}{3-p}}(\Omega)}\right), \tag{4.7}$$

where C is a positive constant independent of n and λ.

(ii) If $\inf_{(x,y)\in\Omega^2} K(x, y) \ge \kappa > 0$, then for any $p \in [1, +\infty[$,

$$\left\|I_n\mathbf{u}^\star - u^\star\right\|^2_{L^2(\Omega)} \le C\left(\left\|g - I_n\mathbf{g}\right\|^2_{L^2(\Omega)} + \left\|g - I_n\mathbf{g}\right\|_{L^2(\Omega)} + \left\|K - I_n\mathbf{K}\right\|_{L^\infty(\Omega^2)} + \lambda^{1/p}\left\|u^\star - I_nP_nu^\star\right\|_{L^p(\Omega)}\right), \tag{4.8}$$

where C is a positive constant independent of n.

A few remarks are in order before proceeding to the proof.

Remark 4.5 (i) Observe that $2/(3 - p) \le p$ for $p \in [1, 2]$. Thus, by standard embeddings of $L^q(\Omega)$ spaces for Ω bounded, we have for $p \in [1, 2]$

$$\left\|K - I_n\mathbf{K}\right\|_{L^{\frac{2}{2-p}}(\Omega^2)} \le \left\|K - I_n\mathbf{K}\right\|_{L^\infty(\Omega^2)} \text{ and}$$

$$\left\|u^\star - I_nP_nu^\star\right\|_{L^{\frac{2}{3-p}}(\Omega)} \le \left\|u^\star - I_nP_nu^\star\right\|_{L^p(\Omega)},$$

which means that our bound in (4.7) not only does not require an extra assumption on K but is also sharper than (4.8). The assumption on K in the second statement seems difficult to remove or weaken. Whether this is possible or not is an open question that we leave to a future work.

(ii) We have made the dependence of the bound on λ explicit on purpose. To see our motivation, assume that $g = u^\dagger + \varepsilon$, where $u^\dagger \in L^2(\Omega)$ is some true function and $\varepsilon \in L^2(\Omega)$ is some noise. Assume that $\partial R_p(u^\dagger, K) \neq \emptyset$, and let $\eta \in \partial R_p(u^\dagger, K)$, which is known in the inverse problem literature as a dual multiplier or certificate; see Vaiter et al. (2015). Then

$$\|I_n \mathbf{u}^\star - u^\dagger\|_{L^2(\Omega)} \leq \|I_n \mathbf{u}^\star - u^\star\|_{L^2(\Omega)} + \|u^\star - u^\dagger\|_{L^2(\Omega)}.$$

From Scherzer et al. (2009, proposition 3.41), one can show that

$$\|u^\star - u^\dagger\|_{L^2(\Omega)} \leq 2\left(\|\varepsilon\|_{L^2(\Omega)} + \lambda\|\eta\|_{L^2(\Omega)}\right).$$

With the standard choice $\lambda \sim \|\varepsilon\|_{L^2(\Omega)}$ we have $\|u^\star - u^\dagger\|_{L^2(\Omega)} = O(\|\varepsilon\|_{L^2(\Omega)})$, and thus $\|u^\star - u^\dagger\|_{L^2(\Omega)} \to 0$ as $\|\varepsilon\|_{L^2(\Omega)} \to 0$. Combining this with Theorem 4.4 and the fact that

$$\|g - I_n \mathbf{g}\|_{L^2(\Omega)} \leq \|u^\dagger - I_n P_n u^\dagger\|_{L^2(\Omega)} + 2\|\varepsilon\|_{L^2(\Omega)},$$

one obtains an error bound of $\|I_n \mathbf{u}^\star - u^\dagger\|_{L^2(\Omega)}$ as a function of $\|\varepsilon\|_{L^2(\Omega)}$ and the discretization error of $u^\dagger$ and K. This error bound is dominated by that of $u^\dagger$ and K as $\|\varepsilon\|_{L^2(\Omega)} \to 0$ fast enough. Having said this, as our focus here is on numerical consistency; in the rest of the Element, the dependence of the error bound on λ will be absorbed in the constants.

PROOF:

(i) Since $E_\lambda(\cdot, g, K)$ is a strongly convex function, we have

$$\begin{aligned}\frac{1}{2\lambda}\|I_n \mathbf{u}^\star - u^\star\|^2_{L^2(\Omega)} &\leq E_\lambda(I_n \mathbf{u}^\star, g, K) - E_\lambda(u^\star, g, K) \\ &\leq \left(E_\lambda(I_n \mathbf{u}^\star, g, K) - \mathbf{E}_\lambda(\mathbf{u}^\star, \mathbf{g}, \mathbf{K})\right) - \left(E_\lambda(u^\star, g, K) - \mathbf{E}_\lambda(\mathbf{u}^\star, \mathbf{g}, \mathbf{K})\right).\end{aligned} \tag{4.9}$$

It is straightforward to see

$$E_\lambda(I_n \mathbf{u}^\star, I_n \mathbf{g}, I_n \mathbf{K}) = \mathbf{E}_\lambda(\mathbf{u}^\star, \mathbf{g}, \mathbf{K}). \tag{4.10}$$

Now, applying the Cauchy–Schwarz inequality and using (4.10), we have

$$\begin{aligned}E_\lambda(I_n \mathbf{u}^\star, g, K) &= \frac{1}{2\lambda}\|I_n \mathbf{u}^\star - I_n \mathbf{g}\|^2_{L^2(\Omega)} + \frac{1}{\lambda}\langle I_n \mathbf{u}^\star - I_n \mathbf{g}, I_n \mathbf{g} - g\rangle_{L^2(\Omega)} \\ &\quad + \frac{1}{2\lambda}\|I_n \mathbf{g} - g\|^2_{L^2(\Omega)} + R_p(I_n \mathbf{u}^\star, K) \\ &\leq \mathbf{E}_\lambda(\mathbf{u}^\star, \mathbf{g}, \mathbf{K}) + \frac{1}{\lambda}\|I_n \mathbf{u}^\star - I_n \mathbf{g}\|_{L^2(\Omega)}\|I_n \mathbf{g} - g\|_{L^2(\Omega)} + \frac{1}{2\lambda}\|I_n \mathbf{g} - g\|^2_{L^2(\Omega)} \\ &\quad + \left(R_p(I_n \mathbf{u}^\star, K) - R_p(I_n \mathbf{u}^\star, I_n \mathbf{K})\right)\end{aligned}$$

$$\leq \mathbf{E}_\lambda(\mathbf{u}^\star,\mathbf{g},\mathbf{K}) + \frac{1}{\lambda}\left\|I_n\mathbf{u}^\star - I_n\mathbf{g}\right\|_{L^2(\Omega)}\left\|I_n\mathbf{g} - g\right\|_{L^2(\Omega)} + \frac{1}{2\lambda}\left\|I_n\mathbf{g} - g\right\|^2_{L^2(\Omega)}$$
$$+ \frac{1}{2p}\left|\int_{\Omega^2}(K(x,y) - I_n\mathbf{K}(x,y))|I_n\mathbf{u}^\star(y) - I_n\mathbf{u}^\star(x)|^p\,dxdy\right|. \tag{4.11}$$

As we suppose that $g \in L^2(\Omega)$ and since $\mathbf{u}^\star$ is the (unique) minimizer of $\mathbf{E}_\lambda(\cdot,\mathbf{g},\mathbf{K})$, it is immediate to see, using (4.10) and (2.8), that

$$\frac{1}{2\lambda}\left\|I_n\mathbf{u}^\star - I_n\mathbf{g}\right\|^2_{L^2(\Omega)} \leq \mathbf{E}_\lambda(\mathbf{u}^\star,\mathbf{g},\mathbf{K}) \leq E_\lambda(0,I_n\mathbf{g},I_n\mathbf{K}) \leq \frac{1}{2\lambda}\|g\|^2_{L^2(\Omega)} < +\infty$$

and thus

$$\left\|I_n\mathbf{u}^\star - I_n\mathbf{g}\right\|_{L^2(\Omega)} \leq \|g\|_{L^2(\Omega)} \stackrel{\text{def}}{=} C_1. \tag{4.12}$$

Since $p \in [1,2]$, by the Hölder and triangle inequalities, and (4.3) applied to $I_n\mathbf{u}^\star$, we have that

$$\begin{aligned}
&\left|\int_{\Omega^2}(K(x,y) - I_n\mathbf{K}(x,y))|I_n\mathbf{u}^\star(y) - I_n\mathbf{u}^\star(x)|^p\,dxdy\right| \\
&\leq \left\|K - I_n\mathbf{K}\right\|_{L^{\frac{2}{2-p}}(\Omega^2)}\left(\int_{\Omega^2}|I_n\mathbf{u}^\star(y) - I_n\mathbf{u}^\star(x)|^2\,dxdy\right)^{p/2} \\
&\leq 2^p\left\|I_n\mathbf{u}^\star\right\|^p_{L^2(\Omega)}\left\|K - I_n\mathbf{K}\right\|_{L^{\frac{2}{2-p}}(\Omega^2)} \\
&\leq 2^{2p}\|g\|^p_{L^2(\Omega)}\left\|K - I_n\mathbf{K}\right\|_{L^{\frac{2}{2-p}}(\Omega^2)} = C_2\left\|K - I_n\mathbf{K}\right\|_{L^{\frac{2}{2-p}}(\Omega^2)},
\end{aligned} \tag{4.13}$$

where $C_2 \stackrel{\text{def}}{=} 2^{2p}C_1^p$.

We now turn to bounding the second term on the right-hand side of (4.9). Using (2.8) and the fact that $\mathbf{u}^\star$ is the (unique) minimizer of ($\mathcal{VP}^d_{\text{nloc}}$), we have

$$\begin{aligned}
E_\lambda(I_n\mathbf{u}^\star, I_n\mathbf{g}, I_n\mathbf{K}) &\leq E_\lambda(I_nP_nu^\star, I_n\mathbf{g}, I_n\mathbf{K}) \\
&\leq \frac{1}{2\lambda}\|u^\star - g\|^2_{L^2(\Omega)} + R_p(u^\star,K) + R_p(I_nP_nu^\star, I_n\mathbf{K}) - R_p(u^\star,K) \\
&\leq E_\lambda(u^\star,g,K) + \left(R_p(I_nP_nu^\star,K) - R_p(u^\star,K)\right) \\
&\quad + (R_p(I_nP_nu^\star, I_n\mathbf{K}) - R_p(I_nP_nu^\star,K)).
\end{aligned} \tag{4.14}$$

We bound the second term on the right-hand side of (4.14) by applying the mean value theorem on $[a(x,y), b(x,y)]$ to the function $t \in \mathbb{R}^+ \mapsto t^p$ with $a(x,y) = |\nabla^{\text{NL}}u^\star(x,y)|$ and $b(x,y) = |\nabla^{\text{NL}}I_nP_nu^\star(x,y)|$. Let $\eta(x,y) \stackrel{\text{def}}{=} \rho a(x,y) + (1-\rho)b(x,y)$, $\rho \in [0,1]$, be an intermediate value between $a(x,y)$ and $b(x,y)$. We then get

$$
\begin{aligned}
&\left|R_p(I_nP_nu^\star,K) - R_p(u^\star,K)\right| \\
&\quad = \left|\int_{\Omega^2} K(x,y)\left(\left|\nabla^{\mathrm{NL}} I_nP_nu^\star(x,y)\right|^p - \left|\nabla^{\mathrm{NL}} u^\star(x,y)\right|^p\right) dxdy\right| \\
&\quad = p\left|\int_{\Omega^2} K(x,y)\eta(x,y)^{p-1}\left(\left|\nabla^{\mathrm{NL}} I_nP_nu^\star(x,y)\right| - \left|\nabla^{\mathrm{NL}} u^\star(x,y)\right|\right) dxdy\right| \\
&\quad \le pC_3\int_{\Omega^2} \eta(x,y)^{p-1}\left|\left(I_nP_nu^\star(y) - u^\star(y)\right) - \left(I_nP_nu^\star(x) - u^\star(x)\right)\right| dxdy \\
&\quad \le 2pC_3\int_{\Omega^2} \eta(x,y)^{p-1}\left|I_nP_nu^\star(x) - u^\star(x)\right| dxdy, \qquad (4.15)
\end{aligned}
$$

where we used the triangle inequality, symmetry after the change of variable $(x,y) \mapsto (y,x)$, and boundedness of K, say $\|K\|_{L^\infty(\Omega^2)} \stackrel{\text{def}}{=} C_3$. Thus, using the Hölder and Jensen inequalities as well as (2.8), and arguing as in (4.13), leads to

$$
\begin{aligned}
&\left|R_p(I_nP_nu^\star,K) - R_p(u^\star,K)\right| \\
&\quad \le 2pC_3\|\eta\|_{L^2(\Omega^2)}^{p-1}\|u^\star - I_nP_nu^\star\|_{L^{\frac{2}{3-p}}(\Omega)} \\
&\quad \le 2pC_3\left(\rho\|a\|_{L^2(\Omega^2)} + (1-\rho)\|b\|_{L^2(\Omega^2)}\right)^{p-1}\|u^\star - I_nP_nu^\star\|_{L^{\frac{2}{3-p}}(\Omega)} \\
&\quad \le 2pC_3\|a\|_{L^2(\Omega^2)}^{p-1}\|u^\star - I_nP_nu^\star\|_{L^{\frac{2}{3-p}}(\Omega)} \\
&\quad \le 2^{2p-1}pC_3\|g\|_{L^2(\Omega)}^{p-1}\|u^\star - I_nP_nu^\star\|_{L^{\frac{2}{3-p}}(\Omega)} = C_4\|u^\star - I_nP_nu^\star\|_{L^{\frac{2}{3-p}}(\Omega)}, \qquad (4.16)
\end{aligned}
$$

where $C_4 \stackrel{\text{def}}{=} 2^{2p-1}pC_1^{p-1}C_3$.

To bound the last term on the right-hand side of (4.14), we follow the same steps as for establishing (4.13) and get

$$
\left|R_p(I_nP_nu^\star, I_n\mathbf{K}) - R_p(I_nP_nu^\star,K)\right| \le C_2\|K - I_n\mathbf{K}\|_{L^{\frac{2}{2-p}}(\Omega^2)}. \qquad (4.17)
$$

Finally, plugging (4.11), (4.12), (4.13), (4.14), (4.16), and (4.17) into (4.9), we get the desired result.

(ii) The case $p \ge 2$ follows the same proof steps, except that now, we need to modify inequalities (4.13), (4.16), and (4.17), which do not hold anymore. Under our assumption on K, and using (4.4), (4.13) now reads

$$
\begin{aligned}
&\int_{\Omega^2} |K(x,y) - I_n\mathbf{K}(x,y)||I_n\mathbf{u}^\star(y) - I_n\mathbf{u}^\star(x)|^p dxdy \\
&\quad \le \kappa^{-1}\|K - I_n\mathbf{K}\|_{L^\infty(\Omega^2)}\int_{\Omega^2} I_n\mathbf{K}(x,y)|I_n\mathbf{u}^\star(y) - I_n\mathbf{u}^\star(x)|^p dxdy \\
&\quad = \kappa^{-1}\|K - I_n\mathbf{K}\|_{L^\infty(\Omega^2)}R_p(I_n\mathbf{u}^\star, I_n\mathbf{K}) \\
&\quad \le (2\lambda\kappa)^{-1}C_1^2\|K - I_n\mathbf{K}\|_{L^\infty(\Omega^2)}, \qquad (4.18)
\end{aligned}
$$

where $C_1 = \|g\|_{L^2(\Omega)}$ as in the proof of (i).

We embark from the last line of (4.15), to which we apply the Hölder inequality and the Jensen inequality as well as (2.8) to get

$$\begin{aligned}|R_p(I_nP_nu^\star,K)-R_p(u^\star,K)| &\le 2pC_3\|\eta\|^{(p-1)}_{L^p(\Omega^2)}\|u^\star-I_nP_nu^\star\|_{L^p(\Omega)}\\ &\le 2pC_3\|a\|^{(p-1)}_{L^p(\Omega^2)}\|u^\star-I_nP_nu^\star\|_{L^p(\Omega)}\\ &= 2pC_3\|\nabla^{\mathrm{NL}}u^\star\|^{(p-1)}_{L^p(\Omega^2)}\|u^\star-I_nP_nu^\star\|_{L^p(\Omega)}.\end{aligned}$$

Now, by assumption on K and again using (4.4), we obtain

$$\begin{aligned}&|R_p(I_nP_nu^\star,K)-R_p(u^\star,K)|\\ &\le 2\kappa^{(1-p)/p}pC_3\left(\int_{\Omega^2}K(x,y)|\nabla^{\mathrm{NL}}u^\star(x,y)|^p\,dxdy\right)^{(p-1)/p}\|u^\star-I_nP_nu^\star\|_{L^p(\Omega)}\\ &= 2\kappa^{(1-p)/p}pC_3\left(R_p(u^\star,K)\right)^{(p-1)/p}\|u^\star-I_nP_nu^\star\|_{L^p(\Omega)}\\ &\le 2(2\lambda\kappa)^{(1-p)/p}pC_3C_1^{2(p-1)/p}\|u^\star-I_nP_nu^\star\|_{L^p(\Omega)}.\end{aligned}\tag{4.19}$$

To get the new form of (4.17), we use (2.8), (4.4), and the assumption on K to arrive at

$$\begin{aligned}&|R_p(I_nP_nu^\star,I_n\mathbf{K})-R_p(I_nP_nu^\star,K)|\\ &\le \|K-I_n\mathbf{K}\|_{L^\infty(\Omega^2)}\int_{\Omega^2}|u^\star(y)-u^\star(x)|^p\,dxdy\\ &\le \kappa^{-1}\|K-I_n\mathbf{K}\|_{L^\infty(\Omega^2)}R_p(u^\star,K)\le(2\lambda\kappa)^{-1}C_1^2\|K-I_n\mathbf{K}\|_{L^\infty(\Omega^2)}.\end{aligned}\tag{4.20}$$

Plugging (4.11), (4.12), (4.14), (4.18), (4.19) and (4.20), into (4.9), we now conclude the proof. □

Remark 4.6 The error bound of Theorem 4.4 contains three terms: one corresponds to the error in discretizing g; the second is the discretization error of the kernel K; and the last term reflects the discretization error of the minimizer $u^\star$ of the continuum problem $(\mathcal{VP}^{\lambda,p})$. Thus, this form is not convenient to transfer our bounds to networks on graph and establish convergence rates. Clearly, we need a control on the term $\|I_nP_nu^\star-u^\star\|_{L^q(\Omega)}$ on the right-hand side of (4.7)–(4.8). This is what we are about to do in the following key regularity lemma. In a nutshell, it states that if the kernel K only depends on $|x-y|$ (as is the case for many kernels used in data processing), then as soon as the initial data g belongs to some Lipschitz space, so does the minimizer $u^\star$.

Lemma 4.7 *Suppose* $g\in L^\infty(\Omega)\cap \mathrm{Lip}(s,L^q(\Omega))$ *with* $s\in]0,1]$ *and* $q\in[1,+\infty]$. *Suppose, furthermore, that* $K(x,y)=J(|x-y|)$, *where* J *is a nonnegative bounded measurable mapping on* Ω.

(i) If $q \in [1,2]$, *then* $u^\star \in \mathrm{Lip}(sq/2, L^q(\Omega))$.
(ii) If $q \in [2,+\infty]$, *then* $u^\star \in \mathrm{Lip}(s, L^2(\Omega))$.

PROOF: We denote the torus $\mathbb{T} \stackrel{\text{def}}{=} \mathbb{R}/2\mathbb{Z}$. For any function $u \in L^2(\Omega)$, we denote by $\bar{u} \in L^2(\mathbb{T})$ its periodic extension such that

$$\bar{u}(x) = \begin{cases} u(x) & \text{if} \quad x \in [0,1], \\ u(2-x) & \text{if} \quad x \in]1,2]. \end{cases} \tag{4.21}$$

In the rest of the proof, we use letters with bars to indicate functions defined on $\mathbb{T}$.
Let us define

$$\bar{E}_{\lambda/2}(\bar{v},\bar{g},\bar{J}) \stackrel{\text{def}}{=} \frac{1}{\lambda}\|\bar{v}-\bar{g}\|^2_{L^2(\mathbb{T})} + \bar{R}_p(\bar{v},\bar{J})$$

where

$$\bar{R}_p(\bar{v},\bar{J}) \stackrel{\text{def}}{=} \frac{1}{2p}\int_{\mathbb{T}^2} \bar{J}(|x-y|)|\bar{v}(y)-\bar{v}(x)|^p\, dxdy.$$

Consider the following minimization problem:

$$\min_{\bar{v}\in L^2(\mathbb{T})} \bar{E}_{\lambda/2}(\bar{v},\bar{g},\bar{J}), \tag{4.22}$$

which also has a unique minimizer by arguments similar to those of Theorem 4.1. Since $u^\star$ is the unique minimizer of $(\mathcal{VP}^{\lambda,p})$, we have, using (4.21),

$$\begin{aligned} \bar{E}_{\lambda/2}(\overline{u^\star},\bar{g},\bar{J}) &= \frac{2}{\lambda}\|u^\star - g\|^2_{L^2(\Omega)} + 4R_p(u^\star,J) \\ &= 4E_\lambda(u^\star,g,J) \\ &< 4E_\lambda(v,g,J), \forall v \neq u^\star \\ &= \bar{E}_{\lambda/2}(\bar{v},\bar{g},\bar{J}), \forall \bar{v} \neq \overline{u^\star}, \end{aligned} \tag{4.23}$$

which shows that $\overline{u^\star}$ is the unique minimizer of (4.22). Then, we have, via Lemma 4.3,

$$\overline{u^\star} = \mathrm{prox}_{\lambda/2\bar{R}_p(\cdot,\bar{J})}(\bar{g}). \tag{4.24}$$

We define the translation operator

$$(T_h v)(x) = v(x+h), \forall h \in \mathbb{R}.$$

Now, using our assumption on the kernel K, that is, $K(x,y) = J(|x-y|)$ (then invariant by translation), and periodicity of the functions on $\mathbb{T}$, we have

$$\begin{aligned}
\bar{E}_{\lambda/2}(\bar{v}, T_h\bar{g}, \bar{J}) &= \frac{1}{\lambda}\|\bar{v} - T_h\bar{g}\|^2_{L^2(\mathbb{T})} + \bar{R}_p(\bar{v}, \bar{J}) \\
&= \frac{1}{\lambda}\|T_h(T_{-h}\bar{v} - \bar{g})\|^2_{L^2(\mathbb{T})} \\
&+ \int_{\mathbb{T}^2} \bar{J}(|x-y|)|\bar{v}((y+h)-h) - \bar{v}((x+h)-h)|^p\, dxdy \\
&= \frac{1}{\lambda}\|T_{-h}\bar{v} - \bar{g}\|^2_{L^2(\mathbb{T})} + \int_{\mathbb{T}^2} \bar{J}(|x-y|)|T_{-h}\bar{v}(y) \\
&- T_{-h}\bar{v}(x)|^p\, dxdy \\
&= \bar{E}_{\lambda/2}(T_{-h}\bar{v}, \bar{g}, \bar{J}).
\end{aligned}$$

This implies that the unique minimizer $\bar{v}^\star$ of $\bar{E}_{\lambda/2}(\cdot, T_h\bar{g}, \bar{J})$ given by (see Lemma 4.3)

$$\bar{v}^\star = \operatorname{prox}_{\lambda/2\bar{R}_p(\cdot,\bar{J})}(T_h\bar{g}) \tag{4.25}$$

is also the unique minimizer of $\bar{E}_{\lambda/2}(T_{-h}\cdot, \bar{g}, \bar{J})$. But since $\bar{E}_{\lambda/2}(\cdot, \bar{g}, \bar{J})$ has a unique minimizer $\bar{u^\star}$, we deduce from (4.24) and (4.25) that

$$T_h \operatorname{prox}_{\lambda/2\bar{R}_p(\cdot,\bar{J})}(\bar{g}) = \operatorname{prox}_{\lambda/2\bar{R}_p(\cdot,\bar{J})}(T_h\bar{g}). \tag{4.26}$$

That is, the proximal mapping of $\lambda/2\bar{R}_p(\cdot, \bar{J})$ commutes with translation.

We now split the two cases of q.

(i) For $q \in [1,2]$: combining (4.24), (4.26), (4.6), Hafiene et al. (2018, lemma C.1), and $L^2(\Omega) \subset L^q(\Omega)$, we have

$$\begin{aligned}
\|T_h\bar{u^\star} - \bar{u^\star}\|_{L^q(\mathbb{T})} &= \|\operatorname{prox}_{\lambda/2\bar{R}_p(\cdot,\bar{J})}(T_h\bar{g}) - \operatorname{prox}_{\lambda/2\bar{R}_p(\cdot,\bar{J})}(\bar{g})\|_{L^q(\mathbb{T})} \\
&\le 2^{1/q-1/2}\|\operatorname{prox}_{\lambda/2\bar{R}_p(\cdot,\bar{J})}(T_h\bar{g}) - \operatorname{prox}_{\lambda/2\bar{R}_p(\cdot,\bar{J})}(\bar{g})\|_{L^2(\mathbb{T})} \\
&\le 2^{1/q-1/2}\|T_h\bar{g} - \bar{g}\|_{L^2(\mathbb{T})} \\
&\le 2^{1/q-1/2}\left(2\|g\|_{L^\infty(\Omega)}\right)^{1-q/2}\|T_h\bar{g} - \bar{g}\|^{q/2}_{L^q(\mathbb{T})} \\
&= C_1\|T_h\bar{g} - \bar{g}\|^{q/2}_{L^q(\mathbb{T})}.
\end{aligned} \tag{4.27}$$

Let $\Omega_h \stackrel{\text{def}}{=} \{x \in \Omega : x + h \in \Omega\}$. Recalling the modulus of smoothness in (2.10), we have

$$\begin{aligned}
w(u^\star, t)_q \stackrel{\text{def}}{=} \sup_{|h|<t} \|T_h u^\star - u^\star\|_{L^q(\Omega_h)} &\le C_2 \sup_{|h|<t} \|T_h\bar{u^\star} - \bar{u^\star}\|_{L^q(\mathbb{T})} \\
&\le C_1C_2\left(\sup_{|h|<t} \|T_h\bar{g} - \bar{g}\|_{L^q(\mathbb{T})}\right)^{q/2} \\
&= C_1C_2 w(\bar{g}, t)_q^{q/2} \\
&\le C_1C_2(C_3 w(g,t)_q)^{q/2}.
\end{aligned} \tag{4.28}$$

We get the last inequality by applying the Whitney extension theorem (DeVore and Lorentz, 1993, chapter 6, theorem 4.1). Invoking Definition 2.21, there exists a constant $C > 0$ such that

$$\begin{aligned} |u^\star|_{\mathrm{Lip}(sq/2,L^q(\Omega))} &\stackrel{\text{def}}{=} \sup_{t>0} t^{-sq/2} w(u^\star,t)_q \\ &\le C\left(\sup_{t>0} t^{-s} w(g,t)_q\right)^{q/2} \le C\,|g|^{q/2}_{\mathrm{Lip}(s,L^q(\Omega))}, \end{aligned} \tag{4.29}$$

whence the claim follows after observing that $u^\star \in L^2(\Omega) \subset L^q(\Omega)$.

(ii) For $q \in [2,+\infty]$, we combine (4.24), (4.26), (4.6), and that now $L^q(\Omega) \subset L^2(\Omega)$, to get

$$\|T_h\bar{u^\star} - \bar{u^\star}\|_{L^2(\mathbb{T})} \le \|T_h\bar{g} - \bar{g}\|_{L^2(\mathbb{T})} \le 2^{1/2-1/q}\|T_h\bar{g} - \bar{g}\|_{L^q(\mathbb{T})}.$$

The rest of the proof is similar to that of (i).

□

Now, we are in position to establish rates of convergence of the solution of the discrete problems to the solution of the limiting problem, but only for $p \in [1,2]$. Indeed, the approximation bounds of Lemma 2.22 cannot be applied to $u^\star - I_nP_nu^\star$ for $p \ge 2$ since the bound in Theorem 4.4(ii) is in the $L^p(\Omega)$ norm, while Lemma 4.7 proves that $u^\star$ is only in $\mathrm{Lip}(sq/2, L^2(\Omega))$. In particular, one cannot invoke (2.12) since there is no guarantee that $u^\star$ is bounded. This is the reason why in the rest of this section, we will only focus on the case $p \in [1,2]$.

Theorem 4.8 *Let $p \in [1,2[$, and assume that $g \in L^\infty(\Omega) \cap \mathrm{Lip}(s, L^q(\Omega))$, with $s \in]0,1]$ and $q \in [2/(3-p), 2]$. Suppose, moreover, that $K(x,y) = J(|x-y|)$, $\forall (x,y) \in \Omega^2$, with J a nonnegative bounded measurable mapping on Ω. Let $u^\star$ and $\mathbf{u}^\star$ be the unique minimizers of $(\mathcal{VP}^{\lambda,p})$ and $(\mathcal{VP}^d_{\mathrm{nloc}})$, respectively. Then, the following error bounds hold.*

(i) If $p \in [1,2[$, $K \in \mathrm{Lip}(s', L^{q'}(\Omega^2))$ and $(s',q') \in]0,1] \times [1,+\infty[$, then

$$\|I_n\mathbf{u}^\star - u^\star\|^2_{L^2(\Omega)} \le Cn^{-\min(sq/2,s',s'q'(1-p/2))}, \tag{4.30}$$

where C is a positive constant independent of n.
In particular, if $g \in L^\infty(\Omega) \cap \mathrm{BV}(\Omega)$ and $K \in L^\infty(\Omega^2) \cap \mathrm{BV}(\Omega^2)$, then

$$\|I_n\mathbf{u}^\star - u\|^2_{L^2(\Omega)} = O(n^{p/2-1}). \tag{4.31}$$

(ii) If $p \in [1,2]$, $K \in \mathrm{Lip}(s', L^{q'}(\Omega^2))$ and $(s',q') \in]0,1] \times [2/(2-p),+\infty]$, then

$$\|I_n\mathbf{u}^\star - u^\star\|^2_{L^2(\Omega)} \le Cn^{-\min(sq/2,s')}. \tag{4.32}$$

where C is a positive constant independent of n.

In particular, if $g \in L^\infty(\Omega) \cap \mathrm{BV}(\Omega)$, *then*

$$\|I_n \mathbf{u}^\star - u\|^2_{L^2(\Omega)} = O(n^{-\min(1/2,s')}). \tag{4.33}$$

PROOF: In the following, C is any positive constant independent of n. Since $g \in L^\infty(\Omega) \cap \mathrm{Lip}(s, L^q(\Omega))$, $q \leq 2$, and we are dealing with a uniform partition of Ω ($|\Omega_i^{(n)}| = 1/n$, $\forall i \in [n]$), we get, using inequality (2.12), that

$$\|I_n \mathbf{g} - g\|_{L^2(\Omega)} \leq Cn^{-s\min(1,q/2)} = Cn^{-sq/2}. \tag{4.34}$$

By Lemma 4.7(i), we have $u^\star \in \mathrm{Lip}(sq/2, L^q(\Omega))$, and it follows from (2.11) and the fact that $q \geq 2/(3-p)$ that

$$\|I_n P_n u^\star - u^\star\|_{L^{\frac{2}{3-p}}(\Omega)} \leq \|I_n P_n u^\star - u^\star\|_{L^q(\Omega)} \leq Cn^{-sq/2}. \tag{4.35}$$

Combining (4.34) and (4.35), we get

$$\begin{aligned} &\|I_n \mathbf{g} - g\|^2_{L^2(\Omega)} + \|I_n \mathbf{g} - g\|_{L^2(\Omega)} + \|I_n P_n u^\star - u^\star\|_{L^{\frac{2}{3-p}}(\Omega)} \\ &\leq C(n^{-sq} + n^{-sq/2}) \\ &\leq Cn^{-sq/2}. \end{aligned} \tag{4.36}$$

It remains to bound $\|K - I_n \mathbf{K}\|_{L^{\frac{2}{2-p}}(\Omega^2)}$. This is achieved using (2.12) for case (i) and (2.11) for case (ii), which yields

$$\begin{cases} \|K - I_n \mathbf{K}\|_{L^{\frac{2}{2-p}}(\Omega^2)} \leq Cn^{-s'\min(1,q'(1-p/2))} & \text{for case (i)}, \\ \|K - I_n \mathbf{K}\|_{L^{\frac{2}{2-p}}(\Omega^2)} \leq \|K - I_n \mathbf{K}\|_{L^{q'}(\Omega^2)} \leq Cn^{-s'} & \text{for case (ii)}. \end{cases} \tag{4.37}$$

Plugging (4.36) and (4.37) into (4.7), the bounds (4.30) and (4.32) follow.

We know that $\mathrm{BV}(\Omega) \subset \mathrm{Lip}(1/2, L^2(\Omega))$. Thus, setting $s = s' = 1/2$ and $q = q' = 2$ in (4.30), and observing that $1 - p/2 \in [0, 1/2]$, the bound (4.31) follows. That of (4.33) is immediate. □

When $p = 1$ (i.e., nonlocal total variation), $g \in L^\infty(\Omega) \cap \mathrm{Lip}(s, L^2(\Omega))$, and K is a sufficiently smooth function, one can infer from Theorem 4.8 that the solution to the discrete problem ($\mathcal{VP}^d_{\mathrm{nloc}}$) converges to that of the continuum problem ($\mathcal{VP}^{\lambda,p}$) at the rate $O(n^{-s})$. Moreover, if $g \in L^\infty(\Omega) \cap \mathrm{BV}(\Omega)$, then the best convergence rate is $O(n^{-1/2})$, which is attained precisely for $p = 1$.

4.4 Application to Random Inhomogeneous Graph Sequences

We now turn to applying our bounds of Theorem 4.8 to networks on random inhomogeneous graphs of Definition 2.32.

In the rest of this section, the following random variables will be useful. Let $\mathbf{\Lambda} = \{\mathbf{\Lambda}_{ij}\}_{(i,j)\in[n]^2, i\neq j}$ be a collection of independent random variables such that $q_n\mathbf{\Lambda}_{ij}$ follows a Bernoulli distribution with parameter $q_n\hat{\mathbf{K}}^{\boldsymbol{x}}_{ij}$. We consider the independent random variables $\mathbf{\Upsilon}_{ij}$ such that the distribution of $q_n\mathbf{\Upsilon}_{ij}$ conditionally on $\mathbf{X} = \boldsymbol{x}$ is that of $q_n\mathbf{\Lambda}_{ij}$. Thus, $q_n\mathbf{\Upsilon}_{ij}$ follows a Bernoulli distribution with parameter $\mathbb{E}(q_n\hat{\mathbf{K}}^{\mathbf{X}}_{ij})$, where $\mathbb{E}(\cdot)$ is the expectation operator (here with respect to the distribution of $\mathbf{X}$).

4.4.1 Networks on Graphs Generated by Deterministic Nodes

In order to make our reasoning simpler, it will be convenient to assume first that the sequence $\mathbf{X}$ is deterministic. Capitalizing on this result, we will then deal with the totally random model (i.e., generated by random nodes) in Section 4.4.2 by a simple marginalization argument combined with additional assumptions to get the convergence and quantify the corresponding rate. As we have mentioned before, we shall denote $\boldsymbol{x} = (\boldsymbol{x}_1, \cdots, \boldsymbol{x}_n)$, as we assume that the sequence of nodes is deterministic. Relying on this notation, we define the parameter $\delta(n)$ as the maximal size of the spacings of $\boldsymbol{x}$, that is,

$$\delta(n) = \max_{i\in[n]} |\boldsymbol{x}_{(i)} - \boldsymbol{x}_{(i-1)}|, \tag{4.38}$$

where x_i is the ith smallest value.
Next, we consider the discrete counterpart of $(\mathcal{VP}^{\lambda,p})$ on the graph G_n,

$$\min_{\mathbf{u}\in\mathbb{R}^n} \left\{ \mathbf{E}_\lambda(\mathbf{u},\mathbf{g},\mathbf{K}) \stackrel{\text{def}}{=} \frac{1}{2\lambda n}\|\mathbf{u}-\mathbf{g}\|_2^2 + \frac{1}{2pn^2}\sum_{i,j=1}^{n} \mathbf{\Lambda}_{ij}|\mathbf{u}_j - \mathbf{u}_i|^p \right\}, \qquad (\mathcal{VP}^{\lambda,p}_{d,n})$$

where

$$\mathbf{g}_i = \frac{1}{|\Omega^{\boldsymbol{x}}_{ni}|}\int_{\Omega^{\boldsymbol{x}}_{ni}} g(x)dx.$$

Theorem 4.9 *Suppose that $p \in [1,2[$, $g \in L^2(\Omega)$, and K is a nonnegative measurable, symmetric, and bounded mapping. Let $u^\star$ and $\mathbf{u}^\star$ be the unique minimizers of $(\mathcal{VP}^{\lambda,p})$ and $(\mathcal{VP}^{\lambda,p}_{d,n})$, respectively. Let $p' = \frac{2}{2-p}$.*

(i) There exist positive constants C and C_1 that do not depend on n, such that for any $\beta > 0$

$$\|I_n\mathbf{u}^\star - u^\star\|^2_{L^2(\Omega)} \le C\left(\left(\beta\frac{\log(n)}{n} + \frac{1}{q_n^{(p'-1)}n^{p'/2}}\right)^{1/p'} + \|g - I_n\mathbf{g}\|^2_{L^2(\Omega)}\right.$$
$$\left. + \|g - I_n\mathbf{g}\|_{L^2(\Omega)} + \|K - I_n\hat{\mathbf{K}}^{\mathbf{x}}\|_{L^{p'}(\Omega^2)} + \|u^\star - I_nP_nu^\star\|_{L^{\frac{2}{3-p}}(\Omega)}\right), \tag{4.39}$$

with probability at least $1 - 2n^{-C_1 q_n^{2p'-1}\beta}$.

(ii) *Assume, moreover, that* $g \in L^\infty(\Omega) \cap \mathrm{Lip}(s, L^q(\Omega))$, *with* $s \in]0,1]$ *and* $q \in [2/(3-p), 2]$, *that* $K(x,y) = J(|x-y|)$, $\forall (x,y) \in \Omega^2$, *with* J *a nonnegative bounded measurable mapping on* Ω, *and* $K \in \mathrm{Lip}(s', L^{q'}(\Omega^2))$, $(s', q') \in]0,1] \times [p', +\infty]$ *and* $q_n \|K\|_{L^\infty(\Omega^2)} \leq 1$. *Then there exist positive constants* C *and* C_1 *that do not depend on* n, *such that for any* $\beta > 0$

$$\left\|I_n \mathbf{u}^\star - u^\star\right\|^2_{L^2(\Omega)} \leq C\left(\left(\beta\frac{\log(n)}{n} + \frac{1}{q_n^{(p'-1)} n^{p'/2}}\right)^{1/p'} + \delta(n)^{-\min(sq/2, s')}\right), \tag{4.40}$$

with probability at least $1 - 2n^{-C_1 q_n^{2p'-1}\beta}$.

Before delving into the proof, some remarks are in order.

Remark 4.10

(i) The first term in the bounds (4.39)–(4.40) can be replaced by

$$\beta^{1/p'}\left(\frac{\log(n)}{n}\right)^{1/p'} + \frac{1}{q_n^{(1-1/p')} n^{1/2}}.$$

(ii) The last term in the latter bound can be rewritten as

$$n^{-1/2} q_n^{-(1-1/p')} = \begin{cases} (q_n n)^{-1/2} & \text{if } p' = 2, \\ q_n^{1/p'} (q_n^2 n)^{-1/2} & \text{if } p' > 2. \end{cases} \tag{4.41}$$

Thus, if $\inf_{n\geq 1} q_n > 0$, as is the case when the graph is dense, then the term (4.41) is in the order of $n^{-1/2}$ with probability at least $1 - n^{-c\beta}$ for some $c > 0$. If q_n is allowed to be $o(1)$, that is, sparse graphs, then (4.41) is $o(1)$ if either $q_n n \to +\infty$ for $p' = 2$, or $q_n^2 n \to +\infty$ for $p' > 2$. The probability of success is at least $1 - e^{-C_1 \beta \log(n)^{1-\delta}}$, provided that $q_n = \log(n)^{-\delta/(2p'-1)}$, with $\delta \in [0, 1[$. All these conditions on q_n are fulfilled by the inhomogenous graph model discussed previously.

(iii) In fact, if $\inf_{n\geq 1} q_n \geq c > 0$, then we have

$$\sum_{n\geq 1} n^{-C_1 q_n^{2p-1}\beta} \leq \sum_{n\geq 1} n^{-C_1 c^{2p-1}\beta} < +\infty,$$

provided that $\beta > (C_1 c^{2p-1})^{-1}$. Thus, if this holds, invoking the (first) Borel–Cantelli lemma, it follows that the bounds of Theorem 4.9 eventually hold with probability one. The same reasoning carries over for the bounds of Theorem 4.11.

PROOF: In the following, C is any positive constant independent of n.

(i) We start by arguing as in the proof of Theorem 4.4. Similarly to (4.9), we now have

$$\frac{1}{2\lambda}\|I_n\mathbf{u}^\star - u^\star\|^2_{L^2(\Omega)} \leq \left(E_\lambda(I_n\mathbf{u}^\star, g, K) - \mathbf{E}_\lambda(\mathbf{u}^\star, \mathbf{g}, \mathbf{\Lambda})\right) - \left(E_\lambda(u^\star, g, K) - \mathbf{E}_\lambda(\mathbf{u}^\star, \mathbf{g}, \mathbf{\Lambda})\right). \quad (4.42)$$

The first term can be bounded similarly to (4.11)–(4.12) to get

$$\begin{aligned}
&E_\lambda(I_n\mathbf{u}^\star, g, K) - \mathbf{E}_\lambda(\mathbf{u}^\star, \mathbf{g}, \mathbf{\Lambda}) \\
&\leq C\Bigg(\|I_n\mathbf{g} - g\|^2_{L^2(\Omega)} + \|I_n\mathbf{g} - g\|_{L^2(\Omega)} \\
&\qquad + \left|\int_{\Omega^2} (K(x,y) - I_n\mathbf{\Lambda}(x,y))|\nabla^{\mathrm{NL}} I_n\mathbf{u}^\star(x,y)|^p \, dxdy\right|\Bigg) \\
&\leq C\Bigg(\|I_n\mathbf{g} - g\|^2_{L^2(\Omega)} + \|I_n\mathbf{g} - g\|_{L^2(\Omega)} \\
&\qquad + \left|\int_{\Omega^2} (K(x,y) - I_n\hat{\mathbf{K}}^{\mathbf{x}}(x,y))|\nabla^{\mathrm{NL}} I_n\mathbf{u}^\star(x,y)|^p \, dxdy\right| \\
&\qquad + \left|\int_{\Omega^2} (I_n\hat{\mathbf{K}}^{\mathbf{x}}(x,y) - I_n\mathbf{\Lambda}(x,y))|\nabla^{\mathrm{NL}} I_n\mathbf{u}^\star(x,y)|^p \, dxdy\right|\Bigg).
\end{aligned} \quad (4.43)$$

The second term in (4.43) is $O\left(\|K - I_n\hat{\mathbf{K}}^{\mathbf{x}}\|_{L^{p'}(\Omega^2)}\right)$; see (4.13). For the last term, we have, using Jensen and Hölder inequalities,

$$\begin{aligned}
&\left|\int_{\Omega^2} (I_n\hat{\mathbf{K}}^{\mathbf{x}}(x,y) - I_n\mathbf{\Lambda}(x,y))|\nabla^{\mathrm{NL}} I_n\mathbf{u}^\star(x,y)|^p \, dxdy\right| \\
&\leq 2^{p-1}\Bigg(\int_\Omega \left|\int_\Omega (I_n\hat{\mathbf{K}}^{\mathbf{x}}(x,y) - I_n\mathbf{\Lambda}(x,y))dy\right| |I_n\mathbf{u}^\star(x)|^p dx \\
&\qquad + \int_\Omega \left|\int_\Omega (I_n\hat{\mathbf{K}}^{\mathbf{x}}(x,y) - I_n\mathbf{\Lambda}(x,y))dx\right| |I_n\mathbf{u}^\star(y)|^p dy\Bigg) \quad (4.44) \\
&\leq C\Bigg(\left(\int_\Omega \left|\int_\Omega (I_n\hat{\mathbf{K}}^{\mathbf{x}}(x,y) - I_n\mathbf{\Lambda}(x,y))dy\right|^{p'} dx\right)^{1/p'} \\
&\qquad + \left(\int_\Omega \left|\int_\Omega (I_n\hat{\mathbf{K}}^{\mathbf{x}}(x,y) - I_n\mathbf{\Lambda}(x,y))dx\right|^{p'} dy\right)^{1/p'}\Bigg) \\
&= C\left(\|Z_n\|_{p',n} + \|W_n\|_{p',n}\right),
\end{aligned}$$

where

$$\mathbf{Z}_i \stackrel{\text{def}}{=} \frac{1}{n}\sum_{j=1}^{n}\left(\hat{\mathbf{K}}_{ij}^{x} - \mathbf{\Lambda}_{ij}\right) \text{ and } \mathbf{W}_j \stackrel{\text{def}}{=} \frac{1}{n}\sum_{i=1}^{n}\left(\hat{\mathbf{K}}_{ij}^{x} - \mathbf{\Lambda}_{ij}\right).$$

By virtue of Hafiene et al. (2020, lemma A.1), together with ($\mathbf{H}_w^b$.2) and the fact that $p' \geq 2$, there exists a positive constant C_1 such that, for any $\beta > 0$,

$$\mathbb{P}\left(\|\mathbf{Z}\|_{p',n} \geq \varepsilon\right) \leq n^{-C_1 q_n^{2p'-1}\beta},$$

with

$$\varepsilon = \left(\beta\frac{\log(n)}{n} + \frac{1}{q_n^{(p'-1)} n^{p'/2}}\right)^{1/p'}. \tag{4.45}$$

The same bound also holds for $\|\mathbf{W}\|_{p',n}$. A union bound then leads to

$$\|\mathbf{Z}\|_{p',n} + \|\mathbf{W}\|_{p',n} \leq 2\varepsilon, \tag{4.46}$$

with probability at least $1 - 2n^{-C_1 q_n^{2p'-1}\beta}$.
Let us now turn to the second term in (4.42). Using (2.8) and the fact that $\mathbf{u}^\star$ is the unique minimizer of $(\mathcal{VP}_{d,n}^{\lambda,p})$, we have

$$\begin{aligned} E_\lambda(I_n\mathbf{u}^\star, I_n\mathbf{g}, I_n\mathbf{\Lambda}) - E_\lambda(u^\star, g, K) \leq{}& \left(R_p(I_nP_nu^\star, K) - R_p(u^\star, K)\right) \\ &+ \left(R_p(I_nP_nu^\star, I_n\hat{\mathbf{K}}^{\mathbf{x}}) - R_p(I_nP_nu^\star, K)\right) \\ &+ \left(R_p(I_nP_nu^\star, I_n\mathbf{\Lambda}) - R_p(I_nP_nu^\star, I_n\hat{\mathbf{K}}^{\mathbf{x}})\right). \end{aligned} \tag{4.47}$$

The first term is bounded as in (4.16), which yields

$$|R_p(I_nP_nu^\star, K) - R_p(u^\star, K)| \leq C\|u^\star - I_nP_nu^\star\|_{L^{\frac{2}{3-p}}(\Omega)}. \tag{4.48}$$

The second term follows from (4.17)

$$|R_p(I_nP_nu^\star, I_n\hat{\mathbf{K}}^{\mathbf{x}}) - R_p(I_nP_nu^\star, K)| \leq C\|K - I_n\hat{\mathbf{K}}^{\mathbf{x}}\|_{L^{p'}(\Omega^2)}. \tag{4.49}$$

The last term is upper-bounded exactly as in (4.44) and (4.46).
Inserting (4.43), (4.44), (4.46), (4.47), (4.48), and (4.49) into (4.42), we get the claimed bound.

(ii) Insert (4.36) and (4.37) into (4.39) after replacing $1/n$ by $\delta(n)$.

□

4.4.2 Networks on Graphs Generated by Random Nodes

Let us turn now to the totally random model. The discrete counterpart of $(\mathcal{VP}^{\lambda,p})$ on the totally random sequence of graphs $\{G_{q_n}\}_{n\in\mathbb{N}^*}$ is given by

$$\min_{\mathbf{u}\in\mathbb{R}^n}\left\{\mathbf{E}_\lambda(\mathbf{u},\mathbf{g},\mathbf{K}) \stackrel{\text{def}}{=} \frac{1}{2\lambda n}\|\mathbf{u}-\mathbf{g}\|_2^2 + \frac{1}{n^2}\sum_{i,j=1}^{n}\Upsilon_{ij}|\mathbf{u}_j-\mathbf{u}_i|^p\right\}, \qquad (\mathcal{VP}_{r,n}^{\lambda,p})$$

where we recall that the random variables Υ_{ij} are independent, with $q_n\Upsilon_{ij}$ following the Bernoulli distribution with parameter $\mathbb{E}\left(q_n\hat{\mathbf{K}}_{ij}^{\mathbf{X}}\right)$ defined earlier.

Observe that for the totally random model, $\delta(n)$ is a random variable. Thus, we have to derive a bound on it. In Hafiene et al. (2020, lemma 3.2), it was shown that

$$\delta(n) \leq t\frac{\log(n)}{n}, \tag{4.50}$$

with probability at least $1-n^{-t}$, where $t\in]0,e[$.

Combining this bound with Theorem 4.9 (after conditioning and integrating) applied to the totally random sequence $\{G_{q_n}\}_{n\in\mathbb{N}^*}$, we get the following result.

Theorem 4.11 *Suppose that $p\in[1,2[$, $g\in L^2(\Omega)$, and K is a nonnegative measurable, symmetric, and bounded mapping. Let $u^\star$ and $\mathbf{u}^\star$ be the unique minimizers of $(\mathcal{VP}^{\lambda,p})$ and $(\mathcal{VP}_{r,n}^{\lambda,p})$, respectively. Let $p'=\frac{2}{2-p}$.*

(i) There exist positive constants C and C_1 that do not depend on n, such that, for any $\beta>0$,

$$\|I_n\mathbf{u}^\star-u^\star\|_{L^2(\Omega)}^2 \leq C\left(\left(\beta\frac{\log(n)}{n}+\frac{1}{q_n^{(p'-1)}n^{p'/2}}\right)^{1/p'} + \|g-I_n\mathbf{g}\|_{L^2(\Omega)}^2 \right.$$
$$\left. + \|g-I_n\mathbf{g}\|_{L^2(\Omega)} + \|K-I_n\hat{\mathbf{K}}^{\mathbf{X}}\|_{L^{p'}(\Omega^2)} + \|u^\star-I_nP_nu^\star\|_{L^{\frac{2}{3-p}}(\Omega)}\right), \tag{4.51}$$

with probability at least $1-2n^{-C_1q_n^{2p'-1}\beta}$.

(ii) Assume, moreover, that $g\in L^\infty(\Omega)\cap\mathrm{Lip}(s,L^q(\Omega))$, with $s\in]0,1]$ and $q\in[2/(3-p),2]$, that $K(x,y)=J(|x-y|)$, $\forall(x,y)\in\Omega^2$, with J a nonnegative bounded measurable mapping on Ω, and that $K\in\mathrm{Lip}(s',L^{q'}(\Omega^2))$, $(s',q')\in]0,1]\times[p',+\infty]$, and $q_n\|K\|_{L^\infty(\Omega^2)}\leq 1$. Then there exist positive constants C and C_1 that do not depend on n, such that for any $\beta>0$ and $t\in]0,e[$

$$\|I_n\mathbf{u}^\star - u^\star\|^2_{L^2(\Omega)} \leq C\left(\left(\beta\frac{\log(n)}{n} + \frac{1}{q_n^{(p'-1)}n^{p'/2}}\right)^{1/p'} + \left(t\frac{\log(n)}{n}\right)^{\min(sq/2,s')}\right), \tag{4.52}$$

with probability at least $1 - (2n^{-C_1 q_n^{2p'-1}\beta} + n^{-t})$.

PROOF: Again, C will be any positive constant independent of n.

(i) Let

$$\varepsilon' = C\left(\left(\beta\frac{\log(n)}{n} + C\frac{1}{q_n^{(p'-1)}n^{p'/2}}\right)^{1/p'} + \|g - I_n\mathbf{g}\|^2_{L^2(\Omega)} + \|g - I_n\mathbf{g}\|_{L^2(\Omega)}\right.$$
$$\left. + \|K - I_n\hat{\mathbf{K}}^{\mathbf{X}}\|_{L^{p'}(\Omega^2)} + \|u^\star - I_n P_n u^\star\|_{L^{\frac{2}{3-p}}(\Omega)}\right).$$

Using (4.39), and independence of this bound from $\boldsymbol{x}$, we have

$$\mathbb{P}\left(\|I_n\mathbf{u}^\star - u^\star\|^2_{L^2(\Omega)} \geq \varepsilon'\right) = \frac{1}{|\Omega|^n}\int_{\Omega^n}\mathbb{P}\left(\|I_n\mathbf{u}^\star - u^\star\|^2_{L^2(\Omega)} \geq \varepsilon' | \mathbf{X} = \boldsymbol{x}\right)d\boldsymbol{x}$$
$$\leq \frac{1}{|\Omega|^n}\int_{\Omega^n} 2n^{-C_1 q_n^{2p'-1}\beta}d\boldsymbol{x} = 2n^{-C_1 q_n^{2p'-1}\beta}.$$

(ii) Recall ε in (4.45) and $\kappa = C\left(t\frac{\log(n)}{n}\right)^{\min(sq/2,s')}$. Denote the event

$$A_1 : \left\{\|g - I_n\mathbf{g}\|^2_{L^2(\Omega)} + \|g - I_n\mathbf{g}\|_{L^2(\Omega)} + \|K - I_n\hat{\mathbf{K}}^{\mathbf{X}}\|_{L^{p'}(\Omega^2)} + \|u^\star - I_n P_n u^\star\|_{L^{\frac{2}{3-p}}(\Omega)} \leq \kappa\right\}.$$

In view of (4.36), (4.37), and (4.50), and that under our assumptions $\hat{\mathbf{K}}^{\mathbf{X}} = \mathbf{K}^{\mathbf{X}}$, we have

$$\mathbb{P}(A_1) \geq \mathbb{P}\left(\delta(n) \leq t\frac{\log(n)}{n}\right) \geq 1 - n^{-t}.$$

Let the event

$$A_2 : \left\{\|\mathbf{Z}\|_{p',n} + \|\mathbf{W}\|_{p',n} < 2\varepsilon\right\},$$

and denote A_i^c the complement of the event A_i. It then follows from (4.46) and the union bound that

$$\mathbb{P}\left(\|I_n\mathbf{u}^\star - u^\star\|^2_{L^2(\Omega)} \leq 2C\varepsilon + \kappa\right) \geq \mathbb{P}(A_1 \cap A_2) = 1 - \mathbb{P}(A_1^c \cup A_2^c)$$
$$\geq 1 - \sum_{i=1}^{2}\mathbb{P}(A_i^c) \geq 1 - \left(2n^{-C_1 q_n^{2p'-1}\beta} + n^{-t}\right),$$

which leads to the claimed result. □

When $p = 1$ (i.e., nonlocal total variation), $g \in L^\infty(\Omega) \cap \mathrm{Lip}(s, L^2(\Omega))$, and K is a sufficiently smooth function, one can deduce from Theorem 4.11 that with high probability, the solution to the discrete problem ($\mathcal{VP}^{\lambda,p}_{r,n}$) converges to that of the continuum problem ($\mathcal{VP}^{\lambda,p}$) at the rate $O\left(\left(\frac{\log(n)}{n}\right)^{-\min(1/2,s)}\right)$. Compared to the deterministic graph model, there is overhead due to the randomness of the graph model, which is captured in the rate and the extralogarithmic factor.

5 Nonlocal p-Laplacian Dirichlet Problem on Graphs

5.1 Problem Statement

Let Ω be a bounded domain of $\mathbb{R}^d$, $d \geq 1$, and $p \in]1, +\infty[$. Let us recall the boundary value problem introduced in Section 1:

$$\begin{cases} -\Delta_p^K u = f, & \text{in } U, \\ u = g, & \text{on } \Gamma, \end{cases} \tag{$\mathcal{P}_D$}$$

where K is a kernel, Δ_p^K is the nonlocal p-Laplacian given by (1.1), U is a subdomain of Ω, $\Gamma = \Omega \setminus U$, $g \in L^p(\Omega)$, and $f \in L^q(\Omega)$, where q is the Hölder conjugate of p. Throughout, we assume that U is a subdomain of Ω such that $U + \mathbb{B}_r \subset \Omega$ for some $r > 0$, where $\mathbb{B}_r$ is the open ball with radius r at the origin.

Our chief goal in this section is to study numerical approximations of the nonlocal boundary value problem ($\mathcal{P}_D$), which, in turn, will allow us to establish consistency estimates of the discrete counterpart of this problem on graphs, which reads

$$\begin{cases} \frac{1}{n^d} \sum_{y \in V_n(\Omega)} \mathbf{K}_{xy} |\mathbf{u}_y - \mathbf{u}_x|^{p-2} (\mathbf{u}_y - \mathbf{u}_x) = \mathbf{f}_x, & x \in A_n, \\ \mathbf{u}_x = \mathbf{g}_x, & x \in A_n^c, \end{cases} \tag{$\mathcal{P}_n^d$}$$

where $V_n(\Omega)$ is the vertex set, $\mathbf{u}, \mathbf{f}, \mathbf{g} \in \mathbb{R}^{V_n(\Omega)}$, and $\mathbf{K} \in \mathbb{R}^{V_n(\Omega) \times V_n(\Omega)}$; see Section 5.4 for more detail.

We impose the following assumptions on the kernel we consider, which will be useful in order to make the statements of our result brief and clear (for some results only a subset will be necessary):

(H.1) K is a nonnegative measurable function.
(H.2) K is symmetric, that is, $K(x, y) = K(y, x)$.
(H.3) $\sup_{x \in \Omega} \int_\Omega |K(x, y)| dy < +\infty$.

(H.4) There exist $m,\ r_0 > 0$ such that $|K(\boldsymbol{x},\boldsymbol{y})| \geq m\chi_{[0,r_0[}(\|\boldsymbol{x}-\boldsymbol{y}\|)$ for all $\boldsymbol{x},\ \boldsymbol{y} \in \Omega$.

(H.5) K belongs to $L^\infty(\Omega^2)$.

Observe that, the assumptions **(H.1)**–**(H.3)** are exactly the same assumptions considered in the preceding section.
When the kernel is such that $K(\boldsymbol{x},\boldsymbol{y}) = J(\boldsymbol{x}-\boldsymbol{y})$, where $J\colon \mathbb{R}^N \to \mathbb{R}$, then **(H.1)**–**(H.5)** read as follows:

(H'.1) J is a nonnegative measurable function.
(H'.2) J is symmetric, that is, $J(\boldsymbol{x}) = J(-\boldsymbol{x})$.
(H'.3) $\int_{\Omega-\Omega} |J(\boldsymbol{x})| d\boldsymbol{x} < +\infty$.
(H'.4) There exist $m,\ r_0 > 0$ such that $|J(\boldsymbol{x})| \geq m\chi_{[0,r_0[}(\|\boldsymbol{x}\|)$ for all $\boldsymbol{x} \in \Omega-\Omega$.
(H'.5) J belongs to $L^\infty(\Omega-\Omega)$.

Recall that $\Omega-\Omega$ is the Minkowski sum of Ω and $-\Omega$.

Let $K_n,\ K$ be a sequence of measurable functions in $L^{\infty,p}(\Omega^2)$. We say that the sequence $\{K_n,\ K\colon n \in \mathbb{N}\}$ satisfies hypothesis $(\mathcal{A}_{ker})$ if the following hold:

$(\mathcal{A}_{ker})$ The functions $K_n,\ n \in \mathbb{N}$ and K are symmetric (i.e., satisfy **(H.2)**), and $\{K_n\}_{n\in\mathbb{N}}$ converges pointwise to K almost everywhere on Ω^2 and $\{K_n\}_{n\in\mathbb{N}}$ converges strongly to K in $L^{\infty,p}(\Omega^2)$.

We say that the sequence $\{K_n,\ K\colon n \in \mathbb{N}\}$ satisfies hypothesis $(\mathcal{B}_{ker})$ if the following hold:

$(\mathcal{B}_{ker})$ The sequence $\{K_n,\ K\colon\ n \in \mathbb{N}\}$ is uniformly bounded in $L^\infty(\Omega^2)$, and $\{K_n\}_{n\in\mathbb{N}}$ converges pointwise to K almost everywhere on Ω^2.

If the kernels $K,\ K_n,\ n \in \mathbb{N}$ are such that $K(\boldsymbol{x},\boldsymbol{y}) = J(\boldsymbol{x}-\boldsymbol{y}),\ K_n(\boldsymbol{x},\boldsymbol{y}) = J_n(\boldsymbol{x}-\boldsymbol{y})$, where $J,\ J_n\colon \mathbb{R}^N \to \mathbb{R},\ n \in \mathbb{N}$, the assumptions $(\mathcal{A}_{ker})$ and $(\mathcal{B}_{ker})$ read respectively:

$(\mathcal{A}'_{rad})$ The functions $J_n,\ n \in \mathbb{N}$ and J are symmetric (i.e., satisfy **(H'.2)**), and $\{J_n\}_{n\in\mathbb{N}}$ converges pointwise to J almost everywhere on $\Omega-\Omega$ and $\{J_n\}_{n\in\mathbb{N}}$ converges strongly to J in $L^p(\Omega-\Omega)$.

$(\mathcal{B}'_{rad})$ The sequence $\{J_n,\ J\colon n \in \mathbb{N}\}$ is uniformly bounded in $L^\infty(\Omega-\Omega)$, and $\{J_n\}_{n\in\mathbb{N}}$ converges pointwise to J almost everywhere on $\Omega-\Omega$.

A key intermediate step to achieve our goal is to use the Dirichlet principle and transform $(\mathcal{P}_n^d)$ into an equivalent sequence of variational problems

$$\min_{u \in \mathbb{A}_{g_n}(V_n(\Omega),\Gamma_n)} F_n(\nabla_{K_n}^{\mathrm{NL}} u) + \int_\Omega f_n(x)u(x)dx, \qquad (\mathcal{VP}_n)$$

where ∇_K^{NL} is the nonlocal gradient operator, F_n is an integral functional, and $\mathbb{A}_{g_n}(V_n(\Omega), \Gamma_n)$ is an affine subspace of $L^p(\Omega)$, which will be made precise later.

To make this asymptotic analysis precise, we use the notation and methods of Γ-convergence and Mosco-convergence of De Giorgi and Mosco respectively; see Dal Maso (1993); Braides et al. (2002); Beer and Lucchetti (1992); Azé et al. (1988); Borwein and Fitzpatrick (1989). We will in particular show that $(\mathcal{VP}_n)$ has a Γ-limit that takes the form

$$\min_{u \in L_g^p(\Omega,U)} F(\nabla_K^{\mathrm{NL}} u) + \int_\Omega f(x)u(x)dx, \qquad (\mathcal{VP})$$

where $g \in L^p(\Omega)$, $f \in L^q(\Omega)$, and F is an appropriate integral functional and

$$L_g^p(\Omega, U) = \{u \in L^p(\Omega) : u = g \text{ on } \Gamma = \Omega \setminus U\}, \qquad (5.1)$$

5.2 Convergence of Minima of Integral Functionals

This section is devoted to studying the well-posedness of the problem $(\mathcal{VP})$. We study also the Mosco-convergence and Γ-convergence of the sequence of the energy functionals and the sequence of geometry constraints given in $(\mathcal{VP}_n)$.

5.2.1 Mosco-Convergence of Convex Functionals

Let $\mathcal{U}$ be a bounded domain of $\mathbb{R}^N$, $N \geq 1$, and $p \in]1, +\infty[$. We consider the integral functional

$$\begin{aligned} F: \quad & L^p(\mathcal{U}) \to \mathbb{R} \\ & v \mapsto \int_{\mathcal{U}} f(x, v(x))dx, \end{aligned} \qquad (5.2)$$

where $f : \mathcal{U} \times \mathbb{R} \to \mathbb{R}$ is a function satisfying the following requirements:

(A.1) for every $s \in \mathbb{R}$, the function $f(\cdot, s)$ is Lebesgue measurable on $\mathcal{U}$.

(A.2) for a.e. $x \in \mathcal{U}$, the function $f(x, \cdot)$ is convex on $\mathbb{R}$.

(A.3) there exist $C_2 \geq C_1 > 0$ and a positive function $a \in L^1(\mathcal{U})$ such that

$$-a(x) + C_1|s|^p \leq f(x, s) \leq a(x) + C_2(|s|^p + 1), \qquad (5.3)$$

for a.e. $x \in \mathcal{U}$ and for all $s \in \mathbb{R}$.

We denote by $\mathcal{F}(a, C_1, C_2, p)$ the set of all functionals F of the form (5.2) where the corresponding integrands satisfy the assumptions (**A.1**), (**A.2**), and (**A.3**) for the same function $a \in L^1(\mathcal{U})$ and the same constants C_2, C_1.

We denote by $\mathcal{F}'(a, C_1, C_2, p)$ the set of all functionals $F \in \mathcal{F}(a, C_1, C_2, p)$ such that the assumption (**A.2**) of the corresponding integrand is replaced by

(**A'.2**) for a.e. $x \in \mathcal{U}$, the function $f(x, \cdot)$ is strictly convex on $\mathbb{R}$.

Let $F, \; F_n, \; n \in \mathbb{N}$ be integral functionals taking the form of (5.2) with $f, f_n, n \in \mathbb{N}$ the corresponding integrands. We say that the sequence $\{F, F_n : n \in \mathbb{N}\}$ satisfies hypothesis $(\mathcal{H}_{seq})$ if the following holds:

$(\mathcal{H}_{seq})$ There exists a positive function $a \in L^1(\mathcal{U})$ and $C_2 \geq C_1 > 0$ such that $F, \; F_n, \in \mathcal{F}(a, C_1, C_2, p)$, $n \in \mathbb{N}$, and for every $s \in \mathbb{R}$, $\{f_n(\cdot, s))\}_{n \in \mathbb{N}}$ converges to $f(\cdot, s)$ pointwise a.e. on $\mathcal{U}$.

By standard convex analysis arguments, we obtain the following properties of functions of these classes of functionals.

Proposition 5.1 *Let $F \in \mathcal{F}(a, C_1, C_2, p)$ (reps. $F \in \mathcal{F}'(a, C_1, C_2, p)$), where $C_2 \geq C_1 > 0$ and a positive function $a \in L^1(\mathcal{U})$. Then F satisfies the following properties:*

(i) F is convex (resp. strictly convex) and continuous on $L^p(\mathcal{U})$;
(ii) F is weakly lower semicontinuous on $L^p(\mathcal{U})$;
(iii) F is coercive on $L^p(\mathcal{U})$ induced by the weak topology.

Let us announce a first-result Mosco-convergence for sequences in these classes.

Theorem 5.2 *Let $\{F, F_n : n \in \mathbb{N}\}$ be a sequence of integral functionals given by (5.2), which satisfies $(\mathcal{H}_{seq})$. Then*

(i) $\{F_n\}$ Mosco-converges to F on $L^p(\mathcal{U})$;
(ii)

$$\min_{L^p(\mathcal{U})} F = \lim_n \min_{L^p(\mathcal{U})} F_n.$$

Moreover, if $\{u_n\}_{n \in \mathbb{N}}$ is a sequence such that $\lim_n F_n(u_n) = \lim_n \inf_{L^p(\mathcal{U})} F_n$, then $\{u_n\}_{n \in \mathbb{N}}$ is weakly precompact in $L^p(\mathcal{U})$ and every weak cluster point of $\{u_n\}_{n \in \mathbb{N}}$ is a minimum point for F.

PROOF: It is enough to show point (i). Point (ii) is a consequence of (i), Theorem 2.6, Proposition 5.1, and the equicoercivity of the sequence $\{F_n\}_{n\in\mathbb{N}}$, which is a trivial result of Proposition 2.5 and the growth condition (**A.3**) of the integrands. By the dominated convergence theorem, the sequence $\{F_n(u)\}_{n\in\mathbb{N}}$ converges to $F(u)$ for every $u \in L^p(\mathcal{U})$. The conclusion is achieved if we prove (ii) of Definition 2.7.

On the other hand, we have that F, F_n, $n \in \mathbb{N}$ are closed convex functions, then by Theorem 2.8, the proof of the Mosco-convergence amounts to proving that the sequence $\{F_n\}_{n\in\mathbb{N}}$ is equi-lsc. By the assumption $(\mathcal{H}_{seq})$ we have that

$$|F_n(u)| \leq \|a\|_{L^1(\mathcal{U})} + C_2(R^p + |\mathcal{U}|),$$

for all $u \in \mathbb{B}_R \subset L^p(\mathcal{U})$ and all $n \in \mathbb{N}$. Then the sequence $\{F_n\}_{n\in\mathbb{N}}$ is locally uniformly Lipschitz, thanks to Proposition 2.2; in particular, it is equi-lsc. □

5.2.2 Mosco-Convergence of Geometry Constraints

Let us turn to approximate $L^p_g(\Omega, U)$ by a sequence of finite affine subspaces. Throughout, we denote, for $n \in \mathbb{N}^\star$,

$$V_n(\Omega) = \{x \in \frac{1}{n}\mathbb{Z}^d : \Omega_x^{(n)} \subset \Omega\}, \tag{5.4}$$

where $\Omega_x^{(n)} = x + \frac{1}{n}[0,1[^d$, and

$$\mathbb{A}(V_n(\Omega)) = \{u \in L^1(\Omega) \colon \; u = \sum_{x\in V_n(\Omega)} \alpha_x \chi_{\Omega_x^{(n)}}, \; \alpha_x \in \mathbb{R}\}.$$

We fix $n \in \mathbb{N}^\star$. Set

$$U_n = \bigcup_{\Omega_x^{(n)} \subset U \,:\, x\in V_n(\Omega)} \Omega_x^{(n)} \textit{ and } \Gamma_n = \Omega \setminus U_n,$$

$$U_n' = \bigcup_{\Omega_x^{(n)} \cap U \neq \emptyset \,:\, x\in V_n(\Omega)} \Omega_x^{(n)} \textit{ and } \Gamma_n' = \Omega \setminus U_n'.$$

For $g_n \in \mathbb{A}(V_n(\Omega))$, we denote

$$\mathbb{A}_{g_n}(V_n(\Omega), \Gamma_n) \stackrel{\text{def}}{=} \{u \in \mathbb{A}(V_n(\Omega)) \colon \; u = g_n \text{ on } \Gamma_n\}, \tag{5.5}$$

$$\mathbb{A}'_{g_n}(V_n(\Omega), \Gamma_n') \stackrel{\text{def}}{=} \{u \in \mathbb{A}(V_n(\Omega)) \colon \; u = g_n \text{ on } \Gamma_n'\}. \tag{5.6}$$

The sets $\mathbb{A}_{g_n}(V_n(\Omega), \Gamma_n)$ and $\mathbb{A}_{g_n}(V_n(\Omega), \Gamma_n)$ correspond to the geometry constraints of the variational problem $(\mathcal{VP}_n)$.

We have the following approximation of $L^p_g(\Omega, U)$.

Proposition 5.3 *Let* g_n, Γ_n, Γ_n', $\mathbb{A}_{g_n}(V_n(\Omega), \Gamma_n)$, $\mathbb{A}'_{g_n}(V_n(\Omega), \Gamma_n')$, *as earlier. Assume that the sequence* $\{g_n\}_{n\in\mathbb{N}}$ *converges strongly to some function* g

in $L^p(\Omega)$. Then the sequences $\{\mathbb{A}_{g_n}(V_n(\Omega),\Gamma_n)\}_{n\in\mathbb{N}}$ and $\{\mathbb{A}'_{g_n}(V_n(\Omega),\Gamma'_n)\}_{n\in\mathbb{N}}$ Mosco-converge to $L^p_g(\Omega,U)$ in $L^p(\Omega)$.

PROOF: We show that $\{\mathbb{A}_{g_n}(V_n(\Omega),\Gamma_n)\}$ Mosco-converges to $L^p_g(\Omega,U)$ in $L^p(\Omega)$; by similar argument, we show the Mosco-convergence of $\{\mathbb{A}'_{g_n}(V_n(\Omega),\Gamma'_n)\}$.

Let $f_n \in \mathbb{A}_{g_n}(V_n(\Omega),\Gamma_n)$, $n \in \mathbb{N}$, such that $f_n \rightharpoonup f$ in $L^p(\Omega)$ for some $f \in L^p(\Omega)$. It is easy to see that

$$\int_\Omega |f_n\chi_{\Gamma_n} - g\chi_\Gamma|dx \le \int_\Omega \left[|g_n - g| + |g|\chi_{\Gamma\Delta\Gamma_n}\right] dx.$$

By assumption, the terms in the right-hand side of the preceding inequality tend to 0, since $|U_n\Delta U| \to 0$ by construction. Therefore, $f_n\chi_{\Gamma_n} \rightharpoonup g\chi_\Gamma$ in $L^1(\Omega)$; hence $f = g$ a.e. on Γ, that is, $f \in L^p_g(\Omega,U)$.

Now, let $f \in L^p_g(\Omega,U)$. For $n \in \mathbb{N}^\star$, we consider

$$\hat{f}_n = I_nP_nf = \sum_{x\in V_n(\Omega)} \frac{1}{|\Omega_x^{(n)}|}\int_{\Omega_x^{(n)}} f(y)dy \cdot \chi_{\Omega_x^{(n)}}$$

and define

$$f_n(y) = \begin{cases} g_n(y), & \text{if } y \in \Gamma_n, \\ \hat{f}_n(y), & \text{otherwise.} \end{cases}$$

By the Lebesgue differentiation theorem, we have that $\{\hat{f}_n\}_{n\in\mathbb{N}}$ converges pointwise to f a.e. on Ω; since $\|\hat{f}_n\|_{L^p(\Omega)} \le \|f\|_{L^p(\Omega)}$ for all $n \in \mathbb{N}$, we conclude by the Riesz–Scheffé lemma (Kusolitsch, 2010, lemma 2) that $\{\hat{f}_n\}_{n\in\mathbb{N}}$ converges strongly to f in $L^p(\Omega)$. By construction, we have $f_n \in \mathbb{A}_{g_n}(V_n(\Omega),\Gamma_n)$, for all $n \in \mathbb{N}$, and (f_n) converges strongly to f in $L^p(\Omega)$. Indeed, we have

$$\begin{aligned}
|f - f_n| &\le |f - \hat{f}_n| + |\hat{f}_n - f_n| \\
&\le |f - \hat{f}_n| + |(\hat{f}_n - f_n)\cdot\chi_{\Gamma_n}| \\
&\le |f - \hat{f}_n| + |(\hat{f}_n - g_n)\cdot\chi_{\Gamma_n}| \\
&\le |f - \hat{f}_n| + |(\hat{f}_n - f)\cdot\chi_{\Gamma_n}| + |(f-g)\cdot\chi_{\Gamma_n}| + |(g - g_n)\cdot\chi_{\Gamma_n}| \\
&\le 2|f - \hat{f}_n| + |g - g_n| + |(f-g)\cdot\chi_{\Gamma_n\Delta\Gamma}|,
\end{aligned}$$

and so

$$\|f - f_n\|_{L^p(\Omega)} \le 2\|f - \hat{f}_n\|_{L^p(\Omega)} + \|g - g_n\|_{L^p(\Omega)} + \|(f-g)\cdot\chi_{\Gamma_n\Delta\Gamma}\|_{L^p(\Omega)}.$$

Hence, we get the result, since the terms in the right-hand side of the preceding inequality tend to zero. □

5.2.3 Convergence of Minimum Problems

In the rest of the section, we assume that $N = 2d$ and $\mathcal{U} = \Omega\times\Omega$. Let $L^p_g(\Omega, U)$ the affine space given by (5.1), where $g \in L^p(\Omega)$.

Lemma 5.4 *Let $K \in L^1(\Omega^2)$ satisfies* **(H.1)**, **(H.2)**, *and* **(H.4)**, *and let $g \in L^p(\Omega)$.*

(i) *We have the following nonlocal Poincaré's inequality. There exists $\lambda = \lambda(K, \Omega, \Gamma, r_0) > 0$ such that*

$$\lambda \int_\Omega |u(x)|^p\,dx \le \int_{\Omega^2} K(x,y)|u(y)-u(x)|^p\,dx\,dy + \int_\Gamma |g(x)|^p\,dx, \quad (5.7)$$

for all $u \in L^p_g(\Omega, U)$.

(ii) *Moreover, if $K \in L^{\infty,1}(\Omega^2)$, then there exists a positive constant $C > 0$ such that*

$$\|v-u\|_{L^p(\Omega)}^{p/\max(1,\frac{2}{p})} \le C\int_\Omega \left(\Delta^K_p v - \Delta^K_p u\right)(x)\,(v-u)\,(x)dx, \quad (5.8)$$

for all u, $v \in L^p_g(\Omega, U)$,

Proof: (i) See Hinds and Radu (2012, lemma 3.5).

(ii) Combining Proposition 3.2 (v) and the nonlocal Poincaré's inequality, we get the desired result. □

Proposition 5.5 *Let $F \in \mathcal{F}(a, C_1, C_2, p)$, $g \in L^p(\Omega)$ and let K be a function in $L^{\infty,p}(\Omega^2)$. We assume that K satisfies* **(H.2)** *or* **(H.5)**.

Consider the function $\mathcal{G}: L^p(\Omega) \to \mathbb{R}$ defined by

$$\mathcal{G} = F \circ \nabla^{\mathrm{NL}}_K.$$

Then

(i) *$\mathcal{G}$ is convex and continuous on $L^p(\Omega)$. In particular, $\mathcal{G}$ is weakly lower semicontinuous on $L^p(\Omega)$.*

Moreover, if K satisfies **(H.4)**, *then*

(ii) *$\mathcal{G}$ is coercive on $L^p_g(\Omega, U)$, induced by the weakly topology.*

(iii) *$\mathcal{G}$ attains its minimizer on $L^p_g(\Omega, U)$.*

(iv) *if $F \in \mathcal{F}'(a, C_1, C_2, p)$, then $\mathcal{G}$ is strictly convex on $L^p_g(\Omega, U)$. In particular, $\mathcal{G}$ has a unique minimizer on $L^p_g(\Omega, U)$.*

PROOF: The convexity of the point (i) is evident; therefore, by Proposition 2.2, it is enough to show that $\mathcal{G}$ is locally bounded below on $L^p(\Omega)$, since it is proper. Letting $R > 0$, for all $u \in L^p(\Omega)$ such that $\|u\|_{L^p(\Omega)} \leq R$, we have

$$\|\nabla_K^{\mathrm{NL}} u\|_{L^p(\Omega^2)} \leq \begin{cases} 2\|K\|_{L^{\infty,p}(\Omega^2)} R, & \text{if } K \text{ satisfies } \textbf{(H.2)}, \\ 2\|K\|_{L^{\infty}(\Omega^2)} R, & \text{if } K \text{ satisfies } \textbf{(H.5)}. \end{cases}$$

On the other hand, by assumption **(A.3)** and the definition of $\mathcal{G}$, we get that

$$\begin{aligned} \mathcal{G}(u) &= F(\nabla_K^{\mathrm{NL}} u) \\ &\leq \begin{cases} \|a\|_{L^1(\Omega^2)} + C_2\left(|\Omega^2| + 2^p\|K\|^p_{L^{\infty,p}(\Omega^2)} R^p\right), & \text{if } K \text{ satisfies } \textbf{(H.2)}, \\ \|a\|_{L^1(\Omega^2)} + C_2\left(|\Omega^2| + 2^p|\Omega|\|K\|^p_{L^{\infty}(\Omega^2)} R^p\right), & \text{if } K \text{ satisfies } \textbf{(H.5)}. \end{cases} \end{aligned}$$

For (ii), it is enough to show that, for all $t > 0$, the set $\mathcal{A}_t = \{\mathcal{G} \leq t\} \cap L^p_g(\Omega, U)$ is bounded in $L^p(\Omega)$, since $\mathcal{G}$ is weakly lsc, thanks to point (i). Let $u \in \mathcal{A}_t$; then

$$\begin{aligned} t &\geq \mathcal{G}(u) \\ &\geq C_1 \int_{\Omega^2} |K(x,y)|^p |u(x) - u(y)|^p\, dx\, dy - \int_{\Omega^2} a(x,y)\, dx\, dy. \end{aligned}$$

Applying the Poincaré inequality (see Lemma 5.4) in the preceding inequality, we get

$$t \geq C_1 \lambda^{-1} \int_{\Omega} |u(x)|^p\, dx - C_1 \int_{\Omega} |g(x)|^p\, dx - \|a\|_{L^1(\Omega^2)},$$

where $\lambda = \lambda(r, K, \Omega, p) > 0$. Hence,

$$\int_{\Omega} |u(y)|^p\, dy \leq \frac{\lambda^{-1}}{C_1}(t + \|a\|_{L^1(\Omega^2)}) + \lambda^{-1} \int_{\Gamma} |g(x)|^p\, dx,$$

for all $u \in \mathcal{A}_t$.

Now, we turn to show (iii). Let $\iota_{L^p_g(\Omega,U)}$ be the indicator function of $L^p_g(\Omega, U) \subset L^p(\Omega)$. By (ii) we get that $\mathcal{G}(\cdot) + \iota_{L^p_g(\Omega,U)}(\cdot)$ is coercive. This function is weakly lower semicontinuous by closedness of $L^p_g(\Omega, U)$ and weakly lower semicontinuous of $\mathcal{G}$, hence $\mathcal{G}$ has a minimizer in $L^p_g(\Omega, U)$. For (iv), it is enough to show that $\mathcal{G}$ is strictly convex. Assume that $\mathcal{G}$ is not. Let $u, v \in L^p_g(\Omega, U)$ with $u \neq v$ such that

$$\mathcal{G}(tu + (1-t)v) = t\mathcal{G}(u) + (1-t)\mathcal{G}(v), \quad \text{for } t \in]0,1[.$$

Since F is strictly convex, we have $\nabla_K^{\mathrm{NL}} u = \nabla_K^{\mathrm{NL}} v$, and so $u - v \in \mathrm{Ker}(\nabla_K^{\mathrm{NL}}) \cap L^p_0(\Omega, U) = \{0\}$. Contradiction. □

Theorem 5.6 *Let $F,\ F_n,\ n \in \mathbb{N}$ be a sequence of integral functionals given by (5.2) that satisfy $(\mathcal{H}_{seq})$. Let K_n, K be a sequence of functions in $L^{\infty,p}(\Omega^2)$ such that $\{K_n, K:\ n \in \mathbb{N}\}$ satisfy $(\mathcal{A}_{ker})$ or $(\mathcal{B}_{ker})$. Let $\mathcal{G}, \mathcal{G}_n : L^p(\Omega) \to \mathbb{R}$ be a sequence of functions defined by*

$$\mathcal{G} = F \circ \nabla_K^{\mathrm{NL}} \quad \text{and} \quad \mathcal{G}_n = F_n \circ \nabla_{K_n}^{\mathrm{NL}}, \quad n \in \mathbb{N}.$$

Then, the sequence $(\mathcal{G}_n)$ Mosco-converges to $\mathcal{G}$ on $L^p(\Omega)$.

Let us first state the following result that will be useful for proving the preceding theorem. This result is an immediate consequence of Proposition 2.2 and the Arzelà–Ascoli theorem.

Lemma 5.7 *Let $\{F,\ F_n : n \in \mathbb{N}\}$ as in Theorem 5.6, and let $\{f,\ f_n : n \in \mathbb{N}\}$ be the corresponding integrands. Then, for almost all $(\boldsymbol{x}, \boldsymbol{y}) \in \Omega^2$, the sequence $\{f_n((\boldsymbol{x}, \boldsymbol{y}), \cdot)\}_{n \in \mathbb{N}}$ converges uniformly to $f((\boldsymbol{x}, \boldsymbol{y}), \cdot)$ on every compact subset of $\mathbb{R}$. In particular, the sequence $\{f_n(\cdot, s_n)\}_{n \in \mathbb{N}}$ converges to $f(\cdot, s)$ for every sequence (s_n) converging to s and almost everywhere on Ω^2.*

Proof: First, we prove the pointwise convergence of $\mathcal{G}_n$ to $\mathcal{G}$ on $L^p(\Omega)$, under both the conditions on the sequence of kernels. Let $u \in L^p(\Omega)$; we have $\nabla_{K_n}^{\mathrm{NL}} u$ converge pointwise to $\nabla_K^{\mathrm{NL}} u$ almost everywhere on Ω^2, since K_n are (under the two conditions). By Lemma 5.7, we have that $\{f_n((\boldsymbol{x}, \boldsymbol{y}), \nabla_{K_n}^{\mathrm{NL}}(\boldsymbol{x}, \boldsymbol{y}))\}_{n \in \mathbb{N}}$ converges to $f_n((\boldsymbol{x}, \boldsymbol{y}), \nabla_K^{\mathrm{NL}}(\boldsymbol{x}, \boldsymbol{y}))$ for almost all $(\boldsymbol{x}, \boldsymbol{y})$ in Ω^2. On the other hand, we have

$$|f_n((\boldsymbol{x}, \boldsymbol{y}), \nabla_{K_n}^{\mathrm{NL}} u(\boldsymbol{x}, \boldsymbol{y}))| \le a(\boldsymbol{x}, \boldsymbol{y}) + C_2 \left(\sup_n \|K_n\|_{L^\infty(\Omega^2)}^p |\nabla^{\mathrm{NL}} u(\boldsymbol{x}, \boldsymbol{y})|^p + 1 \right),$$

under the condition $(\mathcal{B}_{ker})$, hence $\{f_n(\cdot, \nabla_{K_n}^{\mathrm{NL}} u \cdot)\}_{n \in \mathbb{N}}$ is equi-integrable, and by the Vitali theorem we get the convergence of $\mathcal{G}_n(u)$ to $\mathcal{G}(u)$. Let us turn to the second case, that is, when the kernels satisfy condition $(\mathcal{A}_{ker})$. In this case, we have that $\{\nabla_{K_n}^{\mathrm{NL}} u\}_{n \in \mathbb{N}}$ converges strongly to $\nabla_{K_n}^{\mathrm{NL}} u$ in $L^p(\Omega^2)$. Indeed, we have

$$\begin{aligned}
\|\nabla_{K_n}^{\mathrm{NL}} u - \nabla_K^{\mathrm{NL}} u\|_{L^p(\Omega^2)}^p &\le 2^{p-1} \int_{\Omega^2} |K_n(\boldsymbol{x}, \boldsymbol{y}) - K(\boldsymbol{x}, \boldsymbol{y})|^p (|u(\boldsymbol{y})|^p + |u(\boldsymbol{x})|^p) d\boldsymbol{x} d\boldsymbol{y} \\
&\overset{\text{symmetry}}{\le} 2^p \int_\Omega |u(\boldsymbol{x})|^p \left(\int_\Omega |K_n(\boldsymbol{x}, \boldsymbol{y}) - K(\boldsymbol{x}, \boldsymbol{y})|^p d\boldsymbol{y} \right) d\boldsymbol{x} \\
&\le 2^p \|u\|_{L^p(\Omega)}^p \|K_n - K\|_{L^{\infty,p}(\Omega^2)}^p.
\end{aligned}$$

We get the convergence by assumption on the kernels. Hence, the sequence $\{|\nabla_{K_n}^{\mathrm{NL}} u|^p\}_{n \in \mathbb{N}}$ is equi-integrable on $L^p(\Omega^2)$, and so is $\{a +$

$C_2\left(|\nabla^{\mathrm{NL}}_{K_n}u|^p+1\right)\}_{n\in\mathbb{N}}$. Therefore, $\{f_n(\cdot,\nabla^{\mathrm{NL}}_{K_n}u\cdot)\}_{n\in\mathbb{N}}$ is equi-integrable. Applying the Vitali convergence theorem again, we get the convergence of $(\mathcal{G}_n(u))$ to $\mathcal{G}(u)$ under condition $(\mathcal{A}_{ker})$.

Now, assume that $\{K_n, K: n\in\mathbb{N}\}$ satisfies $(\mathcal{B}_{ker})$, by arguments similar to those in the proof of Theorem 5.2. We have that $\mathcal{G}$, $\mathcal{G}_n$, $n\in\mathbb{N}$, are closed convex functions in $L^p(\Omega)$ and that

$$\mathcal{G}_n(u)=F_n(\nabla^{\mathrm{NL}}_{K_n}u)\leq\|a\|_{L^1(\Omega^2)}+C_2\left(|\Omega^2|+2^p|\Omega|\sup_n\|K_n\|^p_{L^\infty(\Omega^2)}R^p\right),$$

for all $u\in L^p(\Omega)$ such that $\|u\|_{L^p(\Omega)}\leq R$, $R>0$. Therefore, the sequence $\{\mathcal{G}_n\}_{n\in\mathbb{N}}$ is locally uniformly Lipschitz, thanks again to Proposition 2.2; in particular, it is equi-lower semicontinuous. Invoking Theorem 2.8, we get the Mosco-convergence.

Assume that $\{K_n, K: n\in\mathbb{N}\}$ satisfies $(\mathcal{A}_{ker})$. Since $\mathcal{G}_n$ converge pointwise to $\mathcal{G}$, by definition of Mosco-convergence, it is enough to show point (i) of Definition 2.7. Let $\{u_n\}_{n\in\mathbb{N}}$ be a sequence of functions in $L^p(\Omega)$ weakly converging to u in $L^p(\Omega)$. Since $\{F_n\}_{n\in\mathbb{N}}$ Mosco-converges to F in $L^p(\Omega^2)$, thanks to Theorem 2.8, it amounts to showing that $\{\nabla^{\mathrm{NL}}_{K_n}u_n\}_{n\in\mathbb{N}}$ converges weakly to $\nabla^{\mathrm{NL}}_{K}u$ in $L^p(\Omega^2)$. For $v\in L^q(\Omega^2)$, applying the Hölder inequality and symmetry of the kernels, we obtain

$$\begin{aligned}
&\left|\int_{\Omega^2}v\left(\nabla^{\mathrm{NL}}_{K_n}u_n\right)-v\left(\nabla^{\mathrm{NL}}_{K}u\right)dxdy\right|\\
&\leq\left|\int_{\Omega^2}(v(x,y)+v(y,x))(K_n(x,y)u_n(y)-K(x,y)u(y))\,dxdy\right|\\
&\leq\left|\int_{\Omega}\left(\int_{\Omega}(v(x,y)+v(y,x))K(x,y)dx\right)(u_n(y)-u(y))\,dy\right|\\
&\quad+\left|\int_{\Omega^2}(v(x,y)+v(y,x))\,u_n(y)\,(K_n(x,y)-K(x,y))\,dxdy\right|.
\end{aligned}$$

Hence $\left|\int_{\Omega^2}v\left(\nabla^{\mathrm{NL}}_{K_n}u_n\right)-v\left(\nabla^{\mathrm{NL}}_{K}u\right)\right|\to 0$ as n tends to ∞. Indeed, it is straightforward to see that the function $y\to\int_{\Omega}(v(x,y)+v(y,x))\,K(x,y)dx$ belongs in $L^q(\Omega)$. By weak convergence of (u_n), the first term in the last line of the above inequalities tends to 0; for the second term, we have that

$$\begin{aligned}
&\left|\int_{\Omega^2}(v(x,y)+v(y,x))\,u_n(y)\,(K_n(x,y)-K(x,y))\,dxdy\right|\\
&\leq\|u_n\|_{L^p(\Omega)}\left(\int_{\Omega}\left|\int_{\Omega}(v(x,y)+v(y,x))\,(K_n(x,y)-K(x,y))\,dx\right|^q dy\right)^{1/q}\\
&\leq\|u_n\|_{L^p(\Omega)}\left(\int_{\Omega}\left(\int_{\Omega}|v(x,y)+v(y,x)|^q dx\right)\left(\int_{\Omega}|K_n(x,y)-K(x,y)|^p dx\right)^{q/p}dy\right)^{1/q}\\
&\leq C\|K_n-K\|_{L^{\infty,p}(\Omega^2)},
\end{aligned}\tag{5.9}$$

where $C = 2\|v\|_{L^q(\Omega^2)} \sup_n \|u_n\|_{L^p(\Omega)} < \infty$, since (u_n) is weakly convergent. Passing to the limit as n tends to ∞, in (5.9), we get the desired result. □

Remark 5.8 All the results of this subsection remain true when the kernels are such that $K(x,y) = J(x-y)$ and $K_n(x,y) = J_n(x-y)$, if we replace the hypotheses on the kernels K, K_n, $n \in \mathbb{N}$ by the equivalent ones on the kernels J, J_n, $n \in \mathbb{N}$.

5.3 Well-Posedness of the Boundary Value Problem

Define the energy functional $\mathcal{F} : L^p(\Omega) \to \mathbb{R}$ by

$$\mathcal{F}(u) := \frac{1}{2p} \int_{\Omega^2} K(x,y)|u(y) - u(x)|^p dy dx + \int_{\Omega} f(x)u(x)dx. \tag{5.10}$$

We have the following "integration by parts" identity.

Lemma 5.9 (Hinds and Radu, 2012, lemma 2.2) *Let $K \in L^1(\Omega^2)$ satisfy **(H.2)**. For every $u, v \in L^p(\Omega)$ we have*

$$\int_{\Omega} (\Delta_p^K u)v dx = \frac{1}{2} \int_{\Omega^2} K(x,y)|u(y)-u(x)|^{p-2}(u(y)-u(x))(v(y)-v(x))dy dx. \tag{5.11}$$

Due to the nonlocal property of the operator Δ_p^K, classical boundary conditions (imposed on boundaries of zero volume) will not yield well-posed systems. The authors in Du et al. (2013a) solved this issue and showed well-posedness of $(\mathcal{P}_D)$ for $p = 2$ in the scalar case by using a variational approach based on the Lax–Milgram lemma (see also Du et al., 2012). Since the Lax–Milgram lemma is not applicable for the nonlinear problem $(\mathcal{P}_D)$, Hinds and Radu (2012) proved Dirichlet's principle for the nonlocal setting of $(\mathcal{P}_D)$. Adapted to our setting, this can be stated as follows.

Proposition 5.10 (Dirichlet's principle) *Let $K \in L^1(\Omega^2)$ be a function satisfying **(H.1)** and **(H.2)**. Consider the functional $\mathcal{F} : L^p(\Omega) \to \mathbb{R}$ given in* (5.10)*. Then, the following holds:*

(i) Assume u solves the Dirichlet problem $(\mathcal{P}_D)$. Then

$$\mathcal{F}(u) \le \mathcal{F}(v) \tag{5.12}$$

for every $v \in L_g^p(\Omega, U)$.

(ii) Conversely, if u satisfies (5.12) *for every $v \in L_g^p(\Omega, U)$, then u solves the Dirichlet problem $(\mathcal{P}_D)$.*

Theorem 5.11 *Let $g \in L^p(\Omega)$, $f \in L^q(\Omega)$, with $1 < p, q < +\infty$, and $\frac{1}{p} + \frac{1}{q} = 1$, and $K \in L^1(\Omega^2)$ satisfies **(H.1)**, **(H.2)**, and **(H.4)**. Then the functional $\mathcal{F}$ has a unique minimizer in $L^p_g(\Omega, U)$, that is, the problem $(\mathcal{P}_D)$ has a unique solution.*

PROOF: See Hinds and Radu (2012, theorem 3.11). □

5.4 Consistency and Error Estimates for the Dirichlet Problem

In the numerical analysis literature, consistent numerical approximations have been studied for nonlocal boundary value problems, focusing overwhelmingly on the nonlocal peridynamic model or nonlocal linear diffusion ($p = 2$); see Du (2019) for a recent overview. For instance, so-called asymptotically compatible schemes were proposed in Tian and Du (2014, 2020) as an abstract framework for the study of robust numerical methods for nonlocal models and their continuum local limits. They studied, in particular, consistency of Galerkin finite element discretizations of the boundary value problem, with $p = 2$ (i.e., nonlocal linear diffusion) and $K(x, y) = \varepsilon^{-N} J(|x - y|/\varepsilon)$, $\varepsilon > 0$, and established its continuum limit as both the mesh size and ε vanish. These results do not allow one to cover the case of the p-Laplacian.

5.4.1 General Consistency Estimates

Fix $n \in \mathbb{N}$. We denote by $\mathbb{H}(V_n(\Omega))$ the set of real functions defined on $V_n(\Omega)$, where $V_n(\Omega)$ is given by (5.4), and similarly for $\mathbb{H}(V_n(\Omega) \times V_n(\Omega))$. Let K be a nonnegative symmetric function in $L^{\infty,1}(\Omega^2)$, $g \in L^p(\Omega)$, and $f \in L^q(\Omega)$, with $\frac{1}{p} + \frac{1}{q} = 1$.

Recall the discrete Dirichlet problem introduced at the beginning of this section,

$$\begin{cases} \frac{1}{n^d} \sum_{y \in V_n(\Omega)} \mathbf{K}_{xy} |\mathbf{u}_y - \mathbf{u}_x|^{p-2}(\mathbf{u}_y - \mathbf{u}_x) = \mathbf{f}_x, & x \in A_n \\ \mathbf{u}_x = \mathbf{g}_x, & x \in A_n^c, \end{cases} \qquad (\mathcal{P}_n^d)$$

where $\mathbf{g} = P_n g$, $\mathbf{f} = P_n f$, $\mathbf{K} = P_n K$, $A_n = \{x \in V_n(\Omega) \colon \Omega_x^{(n)} \subset U\}$, and $A_n^c = V_n(\Omega) \setminus A_n$.

The problem $(\mathcal{P}_n^d)$ is equivalent to solving the following minimization problem:

$$\min\{\mathcal{G}_n(\mathbf{u}), \text{ on } \mathbb{H}_{\mathbf{g}}(V_n(\Omega), A_n)\}, \qquad (\mathcal{VP}_n^{d,D})$$

where

$$\mathcal{G}_n(\mathbf{u}) \stackrel{\text{def}}{=} \frac{1}{2p} \sum_{x,y \in V_n(\Omega)} \mathbf{K}_{xy} |\mathbf{u}_y - \mathbf{u}_x|^p + \sum_{x \in V_n(\Omega)} \mathbf{u}_x \mathbf{f}_x$$

and

$$\mathbb{H}_{\mathbf{g}}(V_n(\Omega), A_n) = \{\mathbf{u} \in \mathbb{H}(V_n(\Omega)) : \ \mathbf{u} = \mathbf{g} \text{ on } A_n^c\}.$$

Our aim is to compare the solutions of the problems $(\mathcal{P}_D)$ and $(\mathcal{P}_n^d)$. For this purpose, we introduce an intermediate model, which is the continuous extension of the discrete problem $(\mathcal{P}_n^d)$, which has discrete solutions.

It is immediate to see that a function is a solution of the problem $(\mathcal{P}_n^d)$ if and only if its continuous extension is a solution of the following problem:

$$\begin{cases} -\Delta_p^{K_n} u_n = f_n, & \text{in } U_n \\ u_n = g_n, & \text{on } \Gamma_n = \Omega \setminus U_n, \end{cases} \qquad (\mathcal{P}_n^c)$$

which, in turn, is equivalent to minimizing the functional

$$\mathcal{F}_n \colon v \mapsto \mathcal{F}_n(v) = \frac{1}{2p}\int_{\Omega^2} K_n(x,y)|v(y) - v(x)|^p dydx + \int_{\Omega} v(x) f_n(x) dx, \tag{5.13}$$

on $\mathbb{A}_{g_n}(V_n(\Omega), \Gamma_n)$, where $U_n = \bigcup_{x \in A_n} \Omega_x^{(n)}$ and

$$f_n = I_n \mathbf{f}, \quad g_n = I_n \mathbf{g}, \quad u_n = I_n \mathbf{u}, \quad \text{and} \quad K_n = I_n \mathbf{K}.$$

Corollary 5.12 *Let $g \in L^p(\Omega)$, $f \in L^q(\Omega)$, and $K \in L^\infty(\Omega^2)$. Assume that K satisfies* **(H.1)**, **(H.2)**, *and* **(H.4)**. *Then, for all $n \in \mathbb{N}$, the problem $(\mathcal{P}_n^d)$ has a unique solution $\mathbf{u} \in \mathbb{H}(V_n(\Omega))$. Moreover, if u is the solution of the problem $(\mathcal{P}_D)$, then $\{I_n \mathbf{u}\}_{n \in \mathbb{N}}$ converges weakly to u in $L^p(\Omega)$.*

PROOF: The existence and uniqueness of the solutions are a consequence of Theorem 5.11.

In view of the definition of the functions f_n, g_n, K_n, by the Lebesgue differentiation theorem (see Pardoux, 2009, theorem 3.4.4), we have that g_n, f_n, and K_n converge pointwise to, respectively, f, g, and K a.e. on Ω and Ω^2. Combining this with Fatou's lemma and (2.8), we get

$$\lim_n \|g_n\|_{L^p(\Omega)} = \|g\|_{L^p(\Omega)} \quad \text{and} \quad \lim_n \|f_n\|_{L^q(\Omega)} = \|f\|_{L^q(\Omega)}.$$

Hence, by the Riesz–Scheffé lemma, we have that $I_n P_n g \to g$ strongly in $L^p(\Omega)$ and $I_n P_n f \to f$ strongly in $L^q(\Omega)$, thus the sequence $\{u \mapsto \int_\Omega f_n u\}_{n \in \mathbb{N}}$ is Mosco-convergent to $u \mapsto \int_\Omega f_n u$ in $L^p(\Omega)$. On the other hand, by the assumption **(H.4)**, we have $m\chi_{[0,r_0[}(\|x - y\|) \leq I_n \mathbf{K}(x,y) \leq \|K\|_{L^\infty(\Omega^2)}$ for a.e. on Ω^2, whence $\{K_n, K : n \in \mathbb{N}\}$ satisfies the condition $(\mathcal{A}_{ker})$. Therefore, by Theorem 5.6 and Proposition 5.3 and Corollary 2.10, we have $\{\mathcal{E}_n\}_{n\in\mathbb{N}}$ Mosco-convergences to $\mathcal{E}$ in $L^p(\Omega)$, where

$$\mathcal{E}(u) = \frac{1}{2p}\int_{\Omega^2} K(x,y)|u(y)-u(x)|^p\,dy\,dx + \int_{\Omega} fu\,dx + \iota_{L^p_g(\Omega,U)}(u);$$
$$\mathcal{E}_n(u) = \frac{1}{2p}\int_{\Omega^2} K_n(x,y)|u(y)-u(x)|^p\,dy\,dx + \int_{\Omega} f_n u\,dx + \iota_{\mathbb{A}_{g_n}(V_n(\Omega),\Gamma_n)}(u).$$

In particular, $\{\mathcal{E}_n\}_{n\in\mathbb{N}}$ Γ-converges to $\mathcal{E}$ in $L^p(\Omega)$ endowed with the weak topology.

Moreover, for all $t > 0$, the set $\mathcal{A}_t = \cup_n\{\mathcal{E}_n \le t\}$ is bounded in $L^p(\Omega)$. Indeed, let $u \in \mathcal{A}_t$; there exists $n \in \mathbb{N}$ such that $u \in \mathbb{A}_{g_n}(V_n(\Omega),\Gamma_n)$, hence

$$\begin{aligned}
t &\ge \mathcal{E}_n(u)\\
&= \frac{1}{2p}\int_{\Omega^2} K_n(x,y)|u(y)-u(x)|^p\,dy\,dx + \int_{\Omega} f_n u\,dx\\
&= \frac{1}{2p}\int_{\Omega^2} K(x,y)|u(y)-u(x)|^p\,dy\,dx + \int_{\Omega} f_n u\,dx\\
&\ge \frac{m}{2p}\int_{\Omega^2} \chi_{[0,r_0[}(\|x-y\|)|u(y)-u(x)|^p\,dy\,dx - \int_{\Omega}|f_n u|\,dx\\
&\ge \frac{m}{2p}\left(\lambda\|u\|^p_{L^p(\Omega)} - \|g_n\|^p_{L^p(\Omega)}\right) - \frac{\varepsilon}{2p}\|u\|^p_{L^p(\Omega)} - \frac{2}{q\varepsilon}\|f_n\|^q_{L^q(\Omega)};
\end{aligned}$$

furthermore,

$$\begin{aligned}
\frac{1}{2p}(m\lambda-\varepsilon)\|u\|^p_{L^p(\Omega)} &\le t + \frac{m}{2p}\|g_n\|^p_{L^p(\Omega)} + \frac{2}{q\varepsilon}\|f_n\|^q_{L^q(\Omega)}\\
&\le t + \frac{m}{2p}\sup_n\|g_n\|^p_{L^p(\Omega)} + \frac{2}{q\varepsilon}\sup_n\|f_n\|^q_{L^q(\Omega)},
\end{aligned}$$

where $\lambda = \lambda(r_0, r, p, \Omega) > 0$ is the parameter of Poincaré's inequality given in Lemma 5.4, and ε is a positive real number. By the fundamental theorem of Γ-convergence, we get the result. □

Corollary 5.13 *Let $g \in L^p(\Omega)$, $f \in L^q(\Omega)$, and let $K(x,y) = J(x-y)$, where $J \in L^1(\Omega-\Omega)$ satisfies **(H'.1)**, **(H'.2)**, and **(H'.4)**. Then, for all $n \in \mathbb{N}$, the problem $(\mathcal{P}^d_n)$ has a unique solution $\mathbf{u} \in \mathbb{H}(V_n(\Omega))$. Moreover, if u is the solution of the problem $(\mathcal{P}_D)$, then $\{I_n\mathbf{u}\}_{n\in\mathbb{N}}$ converges weakly to u in $L^p(\Omega)$.*

Proof: We get the results by the same arguments as in the proof of Corollary 5.12, where in this case the sequence of the kernels satisfies the condition $(\mathcal{A}'_{rad})$ (which is equivalent to $(\mathcal{A}_{ker})$ in our case). Indeed, by the Riesz–Scheffé lemma, we have that $\{J_n\}_{n\in\mathbb{N}}$ converges strongly to J in $L^1(\Omega-\Omega)$, whence $\{J^{1/p}, J_n^{1/p}, n \in \mathbb{N}\}$ satisfies the condition $(\mathcal{A}'_{rad})$, since

$$\|J_n^{\frac{1}{p}} - J^{\frac{1}{p}}\|_{L^p(\Omega-\Omega)} \le \|J_n - J\|^{\frac{1}{p}}_{L^1(\Omega-\Omega)}.$$

□

Remark 5.14 The results of Corollary 5.12 and Corollary 5.13 remain true if we replace A_n and A_n^c by $A_n' = \{\boldsymbol{x} \in V_n(\Omega) \colon \Omega_{\boldsymbol{x}}^{(n)} \cap U \neq \emptyset\}$ and $(A_n')^c$, respectively, in $(\mathcal{P}_n^d)$.

5.4.2 A Priori Estimates

In this subsection we give an a priori estimate for the Dirichlet problem. The reason we separate this section from the previous one is that here, we restrict ourselves to the case where the datum g is constant, without loss of generality if we take $g = 0$. The second reason is due to the choice of the boundary set $\Gamma_n \subset \Gamma$ as the set A_n^c defined in $(\mathcal{P}_n^d)$, which ensures the following feasibility conditions of the constraint that $\mathbb{A}_{g_n}(V_n(\Omega), \Gamma_n) \subset L^p_{g_n}(V_n(\Omega), \Gamma_n)$ play a key role to get our estimation.

Theorem 5.15 *Let $(K, f, g, \mathbf{K}, \mathbf{f}, \mathbf{g})$ as is Corollary 5.12, with $g = 0$, $\mathbf{g} = 0$, $\mathbf{K} = P_n K$, and $\mathbf{f} = P_n f$. Let $\mathbf{u}$ be a solution of the discrete problem $(\mathcal{P}_n^d)$ with kernel $\mathbf{K}$, data $(\mathbf{f}, \mathbf{g})$, and the boundary set A_n^c, and u the solution of the continuous problem $(\mathcal{P}_D)$ with kernel K, data (f, g), and the boundary set Γ. Then,*

$$\left\|u - u_n\right\|_{L^p(\Omega)}^{p/\max(1,\frac{2}{p})} \leq C\left(\left\|K - K_n\right\|_{L^{\infty,1}(\Omega^2)}^{\max(2,\frac{p}{p-1})} + \left\|K - K_n\right\|_{L^{\infty,1}(\Omega^2)} \right.$$
$$\left. \left\|I_n P_n u - u\right\|_{L^p(\Omega)} + \begin{cases} \left\|I_n P_n u - u\right\|_{L^p(\Omega)}^{\frac{p}{p-1}} & p \in [2, +\infty[, \\ \left\|I_n P_n u - u\right\|_{L^p(\Omega)}^{\frac{2}{3-p}} & p \in]1, 2]. \end{cases}\right), \tag{5.14}$$

where $C > 0$ independent of n, and K_n, g_n, f_n, and u_n are the continuous extensions of the functions $\mathbf{K}$, $\mathbf{g}$, $\mathbf{f}$, and $\mathbf{u}$ respectively.

Proof: First of all, observe that $\{u_n\}_{n\in\mathbb{N}}$ converges weakly to u in $L^p(\Omega)$, thanks to Corollary 5.12; in particular $\{u_n\}_{n\in\mathbb{N}}$ is bounded in $L^p(\Omega)$.

Let us turn to prove our bound. We denote by $\langle \cdot, \cdot \rangle$ the usual inner product in $L^2(\Omega)$ and $\nabla^{\mathrm{NL}} v(\boldsymbol{x}, \boldsymbol{y}) = v(\boldsymbol{y}) - v(\boldsymbol{x})$, $v \in L^1(\Omega)$. We have

$$\langle \Delta_p^K u, u_n - u \rangle = \langle -f, u_n - u \rangle, \tag{5.15}$$
$$\langle \Delta_p^{K_n} u_n, v - u_n \rangle = \langle -f_n, v - u_n \rangle \quad \textit{for all } v \in \mathbb{A}_{g_n}(V_n(\Omega), \Gamma_n). \tag{5.16}$$

By summing, we deduce from (5.15) and (5.16):

$$\begin{aligned}\langle \Delta_p^{K_n} u_n - \Delta_p^K u, u_n - u \rangle &= \langle \Delta_p^{K_n} u_n, v - u \rangle - \langle -f, u_n - u \rangle - \langle -f_n, v - u_n \rangle \\ &= \langle \Delta_p^{K_n} u_n, v - u \rangle - \langle -f, v - u \rangle\end{aligned}$$

for all $v \in \mathbb{A}_{g_n}(V_n(\Omega), \Gamma_n)$. The last equality comes from the fact that $\langle f, v - u_n\rangle = \langle f_n, v - u_n\rangle$. Since $\Delta_p^K u = -f$ on U and $v = u_n$ on Γ_n, we get

$$\langle \Delta_p^{K_n} u_n - \Delta_p^K u, u_n - u\rangle = \langle \Delta_p^{K_n} u_n - \Delta_p^K u, v - u\rangle,$$

and in turn,

$$\begin{aligned}\langle \Delta_p^K u_n - \Delta_p^K u, u_n - u\rangle = {} & \langle \Delta_p^{K_n} u_n - \Delta_p^K u_n, v - u\rangle + \langle \Delta_p^K u_n - \Delta_p^K u, v - u\rangle \\ & -\langle \Delta_p^{K_n} u_n - \Delta_p^K u_n, u_n - u\rangle. \end{aligned} \tag{5.17}$$

For the term in the left-hand side, we have by Lemma 5.4 (ii) that there exists $C > 0$ independent of n such that

$$\|u - u_n\|_{L^p(\Omega)}^{p/\max(1,\frac{2}{p})} \le C\langle \Delta_p^K u_n - \Delta_p^K u, u_n - u\rangle. \tag{5.18}$$

On the other hand, we start with the last term in the right-hand side of Equation (5.17). By the Hölder inequality, we have

$$\langle \Delta_p^{K_n} u_n - \Delta_p^K u_n, u_n - u\rangle \le \|\Delta_p^{K_n} u_n - \Delta_p^K u_n\|_{L^q(\Omega)}\|u - u_n\|_{L^p(\Omega)}. \tag{5.19}$$

Applying the Jensen inequality on the first term in the right-hand side of the preceding inequality, we get

$$\begin{aligned}
&\|\Delta_p^{K_n} u_n - \Delta_p^K u_n\|_{L^q(\Omega)} \\
&\le \left(\int_\Omega \left(\int_\Omega |K - K_n|(\boldsymbol{x},\boldsymbol{y})|\nabla^{\mathrm{NL}} u_n(\boldsymbol{x},\boldsymbol{y})|^{p-1} d\boldsymbol{y}\right)^q d\boldsymbol{x}\right)^{1/q} \\
&\overset{Jensen}{\le} \left(\int_\Omega\left(\int_\Omega |K - K_n|(\boldsymbol{x},\boldsymbol{y}) d\boldsymbol{y}\right)^{q-1} \int_\Omega |K - K_n|(\boldsymbol{x},\boldsymbol{y})|\nabla^{\mathrm{NL}} u_n(\boldsymbol{x},\boldsymbol{y})|^p d\boldsymbol{y} d\boldsymbol{x}\right)^{1/q} \\
&\le 2^p \|K - K_n\|_{L^{\infty,1}(\Omega^2)}^{\frac{q-1}{q}} \left(\int_{\Omega^2} |K - K_n|(\boldsymbol{x},\boldsymbol{y})|u_n(\boldsymbol{y})|^p d\boldsymbol{y} d\boldsymbol{x}\right)^{1/q} \\
&\le C_1 \|K - K_n\|_{L^{\infty,1}(\Omega^2)},
\end{aligned} \tag{5.20}$$

where $C_1 = 2^p |\Omega|^{\frac{p-1}{p}} \sup_n \|u_n\|_{L^p(\Omega)}^{p-1} < \infty$. Plugging (5.20) into (5.19), we get

$$\langle \Delta_p^{K_n} u_n - \Delta_p^K u_n, u_n - u\rangle \le C_1 \|K - K_n\|_{L^{\infty,1}(\Omega^2)}\|u - u_n\|_{L^p(\Omega)}. \tag{5.21}$$

Similarly, for the second term in the right-hand side of Equation (5.17), we have

$$|\langle \Delta_p^{K_n} u_n - \Delta_p^K u_n, v - u\rangle| \le C_1 \|K - K_n\|_{L^{\infty,1}(\Omega^2)}\|v - u\|_{L^p(\Omega)}. \tag{5.22}$$

Let's turn to the first term in the right-hand side of Equation (5.17); we have

$$|\langle \Delta_p^K u_n - \Delta_p^K u, v - u\rangle| \le \|\Delta_p^K u_n - \Delta_p^K u\|_{L^q(\Omega)}\|v - u\|_{L^p(\Omega)}. \tag{5.23}$$

For the case when $p \in]1,2]$, using inequality (3.6) and the Jensen inequality, we get

$$\|\Delta_p^K u_n - \Delta_p^K u\|_{L^q(\Omega)} \leq \left(\int_\Omega \left(\int_\Omega K(x,y)|(u-u_n)(x)-(u-u_n)(y)|^{p-1}dy\right)^q dx\right)^{\frac{1}{q}}$$
$$\leq C\|K\|_{L^{\infty,1}(\Omega^2)}\|u-u_n\|^{p-1}_{L^p(\Omega)}, \tag{5.24}$$

where $C = 2^{p-1}|\Omega|^{\frac{p-1}{p}}$. In the case when $p > 2$, we apply inequality (3.6) and the Hölder inequality twice; we obtain

$$\begin{aligned}
&\|\Delta_p^K u_n - \Delta_p^K u\|_{L^q(\Omega)} \\
&\leq \left(\int_\Omega \left(\int_\Omega K(x,y)\left(|\nabla^{NL}u_n(x,y)|+|\nabla^{NL}u(x,y)|\right)^{p-2}|\nabla^{NL}(u-u_n)(x,y)|dy\right)^q dx\right)^{\frac{1}{q}} \\
&\leq \left(\int_\Omega \left(\int_\Omega K(x,y)\left(|\nabla^{NL}u_n(x,y)|+|\nabla^{NL}u(x,y)|\right)^p dy\right)^{\frac{p-2}{p-1}}\right. \\
&\qquad \left.\cdot\left(\int_\Omega K(x,y)|\nabla^{NL}(u-u_n)(x,y)|^p dy\right)^{\frac{1}{p-1}}\left(\int_\Omega K(x,y)dy\right)^{q/p} dx\right)^{1/q} \\
&\leq \|K\|^{1/p}_{L^{\infty,1}(\Omega^2)}\left(\int_{\Omega^2} K(x,y)\left(|\nabla^{NL}u_n(x,y)|+|\nabla^{NL}u(x,y)|\right)^p dydx\right)^{\frac{p-2}{p}} \\
&\qquad \cdot\left(\int_{\Omega^2} K(x,y)|\nabla^{NL}(u-u_n)(x,y)|^p dydx\right)^{\frac{1}{p}} \\
&\leq C\|K\|_{L^{\infty,1}(\Omega^2)}\|u-u_n\|_{L^p(\Omega)},
\end{aligned} \tag{5.25}$$

where $C = 4^p(\sup_n \|u_n\|^{p-2}_{L^p(\Omega)} + \|u\|_{L^p(\Omega)}) < +\infty$. Plugging the inequalities (5.24) and (5.25) into (5.23), one gets

$$|\langle \Delta_p^K u_n - \Delta_p^K u, v-u\rangle| \leq C\begin{cases}\|u_n-u\|_{L^p(\Omega)}\|v-u\|_{L^p(\Omega)} & p\in[2,+\infty[,\\ \|u_n-u\|^{p-1}_{L^p(\Omega)}\|v-u\|_{L^p(\Omega)} & p\in]1,2].\end{cases} \tag{5.26}$$

Assembling the preceding equalities and the inequalities (5.17), (5.18), (5.21), (5.22), and (5.26), we obtain

$$\begin{aligned}
\|u-u_n\|^{p/\max(1,\frac{2}{p})}_{L^p(\Omega)} &\leq C\Bigg(\|K-K_n\|_{L^{\infty,1}(\Omega^2)}\|u_n-u\|_{L^p(\Omega)} + \|K-K_n\|_{L^{\infty,1}(\Omega^2)} \\
&\quad \cdot\|v-u\|_{L^p(\Omega)} + \begin{cases}\|u_n-u\|_{L^p(\Omega)}\|v-u\|_{L^p(\Omega)} & p\geq 2,\\ \|u_n-u\|^{p-1}_{L^p(\Omega)}\|v-u\|_{L^p(\Omega)} & p\in]1,2].\end{cases}\Bigg).
\end{aligned} \tag{5.27}$$

Now, we use Young's inequality and take $v = I_n P_n u$; we obtain the desired result:

$$\|u - u_n\|_{L^p(\Omega)}^{p/\max(1,\frac{2}{p})} \leq$$

$$C \begin{cases} \|K - K_n\|_{L^{\infty,1}(\Omega^2)}^{\frac{p}{p-1}} + \|K - K_n\|_{L^{\infty,1}(\Omega^2)} \|I_n P_n u - u\|_{L^p(\Omega)} \\ \qquad + \|I_n P_n u - u\|_{L^p(\Omega)}^{\frac{p}{p-1}}, \quad p \geq 2, \\ \|K - K_n\|_{L^{\infty,1}(\Omega^2)}^2 + \|K - K_n\|_{L^{\infty,1}(\Omega^2)} \|I_n P_n u - u\|_{L^p(\Omega)} \\ \qquad + \|I_n P_n u - u\|_{L^p(\Omega)}^{\frac{2}{3-p}}, \quad p \in]1,2]. \end{cases} \tag{5.28}$$

□

Theorem 5.16 *Let* $(J, f, g, \mathbf{K}, \mathbf{f}, \mathbf{g})$ *as in Corollary 5.13, with* $g = 0$, $\mathbf{g} = 0$, $\mathbf{K} = P_n K$, *and* $\mathbf{f} = P_n f$. *Let* $\mathbf{u}$ *be a solution of the discrete problem* $(\mathcal{P}_n^d)$ *with kernel* $\mathbf{K}$, *data* $(\mathbf{f}, \mathbf{g})$, *and the boundary set* A_n^c, *and* u *the solution of the continuous problem* $(\mathcal{P}_D)$ *with kernel* J, *data* (f, g), *and the boundary set* Γ. *Then, there exists a positive constant* C *such that*

$$\|u - u_n\|_{L^p(\Omega)}^{p/\max(1,\frac{2}{p})} \leq C \Bigg(\|J - J_n\|_{L^1(\Omega-\Omega)}^{\max(2,\frac{p}{p-1})} + \|J - J_n\|_{L^1(\Omega-\Omega)}$$

$$\|I_n P_n u - u\|_{L^p(\Omega)} + \begin{cases} \|I_n P_n u - u\|_{L^p(\Omega)}^{\frac{p}{p-1}} & p \in [2, +\infty[, \\ \|I_n P_n u - u\|_{L^p(\Omega)}^{\frac{2}{3-p}} & p \in]1, 2], \end{cases} \Bigg), \tag{5.29}$$

where $J_n = I_n P_n J$, *and* g_n, f_n, *and* u_n *are the continuous extensions of the functions* $\mathbf{g}$, $\mathbf{f}$, *and* $\mathbf{u}$ *respectively. In particular,*

$$\lim_n \|u - u_n\|_{L^p(\Omega)} = 0. \tag{5.30}$$

Proof: Observe that $\{u_n\}_{n \in \mathbb{N}}$ converges weakly to u in $L^p(\Omega)$, thanks to Corollary 5.13; in particular, $\{u_n\}_{n \in \mathbb{N}}$ is bounded in $L^p(\Omega)$. By the same argument as in the proof of Theorem 5.15 and the fact that

$$\|K - K_n\|_{L^{\infty,1}(\Omega^2)} \leq \|J - J_n\|_{L^1(\Omega-\Omega)},$$

we get (5.29). For (5.30), we apply the same arguments of the proof of Corollary 5.12; we get that

$$\lim_n \|J - J_n\|_{L^1(\Omega-\Omega)} = 0 \quad \text{and} \quad \lim_n \|I_n P_n u - u\|_{L^p(\Omega)} = 0.$$

Letting n tend to $+\infty$ in (5.29), we get the desired result. □

5.5 Application to Random Graph Sequences

In this section, we study continuum limits of the discrete problem on the random graph model of Definition 2.27. Throughout this section, we suppose that $p \in]1,2]$. Let $\Omega = [0,1]$. Recalling the notation of Section 2.4.3, we define the boundary set $\Gamma = \Omega \setminus U$ where $U =]r, 1-r[$, $r \in]0, 1/2[$. Recall also the construction of the random graph model in Definition 2.27, where each edge (i,j) is independently set to 1 with probability (2.16). This entails that the random matrix $\mathbf{\Lambda}$ is symmetric. However, it is worth emphasizing that the entries of $\mathbf{\Lambda}$ are not independent, but only the entries in each row are mutually independent.

We consider the discrete problem on K-random graphs $\mathbf{G}(n, K, \rho_n)$:

$$\begin{cases} \dfrac{1}{\rho_n n} \displaystyle\sum_{j:(i,j)\in E(\mathbf{G}(n,K,\rho_n))} \Psi(\mathbf{u}_j - \mathbf{u}_i) = \mathbf{f}_i, & x_i \in A_n, \\ \mathbf{u}_i = 0, & \textit{otherwise}, \end{cases} \tag{$\mathcal{P}_n^{d,\mathbf{G}}$}$$

where $\mathbf{u}, \mathbf{f} = P_n f \in \mathbb{R}^n$ and $A_n = \{x_i : [x_i, x_{i+1}[\subset U\}$ with $x_i \overset{\text{def}}{=} \frac{i}{n}$, $i = 0, 1, \cdots, n$. It is important to keep in mind that, since $\mathbf{G}(n, K, \rho_n)$ is a random variable taking values in the set of simple graphs, the boundary value problem $(\mathcal{P}_n^{d,\mathbf{G}})$ must be understood in this sense. Observe that the normalization in $(\mathcal{P}_n^{d,\mathbf{G}})$ by $\rho_n n$ corresponds to the average degree (see Section 2.4.4 for details).

Problem $(\mathcal{P}_n^{d,\mathbf{G}})$ can be equivalently written as

$$\begin{cases} -\mathbf{\Delta}_p^{\widehat{\mathbf{\Lambda}}} \mathbf{u} = \mathbf{f}, & \textit{on } A_n, \\ \mathbf{u} = 0, & \textit{on } A_n^c. \end{cases}$$

We define the continuum extension u_n as in the preceding section. We then see that it satisfies

$$\begin{cases} -\Delta_p^{I_n \mathbf{\Lambda}} u_n(x) = I_n \mathbf{f}(x), & x \in U_n, \\ u_n(x) = 0, & x \in \Gamma_n, \end{cases} \tag{5.31}$$

where $U_n = [r_n, 1 - r_n]$ and $\Gamma_n = [0,1] \setminus U_n$, with $r_n = \min\{x_i : r \leq x_i, i = 0, 1, \cdots, n\}$.

Toward our goal of establishing error bounds, we define $\mathbf{v}$ as the solution of the discrete problem $(\mathcal{P}_n^d)$ with data $(\mathbf{f}, 0)$, boundary set A_n^c, and discrete kernel $\hat{\mathbf{K}}$. Its continuum extension v_n, defined similarly as earlier, fulfills

$$\begin{cases} -\Delta_p^{I_n \hat{\mathbf{K}}} v_n(x) = I_n \mathbf{f}(x), & x \in U_n, \\ v_n(x) = 0, & x \in \Gamma_n. \end{cases} \tag{5.32}$$

We have

$$\left\|u_n - u\right\|_{L^p(\Omega)} \leq \left\|u_n - v_n\right\|_{L^p(\Omega)} + \left\|v_n - u\right\|_{L^p(\Omega)}. \tag{5.33}$$

This bound is composed of two terms: the first one captures the error of random sampling, and the second that of discretization. Assume that $(\mathbf{f}, \mathbf{K}, f, K)$ verify the assumptions of Theorem 5.15. Since $I_n\hat{\mathbf{K}}(x,y) \leq I_n\mathbf{K}(x,y) = I_nP_nK(x,y)$, the assumptions on $\mathbf{K}$ transfer to $\hat{\mathbf{K}}$, and the second term can be bounded using (5.14), replacing I_nP_nK by $I_n\hat{\mathbf{K}}$. It remains to bound the first term by comparing (5.31) and (5.32).

Lemma 5.17 *Assume that $(J, \mathbf{g}, \mathbf{K},, \mathbf{f}, g, f)$ verify the assumptions of Theorem 5.16. Assume also that $\rho_n \to 0$ and $\rho_n n = \omega((\log n)^\gamma)$ for some $\gamma > 1$. Then, for any $\beta \in]0,1[$,*

$$\mathbb{E}(\|u_n - v_n\|_{L^p(\Omega)}) \leq C(\rho_n n)^{1/2}, \tag{5.34}$$

and in turn,

$$\|u_n - v_n\|_{L^p(\Omega)} \leq C(\rho_n n)^{-\beta/2} \tag{5.35}$$

with probability at least $1 - (\rho_n n)^{-(1-\beta)/2}$. In particular,

$$\|u_n - v_n\|_{L^p(\Omega)} \leq o\left((\log n)^{-\gamma\beta/2}\right), \tag{5.36}$$

with probability at least $1 - o\left((\log n)^{-\gamma(1-\beta)/2}\right)$.

To prove this lemma, we need the following deviation inequality that we include for the reader convenience.

Lemma 5.18 (Rosenthal's inequality, Ibragimov and Sharakhmetov, 2002) *Let m be a positive integer, $\gamma \geq 2$, and $\xi_1, \cdots, \xi_m$ be m zero mean independent random variables such that $\sup_i \mathbb{E}(|\xi_i|^\gamma) < \infty$. Then there exists a positive constant C such that*

$$\mathbb{E}\left(\left|\sum_i \xi_i\right|^\gamma\right) \leq C \max\left(\sum_i \mathbb{E}(|\xi_i|^\gamma), \left(\sum_i \mathbb{E}\left(|\xi_i|^2\right)\right)^{\gamma/2}\right).$$

Proof of Lemma 5.17: Denote $f_n = I_n\mathbf{f}$, $\hat{K} = I_n\hat{\mathbf{K}}$, and $\Lambda_n = I_n\mathbf{\Lambda}$. We thus have from (5.31) and (5.32) that a.e.

$$\langle \Delta_p^{\Lambda_n} u_n - \Delta_p^{\Lambda_n} v_n, u_n - v_n\rangle = -\langle \Delta_p^{\Lambda_n} v_n - \Delta_p^{\hat{K}} v_n, u_n - v_n\rangle,$$

since $\langle \Delta_p^{\Lambda_n} u_n - \Delta_p^{\hat{K}} v_n, u_n - v_n\rangle = 0$. Since $p \in]1,2]$ and $m\chi_{[0,r_0[}(\|\boldsymbol{x} - \boldsymbol{y}\|) \leq \Lambda_n(\boldsymbol{x}, \boldsymbol{y})$ almost surely, we have

$$\|u_n - v_n\|^2_{L^p(\Omega)} \leq C\langle \Delta_p^{\Lambda_n} u_n - \Delta_p^{\Lambda_n} v_n, u_n - v_n\rangle,$$

almost surely, thanks to Lemma 5.4 (ii).

On the other hand, let $\mathbf{Z}_i = \frac{1}{n}\sum_j(\hat{\mathbf{K}}_{ij} - \mathbf{\Lambda}_{ij})\Psi(\mathbf{v}_j - \mathbf{v}_i)$. By the Hölder inequality, we have

$$\langle \Delta_p^{\hat{\mathbf{K}}} v_n - \Delta_p^{\Lambda^n} v_n, u_n - v_n\rangle \leq \left\|I_n\mathbf{Z}\right\|_{L^q(\Omega)}\left\|u_n - v_n\right\|_{L^p(\Omega)}, \tag{5.37}$$

where q is the Hölder conjugate of p. In turn,

$$\left\|u_n - v_n\right\|_{L^p(\Omega)} \leq C\left\|I_n\mathbf{Z}\right\|_{L^q(\Omega)}, \tag{5.38}$$

so, it remains to bound the random variable $\left\|I_n\mathbf{Z}\right\|_{L^q(\Omega)}$. For this purpose, we have by the Jensen inequality that

$$\mathbb{E}\left(\left\|I_n\mathbf{Z}\right\|_{L^q(\Omega)}\right) \leq \left(n^{-1}\sum_i \mathbb{E}\left(|\mathbf{Z}_i|^q\right)\right)^{1/q}. \tag{5.39}$$

By independence of $\left(\mathbf{\Lambda}_{ij}\right)_j$ and the fact that $\mathbb{E}(\mathbf{Z}_i) = 0$, for each i, we are then in the position to apply Rosenthal's inequality, whence there exists a positive constant $C_1 > 0$ such that

$$\mathbb{E}\left(|\mathbf{Z}_i|^q\right) \leq C\max\left(\sum_j\left(\frac{1}{\rho_n n}\right)^q \mathbb{E}(|\rho_n\mathbf{\Lambda}_{ij} - \rho_n\hat{\mathbf{K}}_{ij}|^q)|\mathbf{v}_j - \mathbf{v}_i|^p,\right.$$
$$\left.\left(\sum_j\left(\frac{1}{\rho_n n}\right)^2 \mathrm{Var}(\rho_n\mathbf{\Lambda}_{ij})|\mathbf{v}_j - \mathbf{v}_i|^{2(p-1)}\right)^{q/2}\right).$$

Since $\rho_n^{-1}\mathbb{E}(|\rho_n\mathbf{\Lambda}_{ij} - \rho_n\hat{\mathbf{K}}_{ij}|^s) \leq \hat{\mathbf{K}}_{ij}$, for all $s \geq 2$, then we get

$$\mathbb{E}\left(\left\|I_n\mathbf{Z}\right\|_{L^q(\Omega)}\right) \leq C_1\left(n^{-1}\sum_i \max\left(\left(\frac{1}{\rho_n n}\right)^{q-1}\frac{1}{n}\sum_j \hat{\mathbf{K}}_{ij}|\mathbf{v}_j - \mathbf{v}_i|^p,\right.\right.$$
$$\left.\left.\left(\frac{1}{\rho_n n}\right)^{q/2}\left(\frac{1}{n}\sum_j \hat{\mathbf{K}}_{ij}|\mathbf{v}_j - \mathbf{v}_i|^{2(p-1)}\right)^{q/2}\right)\right)^{1/q}. \tag{5.40}$$

Let's start with the first term in the right-hand side of the preceding inequality. We have

$$\begin{aligned}\left(\frac{1}{\rho_n n}\right)^{q-1}\frac{1}{n^2}\sum_{i,j}\hat{\mathbf{K}}_{ij}|\mathbf{v}_j - \mathbf{v}_i|^p &\leq 2\left(\frac{1}{\rho_n n}\right)^{q-1}\int_{\Omega^2}\hat{\mathbf{K}}(x,y)|v_n(y) - v_n(x)|^p\,dydx \\ &\leq 2^{p-1}\left(\frac{1}{\rho_n n}\right)^{q-1}\left\|\hat{\mathbf{K}}\right\|_{L^{\infty,1}(\Omega^2)}\left\|v_n\right\|_{L^p(\Omega)}^p \\ &\leq 2^{p-1}\left(\frac{1}{\rho_n n}\right)^{q-1}\left\|K\right\|_{L^{\infty,1}(\Omega^2)}\left\|v_n\right\|_{L^p(\Omega)}^p,\end{aligned} \tag{5.41}$$

and we get the last inequality by applying Lemma 2.20. For the second term, we have

$$\begin{aligned}
&\left(\frac{1}{\rho_n n}\right)^{q/2} n^{-1}\sum_i \left(n^{-1}\sum_j \hat{\mathbf{K}}_{ij}|\mathbf{v}_j-\mathbf{v}_i|^{2(p-1)}\right)^{q/2}\\
&\le \left(\frac{1}{\rho_n n}\right)^{q/2}\int_\Omega\left(\int_\Omega \hat{\mathbf{K}}(x,y)dy\right)^{q/2}\left(\int_\Omega \frac{\hat{\mathbf{K}}(x,y)|v_n(y)-v_n(x)|^{2(p-1)}}{\int_\Omega \hat{\mathbf{K}}(x,y)dy}dy\right)^{q/2} dx\\
&\overset{\text{Jensen}}{\le} \left(\frac{1}{\rho_n n}\right)^{q/2}\int_\Omega\left(\int_\Omega \hat{\mathbf{K}}(x,y)dy\right)^{q/2-1}\left(\int_\Omega \hat{\mathbf{K}}(x,y)|v_n(y)-v_n(x)|^p\,dy\right)dx\\
&\le \left(\frac{1}{\rho_n n}\right)^{q/2}\|\hat{\mathbf{K}}\|^{q/2-1}_{L^{\infty,1}(\Omega^2)}\int_\Omega\int_\Omega \hat{\mathbf{K}}(x,y)|v_n(y)-v_n(x)|^p\,dydx\\
&\le 2^{p-1}\left(\frac{1}{\rho_n n}\right)^{q/2}\|\hat{\mathbf{K}}\|^{q/2}_{L^{\infty,1}(\Omega^2)}\|v_n\|^p_{L^p(\Omega)} \le 2^{p-1}\left(\frac{1}{\rho_n n}\right)^{q/2}\|K\|^{q/2}_{L^{\infty,1}(\Omega^2)}\|v_n\|^p_{L^p(\Omega)}.
\end{aligned} \tag{5.42}$$

The last inequality follows from Lemma 2.20.
Plugging (5.41) and (5.42) into (5.40) and assembling the last with (5.39), we get

$$\mathbb{E}\left(\|I_n u_n - v_n\|_{L^p(\Omega)}\right) \le C_2\left(\frac{1}{\rho_n n}\right)^{1/2}, \tag{5.43}$$

where

$$C_2 = C_1 2^p \sup_n \|v_n\|^{p-1}_{L^p(\Omega)} \max\left(\|K\|^{1/2}_{L^{\infty,1}(\Omega^2)}, \|K\|^{(p-1)/p}_{L^{\infty,1}(\Omega^2)}\right),$$

and $C_2 < +\infty$, thanks to Theorem 5.16. Now let $\varepsilon > 0$. Using the Markov inequality, we have

$$\begin{aligned}
\mathbb{P}\left(\|I_n u_n - v_n\|_{L^p(\Omega)} \ge \varepsilon\right) &\le \varepsilon^{-1}\mathbb{E}\left(\|I_n u_n - v_n\|_{L^p(\Omega)}\right)\\
&\le \varepsilon^{-1}C_2(\rho_n n)^{-1/2}
\end{aligned} \tag{5.44}$$

Taking $\varepsilon = \frac{C_2}{(\rho_n n)^{\beta/2}}$, we get the desired result. □

Theorem 5.19 *Suppose that $p \in]1,2]$. Let u be a solution of $(\mathcal{P}_D)$ with kernel J, data (f,g), and the boundary set Γ, and let $\{\mathbf{u}\}_{n\in\mathbb{N}}$ be the sequence generated by $(\mathcal{P}_n^{d,\mathbf{G}})$ with $\mathbf{K} = P_n K$, $\mathbf{f} = P_n f$, $\mathbf{g} = 0$, and the boundary set A_n. Assume that $(J, \mathbf{g}, \mathbf{K},, \mathbf{f}, g, K, f)$ verify the assumptions of Theorem 5.16. Then, for any $\beta \in]0,1[$, we have*

$$\mathbb{E}\left(\|u-u_n\|_{L^p(\Omega)}\right) \leq C\Bigg(\|J-J_n\|_{L^1(\Omega-\Omega)} + \|(J-\rho_n^{-1})_+\|_{L^1(\Omega-\Omega)} + (\rho_n n)^{-1/2} +$$

$$\|I_nP_nu-u\|_{L^p(\Omega)}^{\frac{1}{3-p}} + \left(\|(J-\rho_n^{-1})_+\|_{L^1(\Omega-\Omega)}^{\frac{1}{2}} + \|J-J_n\|_{L^1(\Omega-\Omega)}^{\frac{1}{2}}\right)\|I_nP_nu-u\|_{L^p(\Omega)}^{\frac{1}{2}}\Bigg), \tag{5.45}$$

and in turn, with probability at least $1-(\rho_n n)^{-(1-\beta)/2}$*:*

$$\|u-u_n\|_{L^p(\Omega)} \leq C\Bigg(\|J-J_n\|_{L^1(\Omega-\Omega)} + \|(J-\rho_n^{-1})_+\|_{L^1(\Omega-\Omega)} + (\rho_n n)^{-\beta/2} +$$

$$\|I_nP_nu-u\|_{L^p(\Omega)}^{\frac{1}{3-p}} + \left(\|(J-\rho_n^{-1})_+\|_{L^1(\Omega-\Omega)}^{\frac{1}{2}} + \|J-J_n\|_{L^1(\Omega-\Omega)}^{\frac{1}{2}}\right)\|I_nP_nu-u\|_{L^p(\Omega)}^{\frac{1}{2}}\Bigg), \tag{5.46}$$

where $J_n = I_nP_nJ$*, and* g_n*,* f_n*, and* u_n *are the continuous extensions of the functions* **g**, **f**, *and* **u** *respectively.*

PROOF: Embarking from (5.33), for the first term in the right-hand side, we apply the result of Lemma 5.17, and for the second we use the result of Corollary 5.16 on which we apply Jensen's inequality, after observing that

$$\begin{aligned}
\|I_n\hat{\mathbf{K}} - K\|_{L^{\infty,1}(\Omega^2)} &= \|\min(I_nP_nK, \rho_n^{-1}) - K\|_{L^{\infty,1}(\Omega^2)} \\
&\leq \|\min(I_nP_nK, \rho_n^{-1}) - I_nP_nK\|_{L^{\infty,1}(\Omega^2)} + \|I_nP_nK - K\|_{L^{\infty,1}(\Omega^2)} \\
&= \|(I_nP_nK - \rho_n^{-1})_+\|_{L^{\infty,1}(\Omega^2)} + \|I_nP_nK - K\|_{L^{\infty,1}(\Omega^2)} \\
&\leq \|(K - \rho_n^{-1})_+\|_{L^{\infty,1}(\Omega^2)} + 2\|I_nP_nK - K\|_{L^{\infty,1}(\Omega^2)}.
\end{aligned}$$

Since $K(x,y) = J(x-y)$, we have

$$\begin{aligned}
&\|(K - \rho_n^{-1})_+\|_{L^{\infty,1}(\Omega^2)} + 2\|I_nP_nK - K\|_{L^{\infty,1}(\Omega^2)} \\
&\qquad\leq \|(J - \rho_n^{-1})_+\|_{L^1(\Omega-\Omega)} + 2\|I_nP_nJ - J\|_{L^1(\Omega-\Omega)}.
\end{aligned}$$

The fact that $\|(J-\rho_n^{-1})_+\|_{L^1(\Omega-\Omega)} = o(1)$ is because $\rho_n \to 0$. This completes the proof. □

6 Algorithmic Framework Based on Proximal Splitting

6.1 Algorithm for the Variational Problem on Graphs

Let us start by describing an algorithm to solve the variational problem ($\mathcal{VP}^d_{\mathrm{nloc}}$). We remind the reader of the notation used in Section 4.1. The algorithm we propose in this section will be valid for any $p \in [1, +\infty]$.

The minimization problem $(\mathcal{VP}^d_{\text{nloc}})$ can be rewritten in the following form:

$$\min_{\mathbf{u}\in\mathbb{R}^n} \frac{1}{2}\|\mathbf{u}-\mathbf{g}\|_2^2 + \frac{\lambda_n}{p}\|\nabla_{\mathbf{K}}\mathbf{u}\|_p^p, \tag{6.1}$$

where $\lambda_n = \lambda/(2n)$, $p \in [1, +\infty]$,[5] and $\nabla_{\mathbf{K}}$ is the (nonlocal) weighted gradient operator with weights $\mathbf{K}_{ij}$, defined as

$$\nabla_{\mathbf{K}}: \mathbb{R}^n \to \mathbb{R}^{n\times n}$$

$$\mathbf{u} \mapsto \mathbf{V},\ \mathbf{V}_{ij} = \mathbf{K}_{ij}^{1/p}(\mathbf{u}_j - \mathbf{u}_i), \quad \forall (i,j) \in [n]^2.$$

This is a linear operator whose adjoint is the (nonlocal) weighted divergence operator denoted $\mathbf{div}_{\mathbf{K}}$. It is easy to show that

$$\mathbf{div}_{\mathbf{K}}: \mathbb{R}^{n\times n} \to \mathbb{R}^n$$

$$\mathbf{V} \mapsto \mathbf{u},\ \mathbf{u}_i = \sum_{j=1}^{n} \mathbf{K}_{ji}^{1/p}\left(\mathbf{V}_{ji} - \mathbf{V}_{ij}\right), \quad \forall i \in [n].$$

Problem (6.1) can be easily solved using standard duality-based, first-order algorithms. For this, we follow Fadili and Peyré (2010).

By standard conjugacy calculus, the Fenchel–Rockafellar dual problem of (6.1) reads

$$\min_{\mathbf{V}\in\mathbb{R}^{n\times n}} \frac{1}{2}\|\mathbf{g} - \mathbf{div}_{\mathbf{K}}\mathbf{V}\|_2^2 + \frac{\lambda_n}{q}\|\mathbf{V}/\lambda_n\|_q^q, \tag{6.2}$$

where q is the Hölder dual of p, that is, $1/p + 1/q = 1$. One can show with standard arguments that the dual problem (6.2) has a convex compact set of minimizers for any $p \in [1, +\infty[$. Moreover, the unique solution $\mathbf{u}^\star$ to the primal problem (6.1) can be recovered from any dual solution $\mathbf{V}^\star$ as

$$\mathbf{u}^\star = \mathbf{g} - \mathbf{div}_{\mathbf{K}}\mathbf{V}^\star.$$

It remains now to solve (6.2). The latter can be solved with the (accelerated) FISTA iterative scheme (Nesterov, 1983; Beck and Teboulle, 2009; Chambolle and Dossal, 2015), which in this case reads

$$\begin{aligned}
\mathbf{W}^k &= \mathbf{V}^k + \frac{k-1}{k+b}(\mathbf{V}^k - \mathbf{V}^{k-1}) \\
\mathbf{V}^{k+1} &= \mathbf{prox}_{\gamma\frac{\lambda_n}{q}\|\cdot/\lambda_n\|_q^q}\left(\mathbf{W}^k + \gamma\nabla_{\mathbf{K}}(\mathbf{g} - \mathbf{div}_{\mathbf{K}}(\mathbf{W}^k))\right) \\
\mathbf{u}^{k+1} &= \mathbf{g} - \mathbf{div}_{\mathbf{K}}\mathbf{V}^{k+1},
\end{aligned} \tag{6.3}$$

[5] Obviously, $\lim_{p\to+\infty} \frac{1}{p}\|\cdot\|_{p,\mathbb{R}^n}^p = \iota_{\|\mathbf{u}\|_{\infty,\mathbb{R}^n}\le 1}$.

where $\gamma \in \left]0, \left(\sup_{\|u_n\|_2=1} \|\nabla_{\mathbf{K}}\mathbf{u}\|_2\right)^{-1}\right]$, $b > 2$, and we recall that $\mathrm{prox}_{\tau F}$ is the proximal mapping of the proper lsc convex function F with $\tau > 0$, that is,

$$\mathbf{prox}_{\tau F}(\mathbf{W}) = \operatorname*{Argmin}_{\mathbf{V}\in\mathbb{R}^{n\times n}} \frac{1}{2}\|\mathbf{V} - \mathbf{W}\|_2^2 + \tau F(\mathbf{V}).$$

The convergence guarantees of scheme (6.3) are summarized in the following proposition.

Proposition 6.1 *The primal iterates* u_n^k *converge to* $\mathbf{u}^\star$, *the unique minimizer of* $(\mathcal{VP}^d_{\mathrm{nloc}})$, *at the rate*

$$\left\|\mathbf{u}^k - \mathbf{u}^\star\right\|_2 = o(1/k).$$

PROOF: Combine Fadili and Peyré (2010, theorem 2) and Attouch and Peypouquet (2016, theorem 1.1). □

6.2 Algorithm for the Dirichlet Problem on Graphs

Here, we adopt a primal-dual hybrid gradient algorithm to solve the discrete boundary value problems $(\mathcal{P}^d_n)$. We recall the notation of Section 5.4.1. Without loss of generality, we assume that $V_n(\Omega) = \{0, 1, \cdots, n\}$ and $A_n \subset V_n(\Omega)$. Set $V_n = V_n(\Omega)$, $\mathbb{R}^{V_n} = \mathbb{H}(V_n)$, and $\mathbb{R}^{V_n\times V_n} = \mathbb{H}(V_n \times V_n)$.

Problem $(\mathcal{P}^d_n)$ is equivalent to $(\mathcal{VP}^{d,D}_n)$, where the latter takes the form

$$\min_{\mathbb{H}(V_n(\Omega))} F_{d,n}(\nabla_{\mathbf{K}}\mathbf{u}) + G_{d,n}(\mathbf{u}), \tag{6.4}$$

where

$$F_{d,n}(\mathbf{U}) = \frac{1}{p}\|\mathbf{U}\|^p_{p,\mathbb{R}^{V_n\times V_n}} \quad \text{and} \quad G_{d,n}(\mathbf{u}) = \langle \mathbf{u}, \mathbf{f}\rangle_{\mathbb{R}^{V_n}} + \iota_{\boldsymbol{C}_\mathbf{g}}(\mathbf{u}), \tag{6.5}$$

where $\boldsymbol{C}_\mathbf{g} = \{\mathbf{u} \in \mathbb{R}^{V_n} : \mathbf{u} = \mathbf{g} \text{ on } A_n^c\}$, and $\nabla_\mathbf{K}$ and $\mathbf{div}_\mathbf{K}$ are respectively the (nonlocal) weighted gradient operator and the (nonlocal) weighted divergence operator, introduced earlier.

By standard conjugacy calculus, the Fenchel–Rockafellar dual problem of (6.4) reads

$$\min_{\mathbf{U}\in\mathbb{R}^{V_n\times V_n}} \frac{1}{q}\|\mathbf{U}\|^q_{q,\mathbb{R}^{V_n\times V_n}} + \sigma_{\boldsymbol{C}_\mathbf{g}}(-\mathbf{div}_\mathbf{K}\mathbf{U} - \mathbf{f}), \tag{6.6}$$

where $\sigma_{\boldsymbol{C}_\mathbf{g}}$ is the support function of $\boldsymbol{C}_\mathbf{g}$, and q is the Hölder dual of p, that is, $\frac{1}{p} + \frac{1}{q} = 1$. Since strong duality holds, the *primal-dual gap*

$$\mathcal{G}_n(\mathbf{u}, \mathbf{U}) = F_{d,n}(\nabla_\mathbf{K}\mathbf{u}) + G_{d,n}(\mathbf{u}) + G^*_{d,n}(-\mathbf{div}_\mathbf{K}\mathbf{U}) + F^*_{d,n}(\mathbf{U})$$

is a measure of optimality. If it vanishes at $(\mathbf{u}^*, \mathbf{U}^*)$, then $(\mathbf{u}^*, \mathbf{U}^*)$ is a *saddle point* of the *Lagrangian*

$$\mathcal{L}_n(\mathbf{u}, \mathbf{U}) = \langle \mathbf{U}, \nabla_{\mathbf{K}} \mathbf{u} \rangle_{\mathbb{R}^{V_n \times V_n}} - F^*_{d,n}(\mathbf{U}) + G_{d,n}(\mathbf{u}), \tag{6.7}$$

as one has

$$\mathcal{L}_n(\mathbf{u}^*, \mathbf{U}) \leq \mathcal{L}_n(\mathbf{u}^*, \mathbf{U}^*) \leq \mathcal{L}_n(\mathbf{u}, \mathbf{U}^*) \tag{6.8}$$

for all $\mathbf{u} \in \mathbb{R}^{V_n}$, $\mathbf{U} \in \mathbb{R}^{V_n \times V_n}$.
By this optimality, one has that $\nabla_{\mathbf{K}} \mathbf{u}^* - \partial F^*_{d,n}(\mathbf{U}^*) \ni 0$, $\mathbf{div}_{\mathbf{K}} \mathbf{U}^* + \partial G_{d,n}(\mathbf{u}^*) \ni 0$, which may be written

$$0 \in \begin{pmatrix} \partial G_{d,n}(\mathbf{u}) \\ \partial F^*_{d,n}(\mathbf{U}) \end{pmatrix} + \begin{pmatrix} 0 & \mathbf{div}_{\mathbf{K}} \\ -\nabla_{\mathbf{K}} & 0 \end{pmatrix} \begin{pmatrix} \mathbf{u} \\ \mathbf{U} \end{pmatrix}, \tag{6.9}$$

meaning the solution is found by finding the zeros of the sum of two monotone operators.
The latter can be solved with the primal-dual iterative scheme of Chambolle and Pock (2011), which in this case reads

$$\begin{aligned} \mathbf{u}^{k+1} &= \mathbf{prox}_{\tau G_{d,n}}(\mathbf{u}^k - \tau \mathbf{div}_{\mathbf{K}} \mathbf{U}^k) \\ \mathbf{U}^{k+1} &= \mathbf{prox}_{\gamma F^*_{d,n}}(\mathbf{U}^k + \gamma \nabla_{\mathbf{K}}(2\mathbf{u}^{k+1} - \mathbf{u}^k)), \end{aligned} \tag{6.10}$$

where $\tau, \gamma > 0$.

Proposition 6.2 (Chambolle and Pock, 2011) *If* $\tau\gamma \|\nabla_{\mathbf{K}}\|^2 < 1$, *then* $\mathbf{W}^k = (\mathbf{u}^k, \mathbf{U}^k)$, *defined by* (6.10), *converges to a solution of* (6.9).

6.3 Computing the Proximal Operators

Let us turn to the computation of the proximal mapping $\mathbf{prox}_{\sigma \frac{1}{q} \|\cdot/\lambda\|_q^q}$. Since $\|\cdot\|_q^q$ is separable, one has that

$$\mathbf{prox}_{\sigma \frac{1}{q} \|\cdot/\lambda\|_q^q}(\mathbf{v}) = \left(\mathbf{prox}_{\sigma \frac{1}{q} |\cdot/\lambda|^q}(\mathbf{v}_x)\right)_{x \in V}.$$

Moreover, as $|\cdot|^q$ is an even function on $\mathbb{R}$, $\mathbf{prox}_{\sigma \frac{1}{q} |\cdot|^q}$ is an odd mapping on $\mathbb{R}$, that is,

$$\mathbf{prox}_{\sigma \frac{1}{q} |\cdot|^q}(\mathbf{v}_x) = \mathbf{prox}_{\sigma \frac{1}{q} |\cdot|^q}(|\mathbf{v}_x|) \operatorname{sign}(\mathbf{v}_x).$$

Hence, one has to compute $\mathbf{prox}_{\sigma \frac{1}{q} |\cdot|^q}(t)$[6] for $t \in \mathbb{R}^+$. We distinguish different situations depending on the value of q:

[6] Recall that $\lim_{q \to \infty} \frac{1}{q} |\cdot|^q = \iota_{[-1,1]}(\cdot)$.

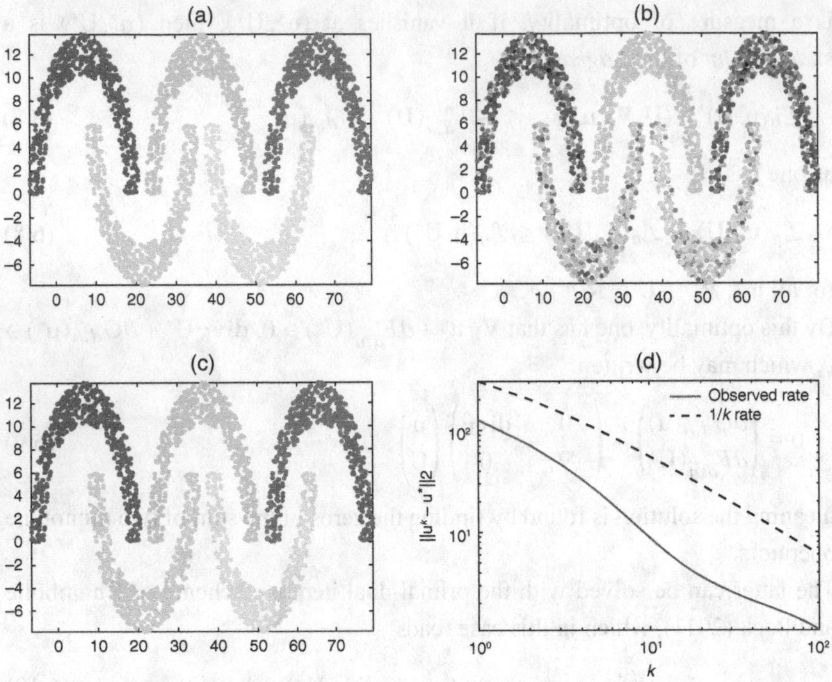

Figure 6.1 Denoising results with $p = 1$. (a) Original point cloud. (b) Noisy point cloud. (c) Point cloud recovered by solving (6.1). (d) Primal convergence criterion $\|\mathbf{u}^k - \mathbf{u}^\star\|_2$ as a function of the iteration counter k.

- $q = +\infty$ (i.e., $p = 1$): this case amounts to computing the orthogonal projector on $[-\lambda, \lambda]$, which reads

$$t \in \mathbb{R}^+ \to \mathbf{P}_{[-\lambda,\lambda]}(t) = \min(t, \lambda).$$

- $q = 1$ (i.e., $p = +\infty$): this case corresponds to the well-known soft-thresholding operator, which is given by

$$t \in \mathbb{R}^+ \to \mathbf{prox}_{\sigma|\cdot|}(t) = \max(t - \sigma, 0).$$

- $q = 2$ (i.e., $p = 2$): it is immediate to see that

$$\mathbf{prox}_{\sigma\frac{1}{2}|\cdot|^2}(t) = \frac{t}{1+\sigma}.$$

- $q \in]1, +\infty[$: in this case, as $|\cdot|^q$ is differentiable, the proximal point $\mathbf{prox}_{\sigma\frac{1}{q}|\cdot|^q}(t)$ is the unique solution $\alpha^\star$ on $\mathbb{R}^+$ of the nonlinear equation:

$$\alpha - t + \sigma\alpha^{q-1} = 0.$$

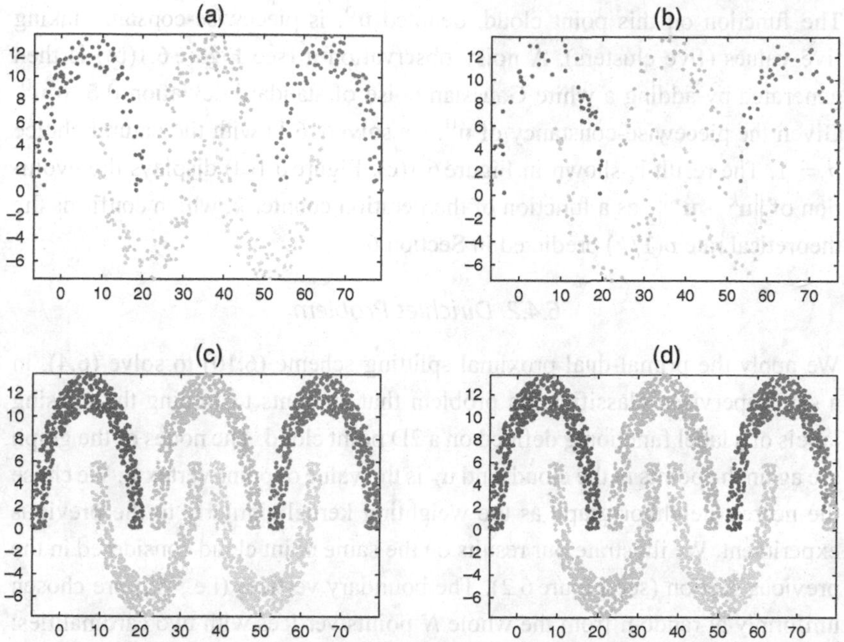

Figure 6.2 Label propagation with $p = 1$. (a) Subsampled (boundary) data with $N/5$ points. (b) Subsampled (boundary) data with $N/10$ points. (c) Result obtained from the boundary data (a). (d) Result obtained from the boundary data (b).

The proximal mapping $\mathbf{prox}_{\tau G_{d,n}}$ is given as

$$\mathbf{prox}_{\tau G_{d,n}}(\mathbf{u}) = \mathbf{P}_{C_{\mathrm{g}}}(\mathbf{u} - \tau \mathbf{f}) \stackrel{\text{def}}{=} \begin{cases} \mathbf{u}_{x} - \tau \mathbf{f}_{x}, & \textit{if } x \in A_n, \\ \mathbf{g}_{x}, & \textit{if } x \in A_n^c, \end{cases}$$

where $\mathbf{P}_{C_{\mathrm{g}}}$ is the projection function on the set C_{g}.

6.4 Numerical Results

6.4.1 Variational Problem

We apply the accelerated forward-backward proximal splitting scheme (6.3) to solve (6.1) for denoising a function defined on a 2D point cloud. In this setting, the nodes of the graph are the points in the cloud, and $\mathbf{u}_x$ the value of point/vertex index x. We choose the nearest-neighbor graph with the standard weighting kernel $\exp(-|\boldsymbol{i}_x - \boldsymbol{i}_y|)$ when $|\boldsymbol{i}_x - \boldsymbol{i}_y| \leq \delta$ and 0 otherwise, where $\boldsymbol{i}_x$ and $\boldsymbol{i}_y$ are the 2D spatial coordinates of the points for the point cloud.

The original point cloud used in our numerical experiments is shown in Figure 6.1(a). It consists of $N = 2,500$ points that are not on a regular grid.

The function on this point cloud, denoted $\mathbf{u}^0$, is piecewise-constant, taking five values (five clusters). A noisy observation g (see Figure 6.1(b)) is then generated by adding a white Gaussian noise of standard deviation 0.5 to $\mathbf{u}^0$. Given the piecewise-constancy of $\mathbf{u}^0$, we solved (6.1) with the natural choice $p = 1$. The result is shown in Figure 6.1(c). Figure 6.1(d) displays the evolution of $\|\mathbf{u}^k - \mathbf{u}^\star\|_2$ as a function of the iteration counter k, which confirms the theoretical rate $o(1/k)$ predicted in Section 6.

6.4.2 Dirichlet Problem

We apply the primal-dual proximal splitting scheme (6.10) to solve (6.4), in a semisupervised classification problem that amounts to finding the missing labels of a label function g defined on a 2D point cloud. The nodes of the graph are again the points in the cloud, and $\mathbf{u}_{\boldsymbol{x}}$ is the value of point/vertex $\boldsymbol{x}$. We chose the nearest-neighbor graph as the weighting kernel similarly to the previous experiment. We illustrate our results on the same point cloud considered in the previous section (see Figure 6.2). The boundary vertices (i.e., A_n^c) are chosen uniformly at random from the whole N points/vertices with two cardinalities: $|A_n^c| = N/5$ and $|A_n^c| = N/10$. Obviously, the label function $\mathbf{u}$ to be recovered agrees with g on A_n^c according to (6.4). In our experiments, for each A_n^c, we solve (6.4) with $\mathrm{f} = 0$ and $p = 1$.

References

Aksoylu, Burak, and Mengesha, Tadele. 2010. Results on nonlocal boundary value problems. *Numerical Functional Analysis and Optimization*, **31**(12), 1301–1317.

Alali, Bacim, Liu, Kuo, and Gunzburger, Max. 2015. A generalized nonlocal vector calculus. *Zeitschrift für angewandte Mathematik und Physik*, **66**(5), 2807–2828.

Andreu, Fuensanta, Mazón, José, Rossi, Julio, and Toledo-Melero, Julián. 2008a. The Neumann problem for nonlocal nonlinear diffusion equations. *Journal of Evolution Equations*, **8**(1), 189–215.

Andreu, Fuensanta, Mazón, José, Rossi, Julio, and Toledo-Melero, Julián. 2008b. A nonlocal p-Laplacian evolution equation with Neumann boundary conditions. *Journal de Mathématiques Pures et Appliquées*, **90**(2), 201–227.

Andreu-Vaillo, Fuensanta, Mazón, José, Rossi, Julio, and Toledo-Melero, Julián. 2010. *Nonlocal Diffusion Problems*. Mathematical Surveys and Monographs, vol. 165. American Mathematical Society.

Attouch, Hédy. 1984. *Variational Convergence for Functions and Operators*. Applicable Mathematics Series. Pitman Advanced Publishing Program.

Attouch, Hédy, and Peypouquet, Juan. 2016. The rate of convergence of Nesterov's accelerated forward-backward method is actually faster than 1/k^2. *SIAM Journal on Optimization*, **26**(3), 1824–1834.

Aubert, Gilles, and Kornprobst, Pierre. 2002. *Mathematical Problems in Image Processing*. Applied Mathematical Sciences, vol. 147. Springer.

Ayi, Nathalie, and Pouradier Duteil, Nastassia. 2021. Mean-field and graph limits for collective dynamics models with time-varying weights. *Journal of Differential Equations*, **299**(2), 65–110.

Azé, Dominique, Attouch, Hédy, and Wets, Roger. 1988. Convergence of convex-concave saddle functions: Applications to convex programming and mechanics. *Annales de l'Institut Henri Poincaré C, Analyse non linéaire*, **5**(6), 537–572.

Bates, Peter, and Chmaj, Adam. 1999. An integrodifferential model for phase transitions: Stationary solutions in higher space dimensions. *Journal of Statistical Physics*, **95**(5), 1119–1139.

Bates, Peter, Fife, Paul, Ren, Xiaofeng, and Wang, Xuefeng. 1997. Traveling waves in a convolution model for phase transitions. *Archive for Rational Mechanics and Analysis*, **138**(2), 105–136.

Bauschke, Heinz, and Combettes, Patrick. 2011. *Convex Analysis and Monotone Operator Theory in Hilbert Spaces*. Springer.

Bažant, Zdeněk, and Jirásek, Milan. 2002. Nonlocal integral formulations of plasticity and damage: Survey of progress. *Journal of Engineering Mechanics*, **128**(11), 1119–1149.

Beck, Amir, and Teboulle, Marc. 2009. A fast iterative shrinkage-thresholding algorithm for linear inverse problems. *SIAM Journal on Imaging Sciences*, **2**(1), 183–202.

Beer, Gerald, and Lucchetti, Roberto. 1992. The epi-distance topology: Continuity and stability results with applications to convex optimization problems. *Mathematics of Operations Research*, **17**(3), 715–726.

Bénilan, Philippe. 1972. Solutions intégrales d'équations d'évolution dans un espace de Banach. *Comptes rendus de l'Académie des Sciences Series A–B*, **274**, A47–A50.

Bénilan, Philippe, and Crandall, Michael. 1991. Completely accretive operators. Pages 41–75 of Clément, Philippe, de Pagter, Ben, and Mitidieri, Enzo (eds.), *Semigroup Theory and Evolution Equations*. Lecture Notes in Pure and Applied Mathematics, vol. 135. Dekker.

Biccari, Umberto, Ko, Dongnam, and Zuazua, Enrique. 2019. Dynamics and control for multi-agent networked systems: A finite-difference approach. *Mathematical Models and Methods in Applied Sciences*, **29**(4), 755–790.

Bognar, Gabriella. 2008. Numerical and analytic investigation of some nonlinear problems in fluid mechanics. *Computer and Simulation in Modern Science*, **2**, 172–179.

Bollobás, Béla, and Riordan, Oliver. 2009. Metrics for sparse graphs. Pages 211–288 of Huczynska, Sophie, Mitchell, James, and Roney-Dougal, Colva (eds.), *Surveys in Combinatorics 2009*. London Mathematical Society Lecture Note Series. Cambridge University Press.

Bollobás, Béla, Janson, Svante, and Riordan, Oliver. 2007. The phase transition in inhomogeneous random graphs. *Random Structures & Algorithms*, **31**(1), 3–122.

Borgs, Christian, Chayes, Jennifer, Cohn, Henry, and Zhao, Yufei. 2018. An L^p theory of sparse graph convergence II: LD convergence, quotients and right convergence. *Annals of Probability*, **46**(1), 337–396.

Borgs, Christian, Chayes, Jennifer, Cohn, Henry, and Zhao, Yufei. 2019. An L^p theory of sparse graph convergence I: Limits, sparse random graph models, and power law distributions. *Transactions of the American Mathematical Society*, **372**(5), 3019–3062.

Borgs, Christian, Chayes, Jennifer, Lovász, László, Sós, Vera, and Vesztergombi, Katalin. 2008. Convergent sequences of dense graphs I: Subgraph frequencies, metric properties and testing. *Advances in Mathematics*, **219**(6), 1801–1851.

Borgs, Christian, Chayes, Jennifer, Lovász, László, Sós, Vera, and Vesztergombi, Katalin. 2011. Limits of randomly grown graph sequences. *European Journal of Combinatorics*, **32**(7), 985–999.

Borwein, Jonathan, and Fitzpatrick, Simon. 1989. Mosco convergence and the Kadec property. *Proceedings of the American Mathematical Society*, **106**(3), 843–851.

Braides, Andrea. 2002. *Gamma-Convergence for Beginners*. Oxford Lecture Series in Mathematics and Its Applications, vol. 22. Clarendon Press.

Brézis, Haïm. 1973. *Opérateurs maximaux monotones et semi-groupes de contractions dans les espaces de Hilbert*. North Holland.

Buades, Antoni, Coll, Bartomeu, and Morel, Jean-Michel. 2005. A review of image denoising algorithms, with a new one. *Multiscale Modeling & Simulation*, **4**(2), 490–530.

Bühler, Thomas, and Hein, Matthias. 2009. Spectral clustering based on the graph *p*-Laplacian. Pages 81–88 of *Proceedings of the 26th Annual International Conference on Machine Learning*. ICML '09. Association for Computing Machinery.

Bungert, Leon, Calder, Jeff, and Roith, Tim. 2021. Uniform convergence rates for Lipschitz learning on graphs. *arXiv:2111.12370*.

Byström, Johan. 2005. Sharp constants for some inequalities connected to the *p*-Laplace operator. *Journal of Inequalities in Pure and Applied Mathematics*, **6**(2).

Calder, Jeff. 2018. The game theoretic *p*-Laplacian and semi-supervised learning with few labels. *Nonlinearity*, **32**(1), 301.

Calder, Jeff. 2019. Consistency of Lipschitz learning with infinite unlabeled data and finite labeled data. *SIAM Journal on Mathematics of Data Science*, **1**(4), 780–812.

Calder, Jeff, Slepcev, Dejan, and Thorpe, Matthew. 2020. Rates of convergence for Laplacian semi-supervised learning with low labeling rates. *arXiv:2006.02765*.

Carrillo, C., and Fife, P. 2005. Spatial effects in discrete generation population models. *Journal of Mathematical Biology*, **50**(2), 161–188.

Carrillo, José Antonio, del Pino, Manuel, Figalli, Alessio, Mingione, Giuseppe, and Vázquez, Juan Luis. 2017. *Nonlocal and Nonlinear Diffusions and Interactions: New Methods and Directions*. Lecture Notes in Mathematics, vol. 2186. Springer.

Chambolle, Antonin, and Dossal, Charles. 2015. On the convergence of the iterates of the fast iterative shrinkage/thresholding algorithm. *Journal of Optimization Theory and Applications*, **166**(3), 968–982.

Chambolle, Antonin, and Pock, Thomas. 2011. A first-order primal-dual algorithm for convex problems with applications to imaging. *Journal of Mathematical Imaging and Vision*, **40**(1), 120–145.

Chan, Tony F., and Shen, Jianhong Jackie. 2005. *Image Processing and Analysis*. SIAM.

Clason, Christian. 2017. Nonsmooth analysis and optimization. *arXiv:1708* .04180.

Cortazar, Carmen, Elgueta, Manuel, Rossi, Julio, and Wolanski, Noemi. 2008. How to approximate the heat equation with Neumann boundary conditions by nonlocal diffusion problems. *Archive for Rational Mechanics and Analysis*, **187**(1), 137–156.

Crandall, Michael, and Liggett, Thomas. 1971. Generation of semigroups of nonlinear transformations on general Banach spaces. *American Journal of Mathematics*, **93**(2), 265–298.

Dal Maso, Gianni. 1993. *An Introduction to Gamma-Convergence*. Birkhäuser.

DeVore, Ronald, and Lorentz, George. 1993. *Constructive Approximation*. Grundlehren der Mathematischen, vol. 303. Springer.

Drábek, Pavel. 2007. The p-Laplacian – mascot of nonlinear analysis. *Acta Mathematica Universitatis Comenianae*, **76**(1), 85–98.

Du, Qiang. 2019. *Nonlocal Modeling, Analysis, and Computation: Nonlocal Modeling, Analysis, and Computation*. SIAM.

Du, Qiang, Gunzburger, Max, Lehoucq, Richard, and Zhou, Kun. 2012. Analysis and approximation of nonlocal diffusion problems with volume constraints. *SIAM Review*, **54**(4), 667–696.

Du, Qiang, Gunzburger, Max, Lehoucq, Richard, and Zhou, Kun. 2013a. A nonlocal vector calculus, nonlocal volume-constrained problems, and nonlocal balance laws. *Mathematical Models and Methods in Applied Sciences*, **23**(3), 493–540.

Du, Qiang, Gunzburger, Max, Lehoucq, Richard, and Zhou, Kun. 2013b. A nonlocal vector calculus, nonlocal volume-constrained problems, and nonlocal balance laws. *Mathematical Models and Methods in Applied Sciences*, **23**(3), 493–540.

Dunlop, Matthew, Slepcev, Dejan, and Stuart, Andrew. 2020. Large data and zero noise limits of graph-based semi-supervised learning algorithms. *Applied and Computational Harmonic Analysis*, **49**(2), 655–697.

El Alaoui, Ahmed, Cheng, Xiang, Ramdas, Aaditya, Wainwright, Martin, and Jordan, Michael. 2016. Asymptotic behavior of ℓ_p-based Laplacian regularization in semi-supervised learning. Pages 879–906 of *Conference on Learning Theory*.

El Bouchairi, Imad, Fadili, Jalal, and Elmoataz, Abderrahim. 2020. Continuum limit of p-Laplacian evolution problems on graphs: L^q graphons and sparse graphs. *arXiv:2010.08697*.

El Chakik, Abdallah, Elmoataz, Abdderahim, and Desquesnes, Xavier. 2014. Mean curvature flow on graphs for image and manifold restoration and enhancement. *Signal Processing*, **105**, 449–463.

Elmoataz, Abderrahim, Desquesnes, Xavier, and Lézoray, Olivier. 2012. Non-local morphological PDEs and p-Laplacian equation on graphs with applications in image processing and machine learning. *IEEE Journal of Selected Topics in Signal Processing*, **6**(7), 764–779.

Elmoataz, Abderrahim, Desquesnes, Xavier, Lakhdari, Zakaria, and Lézoray, Olivier. 2014. Nonlocal infinity Laplacian equation on graphs with applications in image processing and machine learning. *Mathematics and Computers in Simulation*, **102**, 153–163.

Elmoataz, Abderrahim, Lezoray, Olivier, Bougleux, Sébastien, and Ta, Vinh Thong. 2008. Unifying local and nonlocal processing with partial difference operators on weighted graphs. Pages 11–26 of *International Workshop on Local and Non-Local Approximation in Image Processing*.

Elmoataz, Abderrahim, Toutain, Matthieu, and Tenbrinck, Daniel. 2015. On the p-Laplacian and ∞-Laplacian on graphs with applications in image and data processing. *SIAM Journal on Imaging Sciences*, **8**(4), 2412–2451.

Erdös, Paul, and Rényi, Alfréd. 1960. On the evolution of random graphs. *Publication of the Mathematical Institute of the Hungarian Academy of Sciences*, **5**, 17–61.

Eringen, Ahmet Cemal, and Wegner, J. L. 2003. Nonlocal continuum field theories. *Applied Mechanics Reviews*, **56**(2), B20–B22.

Fadili, Jalal, Forcadel, Nicolas, Nguyen, Thi Tuyen, and Zantout, Rita. 2021. Limits and consistency of non-local and graph approximations to the Eikonal equation. *arXiv:2105.01977*.

Fadili, Jalal, and Peyré, Gabriel. 2010. Total variation projection with first order schemes. *IEEE Transactions on Image Processing*, **20**(3), 657–669.

Fife, Paul, and Wang, Xuefeng. 1998. A convolution model for interfacial motion: The generation and propagation of internal layers in higher space dimensions. *Advances in Difference Equations*, **3**(1), 85–110.

Fife, Paul. 2002. Some nonclassical trends in parabolic and parabolic-like evolutions. In Fiedler, B. (ed.), *Trends in Nonlinear Analysis*. Springer.

Figalli, Alessio, Peral, Ireneo, and Valdinoci, Enrico. 2018. *Partial Differential Equations and Geometric Measure Theory*. Springer.

Flores, Mauricio, Calder, Jeff, and Lerman, Gilad. 2022. Analysis and algorithms for ℓ_p-based semi-supervised learning on graphs. *Applied and Computational Harmonic Analysis*, **60**, 77–122.

Frieze, Alan, and Kannan, Ravi. 1999. Quick approximation to matrices and applications. *Combinatorica*, **19**(2), 175–220.

Garcia Trillos, Nicolas. 2019. Variational limits of k-NN graph-based functionals on data clouds. *SIAM Journal on Mathematics of Data Science*, **1**(1), 93–120.

Garcia Trillos, Nicolas, and Murray, Ryan. 2020. A maximum principle argument for the uniform convergence of graph Laplacian regressors. *SIAM Journal on Mathematics of Data Science*, **2**(3), 705–739.

Gennip, Yves van, and Bertozzi, Andrea. 2012. Γ-convergence of graph Ginzburg–Landau functionals. *Advances in Differential Equations*, **17**(4), 1115–1180.

Gilboa, Guy, and Osher, Stanley. 2007. Nonlocal linear image regularization and supervised segmentation. *Multiscale Modeling & Simulation*, **6**(2), 595–630.

Gilboa, Guy, and Osher, Stanley. 2008. Nonlocal operators with applications to image processing. *SIAM Journal on Multiscale Modeling and Simulation*, **7**(3), 1005–1028.

Glowinski, Roland, and Marrocco, A. 1975. Sur l'approximation par éléments finis d'ordre un, et la résolution, par pénalisation-dualité, d'une classe de problèmes de Dirichlet non-linéaires. *RAIRO: Analyse Numérique*, **9**(R2), 41–76.

Gunzburger, Max, and Lehoucq, Richard. 2010. A nonlocal vector calculus with applications to nonlocal boundary value problems. *SIAM Journal on Multiscale Modeling and Simulation*, **8**(5), 1581–1620.

Hafiene, Yosra, Fadili, Jalal, and Elmoataz, Abderrahim. 2018. Nonlocal p-Laplacian evolution problems on graphs. *SIAM Journal on Numerical Analysis*, **56**(2), 1064–1090.

Hafiene, Yosra, Fadili, Jalal, and Elmoataz, Abderrahim. 2019. Nonlocal p-Laplacian Variational problems on graphs. *SIAM Journal on Imaging Sciences*, **12**(4), 1772–1807.

Hafiene, Yosra, Fadili, Jalal, Chesneau, Christophe, and Elmoataz, Abderrahim. 2020. Continuum limit of the nonlocal p-Laplacian evolution problem on random inhomogeneous graphs. *ESAIM: Mathematical Modelling and Numerical Analysis*, **54**(2), 565–589.

Hinds, Brittney, and Radu, Petronela. 2012. Dirichlet's principle and well-posedness of solutions for a nonlocal p-Laplacian system. *Applied Mathematics and Computation*, **219**(4), 1411–1419.

Hoeffding, Wassily. 1961. *The Strong Law of Large Numbers for U-Statistics*. Institute of Statistics Mimeograph Series, vol. 302. North Carolina State University.

Ibragimov, Rustam, and Sharakhmetov, Shoturgun. 2002. The exact constant in the Rosenthal inequality for random variables with mean zero. *Theory of Probability & Its Applications*, **46**(1), 127–132.

Janson, Svante. 2013. *Graphons, Cut Norm and Distance, Couplings and Rearrangements*. New York Journal of Mathematics, vol. 4. NYJM Monographs, State University of New York, University at Albany.

Kaliuzhnyi-Verbovetskyi, Dmitry, and Medvedev, Georgi. 2017. The semilinear heat equation on sparse random graphs. *SIAM Journal on Mathematical Analysis*, **49**(2), 1333–1355.

Kawohl, Bernd. 2011. Variations on the p-Laplacian. *Nonlinear Elliptic Partial Differential Equations. Contemporary Mathematics*, **540**, 35–46.

Kindermann, Stefan, Osher, Stanley, and Jones, Peter. 2006. Deblurring and denoising of images by nonlocal functionals. *SIAM Multiscale Modeling and Simulations*, **4**(4), 25.

Koabayashi, Yoshikazu. 1975. Difference approximation of Cauchy problems for quasi-dissipative operators and generation of nonlinear semigroups. *Journal of Mathematical Society of Japan*, **27**(4), 640–665.

Kusolitsch, Norbert. 2010. Why the theorem of Scheffé should be rather called a theorem of Riesz. *Periodica Mathematica Hungarica*, **61**(1–2), 225–229.

Laux, Tim, and Lelmi, Jona. 2021. Large data limit of the MBO scheme for data clustering: Γ-convergence of the thresholding energies. *arXiv:2112.06737*.

Lee, Jong-Sen. 1983. Digital image smoothing and the sigma filter. *Computer Vision, Graphics, and Image Processing*, **24**(2), 255–269.

Lindqvist, Peter. 2017. *Notes on the p-Laplace Equation*. University of Jyväskylä.

Lovász, László. 2012. *Large Networks and Graph Limits*. Colloquium Publications, vol. 60. American Mathematical Society.

Lovász, László, and Szegedy, Balázs. 2006. Limits of dense graph sequences. *Journal of Combinatorial Theory, Series B*, **96**(6), 933–957.

Madenci, Erdogan, and Oterkus, Erkan. 2014. Peridynamic theory. Pages 19–43 of *Peridynamic Theory and Its Applications*. Springer.

McLinden, Lynn, and Bergstrom, Roy. 1981. Preservation of convergence of convex sets and functions in finite dimensions. *Transactions of the American Mathematical Society*, **268**(1), 127–142.

Medvedev, Georgi. 2014a. The nonlinear heat equation on dense graphs. *SIAM Journal on Mathematical Analysis*, **46**(4), 2743–2766.

Medvedev, Georgi. 2014b. The nonlinear heat equation on W-random graphs. *Archive for Rational Mechanics and Analysis*, **212**(3), 781–803.

Medvedev, Georgi. 2019. The continuum limit of the Kuramoto model on sparse random graphs. *Communications in Mathematical Sciences*, **17**(4), 883–898.

Mosco, Umberto. 1969. Convergence of convex sets and of solutions of variational inequalities. *Advances in Mathematics*, **3**(4), 510–585.

Nesterov, Yurii. 1983. A method for solving the convex programming problem with convergence rate $O(1/k^2)$. *Proceedings of the USSR Academy of Sciences*, **269**(3), 543–547.

Nochetto, Ricardo, and Savaré, Giuseppe. 2006. Nonlinear evolution governed by accretive operators in Banach spaces: Error control and applications. *Mathematical Models and Methods in Applied Sciences*, **16**(3), 439–477.

Osher, Stanley, and Paragios, Nikos. 2003. *Geometric Level Set Methods in Imaging, Vision, and Graphics*. Springer.

Pardoux, Etienne. 2009. Cours intégration et probabilité. *Lecture notes (Aix-Marseille Universtité)*, **783**.

Rabczuk, Timon, Ren, Huilong, and Zhuang, Xiaoying. 2019. A nonlocal operator method for partial differential equations with application to electromagnetic waveguide problem. *Computers, Materials & Continua*, **59**(1), 31–55.

Radu, Petronela, Toundykov, Daniel, and Trageser, Jeremy. 2017. A nonlocal biharmonic operator and its connection with the classical analogue. *Archive for Rational Mechanics and Analysis*, **223**(2), 845–880.

Reich, Simeon, and Shoiykhet, David. 2005. *Nonlinear Semigroups, Fixed Points, and Geometry of Domains in Banach Spaces*. Imperial College Press.

Roith, Tim, and Bungert, Leon. 2022. Continuum limit of Lipschitz learning on graphs. *Foundations of Computational Mathematics*, 1–39. DOI: https://doi.org/10.1007/s10208-022-09557-9.

Salinetti, Gabriella, and Wets, Roger. 1977. On the relations between two types of convergence for convex functions. *Journal of Mathematical Analysis and Applications*, **60**(1), 211–226.

Scherzer, Otmar, Grasmair, Markus, Grossauer, Harald, Haltmeier, Markus, and Lenzen, Frank. 2009. *Variational Methods in Imaging*. Applied Mathematical Sciences, vol. 167. Springer.

Silling, Stewart. 2000. Reformulation of elasticity theory for discontinuities and long-range forces. *Journal of the Mechanics and Physics of Solids*, **48**(1), 175–209.

Slepcev, Dejan, and Thorpe, Matthew. 2019. Analysis of p-Laplacian regularization in semisupervised learning. *SIAM Journal on Mathematical Analysis*, **51**(3), 2085–2120.

Tao, Yunzhe, Tian, Xiaochuan, and Du, Qiang. 2017. Nonlocal diffusion and peridynamic models with Neumann type constraints and their numerical approximations. *Applied Mathematics and Computation*, **305**, 282–298.

Tian, Xiaochuan, and Du, Qiang. 2014. Asymptotically compatible schemes and applications to robust discretization of nonlocal models. *SIAM Journal on Numerical Analysis*, **52**(4), 1641–1665.

Tian, Xiaochuan, and Du, Qiang. 2020. Asymptotically compatible schemes for robust discretization of parametrized problems with applications to nonlocal models. *SIAM Review*, **62**(1), 199–227.

Trillos, Nicolás García, and Slepčev, Dejan. 2016. Continuum limit of total variation on point clouds. *Archive for Rational Mechanics and Analysis*, **220**(1), 193–241.

Vaiter, Samuel, Peyré, Gabriel, and Fadili, Jalal. 2015. Low complexity regularization of linear inverse problems. In Pfander, Gotz (ed.), *Sampling Theory, a Renaissance*. Applied and Numerical Harmonic Analysis (ANHA). Birkhäuser/Springer. DOI: https://doi.org/10.1007/978-3-319-19749-4.

Van Gennip, Yves, Guillen, Nestor, Osting, Braxton, and Bertozzi, Andrea. 2014. Mean curvature, threshold dynamics, and phase field theory on finite graphs. *Milan Journal of Mathematics*, **82**(1), 3–65.

Wang, Xuefeng. 2002. Metastability and stability of patterns in a convolution model for phase transitions. *Journal of Differential Equations*, **183**(2), 434–461.

Wijsman, Robert. 1966. Convergence of sequences of convex sets, cones and functions. II. *Transactions of the American Mathematical Society*, **123**(1), 32–45.

You, Huaiqian, Lu, XinYang, Task, Nathaniel, and Yu, Yue. 2020. An asymptotically compatible approach for Neumann-type boundary condition on nonlocal problems. *ESAIM: Mathematical Modelling and Numerical Analysis*, **54**(4), 1373–1413.

Acknowledgments

This work was supported by the ANR (grant GRAPHSIP ANR-14-CE27-0001) and the EU Horizon 2020 research and innovation program (grant NoMADS No. 777826). JF was partly supported by Institut Universitaire de France.

Cambridge Elements

Non-local Data Interactions: Foundations and Applications

Series Editor

Luca Calatroni

Centre National de la Recherche Scientifique (CNRS)

Luca Calatroni is a permanent junior research scientist of the French Centre of Scientific Research (CNRS) at the laboratory I3S of Sophia-Antipolis, France. He got his PhD in applied mathematics in 2016 as part of the Cambridge Centre for Analysis (DTC) and he worked as post-doctoral research fellow at the École Polytechnique (Palaiseau, France) with a *Lecteur Hadamard* fellowship funded by the FMJH. His research interests include variational models for mathematical imaging, inverse problems, non-smooth and non-convex optimization with applications to biomedical imaging, computational neurosciences and digital art restoration.

Associate Editors

Martin Burger
Friedrich-Alexander University Erlangen-Nürnberg, Germany

Raymond Chan
City University of Hong Kong

Ekaterina Rapinchuk
Michigan State University, USA

Carola-Bibiane Schönlieb
University of Cambridge, UK

Daniel Tenbrinck
Friedrich-Alexander University Erlangen-Nürnberg, Germany

About the Series

This series provides a mathematical description of the modelling, the analysis and the optimisation aspects of processing data that features complex and non-local relationships. It is intended for both students and researchers wishing to deepen their understanding of non-local analysis and explore applications to image and data processing.

Cambridge Elements

Non-local Data Interactions: Foundations and Applications

Elements in the Series

Generalized Normalizing Flows via Markov Chains
Gabriele Steidl, Paul Lyonel Hagemann and Johannes Hertrich

Nonlocal Continuum Limits of p*-Laplacian Problems on Graphs*
Imad El Bouchairi, Jalal M. Fadili, Yosra Hafiene and Abderrahim Elmoataz

A full series listing is available at: www.cambridge.org/ENDI